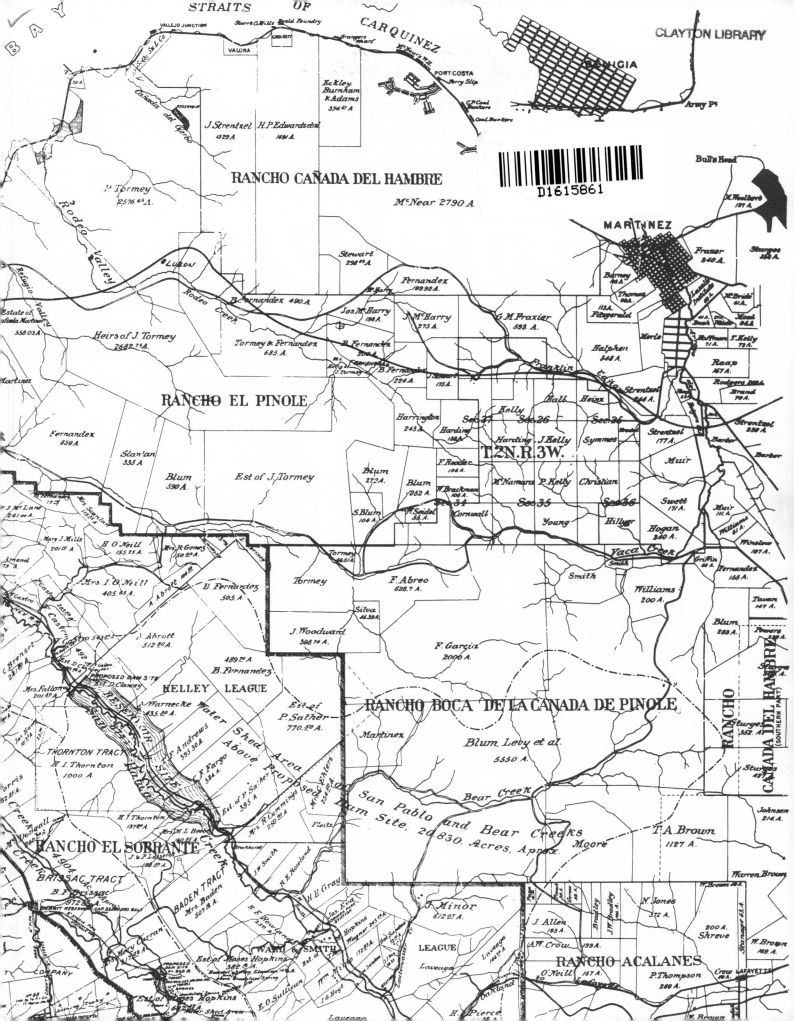

Presented to the

Clayton Community Library

by

THE UPPER CLAYTON VALLEY

CORPORATION

CALIFORNIA'S
CONTRA COSTA COUNTY
AN ILLUSTRATED HISTORY

George Emanuels

W. Mdrews

To CARL 12/29/98

CALIFORNIA'S

CONTRA COSTA COUNTY

AN ILLUSTRATED HISTORY

by
George Emanuels

DIABLO BOOKS—1993

ISBN 0-914330-91-8
Library of Congress Catalog Card Number 86-060766

Distributed by George Emanuels, dba Diablo Books
1317 Canyonwood Court #1
Walnut Creek, California 94595
Telephone (415) 939-8644

Printed in the United States of America

Frontispiece: Downtown Walnut Creek in 1986. Fred Emanuels photograph

Title page: View of Mount Diablo taken on Highway 4, four miles east of Borden Junction, soon after this road to Stockton was completed in 1927. Charles Weeks Collection

This book is dedicated to those unsung heroes, men and women, who give so unselfishly of their time and their abilities to collect, preserve, copy, file and index details of what went on yesterday and year before year that we who read and/or write may enjoy the story of civilization unfolding here in our own backyards.

CONTENTS

Acknowledgements   xi

Introduction   xiii

Central County   1

Martinez, 3   Port Chicago, 15   Clayton, 21   Concord, 27   Pacheco, 39   Pleasant Hill, 45
Walnut Creek, 55   Alamo, 67   Danville, 71   Diablo, 79   San Ramon, 83   Lafayette, 89
Moraga, 99   Canyon, 105   Orinda, 111

West County   119

Kensington, 121   El Cerrito, 125   Richmond, 131   San Pablo, 141   El Sobrante, 149
Pinole, 155   Hercules, 161   Rodeo, 167   Selby, 173   Crockett, 175   Port Costa, 181

East County   187

Byron, 189   Brentwood, 199   Knightsen, 205   Oakley, 209
Antioch, 213   Pittsburg, 225   Coal Mining Towns, 231

Bibliography   241

Index   243

ACKNOWLEDGEMENTS

Everyone who opens this book will soon recognize that only a group of people, not just one person, could bring to life the stories of the birth, the adolescent years, and the maturing of thirty-four communities in Contra Costa County.

The author freely admits that dozens of knowledgeable persons made the text as complete and as accurate as it is. I have tried to list all of those who gave their help and ask forgiveness of any I have overlooked.

Jules Henry Poincare, the famed French mathematician, may have been right when he declared, " . . . a collection of facts is no more a science than a heap of stones is a house," but without collectors' accumulations of evidence historians would be a dying breed.

Thanks be to our collector friends for their tenacity to pick up, sort out, and never throw away even minutiae.

Thanks to that retired pharmacist and lifetime collector of prose and pictures, Louis L. Stein, Jr. His gift to our Contra Costa County Historical Society of more than fifty large photo albums and fifty boxes of newspapers, magazines, and other published material gave this author a rich field of gems and a head start in his research for this work.

Thanks too to Andrew Young, president of the county society, under whose leadership Stein's gift has been well housed and indexed, and a very capable staff of volunteers organized to make it available to researchers. Betty Maffei has led that team since the History Center's opening.

Besides the local historical societies and their collections, three individuals have opened wide their large photographic collections. Each has said, "Here it is, help yourself, copy any pictures you want, return them when you're finished."

One is a retired Western Pacific railroad engineer. After forty years in locomotives, James E. Boynton wrote *Three Barrels of Steam*, a railroad book which has gone through three printings. Beginning in his youth he made railroad photography a serious hobby. He generously gave from his collection of Old Antioch and the Coal Mine trains for this book.

Another generous friend is a former Contra Costa County Public Works employee, George C. Collier. He too is an author. Collier's *A Narrative History of Contra Costa County*, published in 1983, is a well indexed source for local historians. He made his large collection of seven albums available. In addition, he readily assented to my request for a waiver of copyright restrictions on the collection he had given the Bancroft Library.

Out in Eastern Contra Costa County, retired farmer and archivist for the East County Historical Society Charles Weeks pointed to a large box of prints collected over several decades and said, "Take your pick." His photos show early farm life in Contra Costa as well as the development by that Scottish investment firm, Balfour, Guthrie, and others of the productive Delta. Weeks worked for Balfour, Guthrie, farming part of Rancho Los Meganos.

I salute the leaders of the local historical societies in Contra Costa County. They and their volunteers have given me their knowledge. They have found corrections needing my attention, and to them I freely acknowledge my debt.

Never underestimate the value of a copy editor. To mine, Doris Hall—only I know how valuable you have been. Thanks too to the rest of the staff at Panorama West Books. Along with them, I am proud of *Contra Costa County: An Illustrated History.*

The generosity of strangers who became friends in aiding me is one memory which I will retain above all others, for a long time to come. I have met the best, the most generous, and the most unselfish. To you belongs more credit than I give you here. You are:

Marti Aiello	Henry Greenfield	Charlene Perry
Henry Alker	Sheridan Hale	Connie Rehr
Vic Batha	Erle Hansen	Ann Roberts
Charles Bohakel	Lucille Irish	Donna Roselius
Kim Browning	Howard Jamieson	Muir Shank
John Buffo	Virgie Jones	Wm. R. Sharkey III
Sherwood Burgess	Mary Ann Keathley	Ann Shelton
George C. Collier	William Larkins	Maggie Skinner
Vivian Cooper	Anthony Machado	Joseph Smaker
Brother Dennis	Betty Maffei	Louis L. Stein, Jr.
Richard Broyer	Joseph Mariotti	Andy Traverso
Irma Dotson	L. Robert Martin	Charles Weeks
William Ferreira	Lucille Mauzy	June Whiteside
John Fowler	Joan Merryman	Vallie Jo Whitfield
Bernard Freedman	Stanley Nystrom	Tamara Wickland
Ruth Galindo	Victor Parachini	Andrew Young

INTRODUCTION

The temptation to enumerate the things that make Contra Costa County worth writing about is too great to resist. How many counties can say that they were home to the world's largest train ferries, that they mined coal enough in the 1860s to supply San Francisco with almost half its needs, had the fastest shipbuilder in the country and built more ships than any other during World War II? What other county in all of the United States shipped as much grain to Europe during the 1880s as Contra Costa? What other county in the state has a college district with three campuses or has five operating oil refineries and a depository for atom bombs? In this century, what other county had miners mining for quicksilver, silica glass for glass making, and a whaling station which received whales as late as the 1950s?

You may not agree that so many refineries should be here, and you certainly wish the atom bombs had never been brought here; nevertheless, Contra Costa County has them all.

So much for industry, but what about people? Some of the early Anglos—Elam Brown, Nathaniel Jones and John Marsh, just to name a few—let others search for gold. But many, many others who populated our county in the 1850s came down from the mines. Many had farmed at home and they went back to farming in Contra Costa. Others had been merchants back east and they opened shops here after giving up prospecting.

Those of us who lived in Contra Costa in the 1940s will recall three events which took place here in that decade. Just when we could have used it, six months before Pearl Harbor, the Sacramento Northern Railway discontinued passenger service to Oakland and San Francisco.

Four years later, 369 men loading ammunition into two ships at Port Chicago perished when both ships exploded and disappeared.

Beginning about 1946, thousands of war veterans who had passed through Contra Costa on their way to the war in the Pacific returned to our county and stayed. They made history in the 1940s just as earlier settlers had, eighty years before. What a short time between the two periods! Only the span of one lifetime.

The number of new arrivals to our county didn't come gradually, steadily, but in waves. Another wave is washing ashore now, in the late 1980s. It too will make history.

The artist's renditions of Contra Costa County scenes are more than one hundred years old. They appeared first in 1879 in *Illustrations of Contra Costa County*. In 1952 the Contra Costa County Historical Society reprinted the original book. In 1979, Valley Publishers, the predecessor of Panorama West Books, brought out a third edition in a larger format. We regret we cannot give credit to the artist or artists; individual credit has never been given.

The Author

CENTRAL COUNTY

Martinez • Port Chicago • Clayton • Concord
Pacheco • Pleasant Hill • Walnut Creek
Alamo • Danville • Diablo
San Ramon • Lafayette • Moraga
Canyon • Orinda

MARTINEZ

While it is true that a surveyor laid out the town of Martinez in 1849, at that time Vicente Martinez was already living in his two-story adobe on what has become the John Muir National Historic Site.

Martinez asked his brother-in-law, Colonel William M. Smith, to make some of his river frontage into a town. Smith, a partner in a San Francisco general merchandise store, turned the task over to a surveyor, Thomas A. Brown. He plotted 120 acres on the west side of El Hambre Creek into streets and building sites.

Many gold seekers who came overland from southern communities such as Monterey and Pueblo San Jose found many waiting for the ferry ahead of them and had to camp out while awaiting passage. A trading post opened to take advantage of the travelers, and in October 1849, the Bradley House opened.

Martinez' lots sold so well that the same surveyor, in 1850-51, laid out about five hundred acres more for his neighbor, William Welch's widow, the former Maria Galindo. These lots lay across the boundary on the east side of El Hambre Creek, which still identifies the center line of the town.

In a short time new arrivals built more homes, stores, stables and a second hotel.

The constitutional conventions being held in Monterey, San Jose, and Sacramento in anticipation of statehood, in the fall of 1849 and the spring and summer of 1850, brought representatives from most northern California districts to the Sacramento River crossing from Benicia to Martinez. This need estab-

This is the first Contra Costa County Courthouse, in Martinez, completed in 1858. Contra Costa County Historical Society

lished California's earliest continuous transportation system, which for 109 years depended on ferryboats, until the State completed the Benicia-Martinez vehicular bridge on September 15, 1962.

Earlier, in 1846, the first ferry is said to have been a reed boat, the type used by Indians for centuries, operated for a short time by Dr. Semple of Benicia. Next came a flat bottomed "sailing scow," subject to the vagaries of wind and river current. Semple came back to ferrying with a "railway horse-powered" boat, which he ran for a year. A reliable schedule was

3

The Alhambra Hotel, founded in 1855, on the site of the future City Hall, which today is the public parking lot between Main and Ward streets. Ca. 1906. Contra Costa County Historical Society

offered travelers when the little steamer *Ione* went into service. Finally, in August 1850, Oliver C. Coffin brought a larger steam boat out from the east. His ferrying charges were: one dollar, foot passenger; two and a half dollars, man and horse; four dollars, carriage; five dollars, wagon; and fifty cents for each head of livestock.

The earliest stage line established in the growing young town was the one carrying legislators to and from San Jose, California's first capital. The trip took nine hours and the charge to each passenger was two ounces of "dust." A second line connected Martinez to Oakland by way of Rodeo, Pinole, and San Pablo and was operated by Mette and Company. A third line used Martinez as a base for only a few years, running its coaches on a five-and-a-half-hour schedule to Oakland by way of Pacheco, The Corners (later Walnut Creek), and Lafayette.

The discovery of coal in the hills above Clayton brought into being Martinez' most heavily traveled and longest-lived stagecoach line. It ran to the mines by way of Pacheco and Clayton.

Ultimately the Martinez stable owner, Seely J. Bennett, started a service appealing to the leisure class. When the railroad reached Martinez in 1869 it brought visitors from San Francisco desiring to stay in the hotel on Mount Diablo. Bennett carried passengers in his coach-and-four. A description of the resort written in 1878 reads: " . . . is a neat, well-kept hotel, open the year round, with all accommodations. At about 500 feet below the [mountain's] summit, at the roadside, is a never failing spring of pure, soft water."

On April 25, 1850, four and a half months before statehood, Martinez was designated the county seat. The ferryboat owner became postmaster, and F. M.

Above, this is the Jose de los Santos Berryessa adobe. Berryessa's father-in-law was the grantee of Rancho El Pinole, Ignacio Martinez. The home was at the corner of Alhambra and Escobar streets in Martinez. Ca. 1880s. The second floor was used for county businesses before the Courthouse was built. The local Masonic lodge held its first meeting here in 1854. Contra Costa County Historical Society.

Below, the Martinez, Pacheco, Concord and Clayton passenger, mail, and express stage. Ca. 1880. Contra Costa County Historical Society/Stein Collection

Looking north over Martinez. Alhambra Cemetery is next to left border. Residences shown belong to Gabriel Blum, James Hoey, R. M. Jones, R. R. Bunker and William Hale. The Courthouse and De La Salle Institute are out of view to the right. Granger wharf is right of center. National Maritime Museum

Warmcastle sat as the county's first judge. Only two weeks after California became a state, a jury found two Indians, Wampett and Wampett, guilty of manslaughter, but the record fails to record their sentence.

Another Indian stabbed Aparicio Morales, killing him. On August 20, 1852, the Indian was hanged from a sycamore tree on the outskirts of Martinez. The condemned man stood on a barrel in an old cart while deputies fitted the rope around his neck. Then they swiftly drove the cart away, tumbling him off the barrel.

The town's first newspaper, the *Contra Costa Gazette*, published its first issue on September 8, 1858, but it didn't remain in Martinez for long. It moved to Pacheco, a busier town, on September 8, 1861. After most Pacheco residents left their town for Concord, between 1870 and 1872, the *Contra Costa Gazette* moved back to Martinez, in 1873. A second newspaper, *The Contra Costa News*, which began printing in Pacheco in 1874, moved to Martinez in 1877.

One of the strangest sights ever seen in Martinez occurred on July 16, 1864, when thirty-seven camels filed off the ferry and over the hill on their way to Los Angeles. The United States Army had brought them from Africa to Galveston, Texas, and then driven them across country to the arsenal at Benicia. When the Civil War was being fought, camels were expected to be the best animals for carrying supplies or towing

From April 14, 1880, when he married Miss Louie Strentzel, until his death in 1914, John Muir remained Martinez's most famous citizen. In this picture the Muirs' daughters, Wanda and Helen, appear with their parents on the porch of the family's ranch house in 1901. In 1964 the National Park Service bought the home on nine acres and established the John Muir National Historic Site. In 1954 the Ignacio Martinez adobe adjoining Muir's homesite was threatened by developers who planned to clear the neighboring land for a subdivision. Historians Mr. and Mrs. Louis L. Stein, Jr. saved the adobe, which dated from the 1840s, by buying it, re-roofing and making some badly needed repairs. They held it until 1964 when they turned it over to the National Park Service at their cost. Hence it too is a part of the historic site.

The Christian Brothers Novitiate and Junior Seminary, De La Salle Institute, opened in 1879 in what had been a private residence at the head of Pine Street. After fire partially destroyed this building, the brothers renovated the surviving section, making it one wing of the new structure seen above. The school, built on fifty-nine acres, reopened in 1882. That same year the brothers commenced cultivation of their first vineyard in California. In the twentieth century the Christian Brothers vineyards supply the wine the brothers market to finance their schools. De La Salle High School in Concord is one which they support. Martinez Historical Society

wagons in the event an insurrection broke out in the deserts. After the war, the army moved the camels from Benicia to Southern California, to sell them there.

In 1852 the first public school opened, but it served the town only intermittently. Not until 1860 did the Martinez School District provide adequate space and year-round instruction. That year contractors erected a two-story, four-room building with a central stairway. A cupola, housing a belfry, capped the building.

On a hill a half-mile south of the Courthouse, a Catholic order, the Christian Brothers, built a school in which to train teachers for their parochial schools. The De La Salle Institute was housed in a two-and-a-half-story building atop fifty-nine acres, most of which was planted to fruit trees, ornamental trees and shrubbery. Its doors were opened in 1882.

For many years Martinez relied on the county government and the courts for its principal employment opportunities. Somehow it provided business for the livery stables, the hotels, the laundries, the grocery stores and meat markets, and the many saloons. But in 1867 the first flour mill was erected, and flour was shipped up and down the river by freight boats.

As Martinez became a commercial center, Sacramento River boat traffic made more stops at its dock. One particular steamer, the *Cora*, whose captain was A. D. Carpenter, departed Suisun at 7:00 a.m. every day but Sunday, stopped first at Benicia, than at Martinez, and proceeded on to San Francisco's Broadway Wharf. Its return trip began at 3:00 p.m.

When the railroad reached Martinez from Oakland and the San Joaquin Valley in 1869, grain shipping became the major industry. Shippers bought up deep water frontage in preparation for the thousands of tons of wheat to be shipped to Europe from warehouses which would line the river frontage from Martinez to Port Costa. One of the first to build at Martinez was the Granger's Warehouse Association, a cooperative of grain growers. In September 1876 it shipped the first loaded vessel, the *St. Charles*, out of Martinez.

In this view of Martinez, looking south, Shell Oil Company's wharf is at the left. The city wharf is to the right. The ferry slip closest to shore was used until the river silted up. At that time the ferry company built the slip farthest out. Ca. 1960. Martinez Historical Society

Later, three more warehouses lined the waterfront to the west. At harvest time as many as 550 carloads of wheat a day were loaded into sailing ships bound for Europe. To some extent, every business in town benefited from the thousands of railroad men, sailors, teamsters, and stevedores employed in shipping grain.

Another industry, fishing, while not new, grew astronomically in the 1880s, when two fish canneries came to the county seat. It is estimated that in the mid-1880s about eight hundred boats (usually with two-man crews) fished the 120 miles between San Francisco and Sacramento. Nine canneries operated along the river and in Suisun Bay, with more at San Francisco. Two hundred fifty boats fished Carquinez Straits alone. So many salmon reached the river waters, fishermen caught only what they could sell, not what they could catch. Fishermen received thirty-five to sixty-five cents per fish from the canners.

Joseph Black's Cannery and the Martinez Packing Company together employed as many as 150 persons seasonally and shipped nearly a million one-pound cans a month. Their markets were Australia, Europe and the eastern states.

The Martinez population totaled 875 persons in the 1880 census. Three churches served the population then. The Catholic church came first, then the Methodist Episcopal, and lastly the Congregational church, in 1874.

Inter-city telephones first went into use in 1878 between New York and New Haven, Connecticut. In 1881 a telephone line from Oakland reached Martinez with only a single instrument in town, at the Southern Pacific station. The next year, the Contra Costa County Telephone and Telegraph Company applied for a franchise to construct a line between Martinez and Danville. Initially each town along its route was allowed only a single telephone. The railroad gave up its exclusive right to the telephone in 1907 and then six telephone operators were required to handle the calls from the increased number of users.

The first electricity in Martinez was produced by a steam-driven generator for home and office use. Subsequently, the Contra Costa Light and Power Company installed the first street lights in 1905. The Great Western Power Company began delivering electricity to Contra Costa communities in 1910. In March 1911, that company began serving Martinez with electricity for heat and power but the local hospital, Courthouse, and jail didn't receive electricity until 1915.

Just as most students all across America ended their education upon completion of the eighth grade, so did Martinez youngsters until 1902. At the turn of the century, no high school existed in Contra Costa County. In 1901 Mt. Diablo High School in Concord opened its doors for the first time, and in 1902 Alhambra High School in Martinez followed suit.

Manufacturing found Martinez in the late 1890s and within fifteen years tripled the town's population. Several new businesses started operating there after 1900. The Alhambra Water Company started bottling its pure water in 1903. An employer of nearly three hundred men, the Mountain Copper Company came to Martinez in 1905. It smelted copper ore and as a by-product manufactured agricultural fertilizer. The pioneer Bull's Head Oil Company, ca. 1895, became the American Oriental Oil Company in 1910. Three years later the Associated Oil Company began refining oil three miles east of town, employing hundreds.

The Royal Dutch Shell Oil Company began refining petroleum in Martinez in 1914. This refinery was Shell's first in the United States. Its local plant put 2,200 men to work.

With Martinez established as a manufacturing center, all of central Contra Costa County benefited from higher than usual rates of employment.

Above, the first regular eastbound passenger train to cross the Martinez-Benicia bridge, October 15, 1930. C. M. Kurtz Photo, J. E. Boynton Collection

Below, Santa Fe's Chicago-bound San Francisco Chief *crossing Muir trestle in Martinez, ca. 1965.* The Bancroft Library

Alhambra Ranch, property of Dr. John Strentzel, near Martinez.
From Smith & Elliott's "Illustrations of Contra Costa Co."

Property of S. J. Bennett, Martinez. From Smith & Elliott's "Illustrations of Contra Costa Co."

Residence of Dr. J. H. Carothers, Martinez. From Smith & Elliott's "Illustrations of Contra Costa Co."

PORT CHICAGO

Captains of boats carrying freight up the Sacramento River, and bringing down cargoes of produce, fruit, grain and hay, found places to discharge and load far apart in the early days.

In 1848 and 1849 sloops and schooners, drawing only a few feet, carried the shipments. Unique to San Francisco Bay and its tributaries, the flat bottom scows moved easily in and out of the creeks and over river bars.

By 1850 steam vessels were arriving. They didn't replace the scows but rather carried larger and heavier cargoes, but they required deep water docks.

The first practical site upriver from Martinez to berth a steamer was five miles above the county seat at a point called "Seal Bluff." A dock built here was in water deep enough for vessels to come in and load full shipments. The virgin soil of Mount Diablo, Clayton and Ygnacio valleys yielded heavy crops of barley and wheat, and teamsters delivered the yield to the dock at Seal Bluff Landing.

Among the settlers in the early 1850s were four brothers, Newton, Asa, Simeon and Philo Woodruff. Another Woodruff, David S., came in 1858 and taught school in the village.

Samuel S. Bacon took up 160 acres in 1855 and farmed there until 1860, when he moved over to Pacheco to become a shopkeeper. He returned in 1868 and with a partner built a 50- by 100-foot warehouse.

While the surrounding area remained in agriculture for over 100 years, industry came slowly to the community. One of the earliest was a smelter, built in 1890 for Copper King, Ltd. Ore came from a mine twenty-eight miles east of Fresno. Unfortunately the company's assayer was less than competent, and his decisions forced the company into bankruptcy. He ran off with an actress, leaving his wife and seven children in Seal Bluff.

A boost of mammoth proportions came to the village in 1907 when the C. A. Smith Lumber Company of Coos Bay, Oregon, bought 1,500 acres on one and a half miles of river frontage. The company built a planing mill, a dry kiln, and drying sheds and in total had one of the largest finishing mills anywhere in the United States. Its annual payroll came to nearly $300,000. For its employees' convenience the firm established the "City of Bay Point," retiring the name Seal Bluff Landing.

A fire in 1913 destroyed all the improvements, but the company reorganized and opened two years later as the Coos Bay Lumber Company. It operated until 1932, when the demand for lumber ceased as a result of the Great Depression.

Although the fire put a stop to many community improvements, the town already had two churches, Saint Francis' Catholic Church and the Community Congregational Church. To fill the need for a library, the lumber company provided space for the town's 113 books in its hospital room. The Odd Fellows Hall was built in 1911, as was a moving picture theater, established by Andy Shirpke. The two-story California Hotel was built in 1916 by the Heinz Brothers. At

Naval Weapons Station, Concord. Seal Bluff shipways used during 1918 are in lower right corner. Naval Weapons Station, Concord

this time Saturday night dances were a regular feature of the town; they were held at Biel Hall.

One feature of the refinancing out of which came the Coos Bay Lumber Company was a deed restriction written by the former owner prohibiting the sale of liquor on any of its property. The Coos Bay firm got around it by financing the construction of a bar on land not included in the sales agreement. Coos Bay turned the bar over to a club of Bay Point citi-

zens, requiring that all profits " . . . shall be used for the benefit of all the people of Bay Point."

By 1917 Bay Point housed about one thousand people, and that year the biggest change in the town took place. The United States War Department awarded a contract to build ten 10,000-ton freighters to the Pacific Coast Shipbuilding Company. The German U-boats were sinking so many Allied vessels carrying food and war matériel to Europe, replace-

The description of this photo first published with it read: "Among the largest and most important industries on the Coast is the Pacific Coast Smelting Works, located at Suisun Bay, about one mile from the two great railroads, the Southern Pacific and the Santa Fe. It is the property of the Copper King mine, limited, Fresno County, Cal. Since the works went into commission last April they have doubled their capacity, and can now handle over 200 tons of ore per day with an increased capacity of 300 tons per day. They buy gold, silver and copper ore, the plant being fully equipped with sampling mills, ore roasting buildings, smelters and concentrators. The first bar was panned May 1, 1901. They use petroleum exclusively for generating and smelting. As it was the intention to go into the custom business generally and to use ore from the Copper King mine they established their works in their present location." Contra Costa County Historical Society

Only a portion of the C. A. Smith Lumber Company's yard at Port Chicago in 1925.
Contra Costa County Historical Society

Port Chicago, ca. 1942.
Concord Naval Weapons Station

ments were needed even if they came from the Pacific Coast.

On January 6, 1918, the company broke ground for eight ship ways, a plate shop and auxiliary buildings. The Southern Pacific brought workers from Oakland and Berkeley, and the Oakland, Antioch and Eastern carried others from all along its Contra Costa line.

Additional employees meant a need for local housing. The shipyard founded the town of "Clyde," reminiscent of the world's greatest shipbuilding river of the same name in Scotland. The firm built 120 cottages, to provide some housing for its nearly forty-five hundred men. It hired noted architect Bernard Maybeck to design a hotel. When completed, the three-story structure had 176 rooms and a basement with a seventeen-lane bowling alley.

The largest freighter ever built on the Pacific Coast up to the time was launched as the *Diablo*. It slid down the ways on November 30, 1918, nineteen days after the war ended. The Pacific Coast Shipbuilding

Company deserted the town, the Clyde Hotel closed its doors, and the Coos Bay Lumber Company moved to Oakland. But most of the residents, many of whom had opened businesses, stayed on. Others found employment in Concord or at the oil refineries at Avon and Martinez. Even a few new businesses came to town. One, the Bay Point Iron Works, employed men to cast iron, brass, bronze and aluminum. The local school employed six teachers. A newspaper, the *Bay Point Breeze*, was founded by Charles B. Hodgkins, and life went on tranquilly for most inhabitants, with only superficial problems. Yet the town changed its name in 1931 to "Port Chicago."

The change to end all changes began in 1942. In June of that year the War Department established its naval ammunition depot and built its ship loading docks on Port Chicago's waterfront. For two years of World War II, the facility shipped ammunition needed by the armed forces fighting the war in the Pacific.

Two ships, tied up on opposite sides of the loading dock to receive ammunition, exploded on the evening

Sacramento Northern ferry Ramon *shuttling a Sacramento-bound express train from Shell Point, four miles east of Port Chicago to Chipps Island. Ca. 1936.* Moraga Historical Society

of July 17, 1944. In a blinding roar, between five and ten thousand tons of ammunition killed 369 sailors, vaporizing many. Almost all of them were black.

One sailor jumped up and slid down the stairs on his stomach, got over a ten-foot fence topped with barbed wire, scrambled through all kinds of shattered glass in his bare feet, and suffered only a scratched fingernail.

Every seat was filled in the movie house a half mile away, and even though an outer wall buckled, nothing fell on the 192 people under the ceiling. A steward off one of the ships was having a drink at a tavern. The concussion broke his glass and blew him across the room. Nearby an eighteen-month-old infant boy slept in his crib as a fifty-pound piece of ship plate tore a hole through the roof of a house next door and ricocheted through his wall, cutting the legs off his little bed. When the parents, cut and bleeding, found their son, he was still sleeping on the mattress, which was resting on the floor.

Every building in Port Chicago was damaged; phone lines came down; power lines blazed; and gas escaped from open pipes. In Walnut Creek, twelve miles away, folding glass doors of a market blew off their hinges. Windows were blown out even in San Leandro. Three miles away a lookout on a tanker going downstream was blown into the bay.

At the time of the blast Port Chicago contained 660 homes, three hotels, a movie house, and a shopping district.

In spite of all the trauma the residents suffered, few moved away. They rebuilt and went on with their lives, collecting an average of $1,300 each for damage to 300 homes in the town. Twenty years later, when the navy wanted to buy them out, Port Chicago residents resisted with every tool at their disposal. Between 1966 and 1968 the United States government bought 5,000 acres, first some as a buffer zone between the docks and the ammunition depot, and eventually the town itself.

In 1969 the government evicted the last owner and demolished the town.

Residence of Charles and Lafayette I. Fish, Martinez.
From Smith & Elliott's "Illustrations of Contra Costa Co."

CLAYTON

A few of those pioneers not attracted by gold mining in 1850 who guided their gaunt horses or mules down through the Sierra forests to Stockton and were not interested in the treeless mosquito-infested San Joaquin Valley, continued west and followed the trail past John Marsh's home, through a canyon and into Diablo Valley.

At last they reached land free for the taking, not a part of any Mexican land grant, with deep fertile top soil, on both sides of a watercourse fed by numerous springs. The area was described by William H. Brewer in 1862: "[it contains] a considerable stream in winter and spring . . . shaded by willows and grapevines . . . where my companions go to bed at eight or eight-thirty while I sit in the tent . . . reading until cold."

By 1852 about ten families had squatted on several square miles of level land and the canyons adjacent to The Deadfall. Whether named for an accumulation of dead trees or a large bear trap is unrecorded, but Jeremiah Morgan, a resident of the area, reported even later, in 1867, "Bears are so numerous I can shoot one whenever I like."

The residents raised vegetables for themselves, fodder for their milk cows, and hay for the few head of cattle they had brought with them or bought from the Mexican ranchers.

No village was to be seen, only small frame shelters standing well apart, tethered milk cows, a few children scampering about, men and women laboring in the fields. The closest "store" was a small building a mile east of The Deadfall, operated by C. Rhine.

Among the early settlers before 1853 were the brothers Richard and Ebenezer Stranahan, Thomas Johnston, Robert Duncan, E. J. Clark, who sold forty acres to Joel Clayton in 1853, J. W. Crandall, D. D. Dennickson, Alexander Riddell (who died in 1853), and James Kirker.

Not all of those early arrivals had lived as complex a life as James Kirker. Many of those who had, kept their pasts secret, but Kirker's is too well documented to be concealed.

The governor of Chihuahua, Mexico, hired Kirker, an Irish trapper in the lower Rio Grande Valley, and his four companions to guard pack trains and do scout duty for his soldiers. These young volunteers feared the natives more than the Indians feared them and often fled at the sight of a war party. Kirker, once a prisoner of the Apache, remained in the Mexican's employ to take scalps after the Indians ravaged the population down through Zacatecas and as far south as Durango City. The governor offered the Americans $100 for every male and $50 for each female scalp they took. After the first couple of hundred, the hunting became lean; the hunters resorted to taking scalps even in peaceful rancherias. An estimate of the total taken by Kirker and his group was 487.

Just before war between the United States and Mexico broke out, the governor offered "Sebastian Querque," as he called him, the position of colonel if he would fight on Mexico's side. Kirker's answer came one dark night soon after the offer. He and his friends slipped across the border, meeting up with United States troops a few miles north of El Paso.

Kirker, apparently tired of head hunting, stayed only briefly with the troops, rode east and before long embarked on a ship for Ireland, where he visited relatives in 1848.

When he returned to the United States, Kirker slowly made his way westward. In Ohio he "met a party of gentlemen known as the Morgan County and California Rangers of Illinois." They hired him to lead them and he did, riding through the northwest corner of Arkansas, west to Santa Fe, New Mexico, and on to Southern California, where they dispersed.

Kirker took his time deciding where to put down roots but finally came to Contra Costa County and settled in the vicinity of The Deadfall. Possibly the peaceful, slow pace in his newly adopted community was more than he could stand. James Kirker died the following year.

That same year, Joel Clayton, a San Francisco dairyman, loaded his wagon with all his worldly possessions, his wife, Margaret Ellen, and their three children on a sailing scow which set sail for Pacheco Creek. On arrival they found only one house and a warehouse under construction. The only other sign of

View of Main Street from School Hill in 1903.
Contra Costa County Historical Society

Clayton Hotel, ca. 1890. Contra Costa County Historical Society

Old store and saloon at Clayton, 1968. Contra Costa County Historical Society/Roy Bloss Collection

a structure clung to the edge of the bank; it was a platform from which to load sacks of cement burned from deposits in Lime Ridge on the eastern slopes of Ygnacio Valley. Cement was in great demand for the reconstruction of fire-devastated San Francisco.

When Clayton left San Francisco he sold the twenty-five-acre dairy he had established in the area now bounded by Broadway, Pierce, Webster and Clay streets, the part of the city known today as "Cow Hollow."

Clayton bought forty acres in Mitchell Canyon

and built the first of two homes there. As yet no village existed at either Pacheco or Concord. Only a few settlers came to The Deadfall before Joel Clayton laid out a townsite in 1857. The well-delineated streets and lots attracted businesses, and Clayton proudly built his second house in the village to which he gave his name.

The early merchants included a blacksmith and a tavernkeeper. A French immigrant, Romero Mauvais, built the tavern, then built the Clayton Hotel next to it. Charles Rhine moved his store into town, next to the hotel. Frank Such, from Ygnacio Valley, discovered a coal seam on hills northeast of Clayton, and a rush of prospectors made the village their source of supplies. Stages ran from Martinez to Clayton and teamsters hauled tons and tons of freight from Pacheco in the effort to keep up with the demand.

In 1863 a great excitement was created by the discovery of copper in Mount Zion, only two miles southwest of the village. The reports came in that the mountain had ore of untold richness. Suddenly every unemployed man turned prospector. Blankets, beans, bacon and hard bread rose to premium prices. The hills around Mitchell Canyon lighted up at night with reportedly hundreds of campfires. Hammers and picks were in great demand; it seemed as if the whole community had been bitten by the mining tarantula. Another hotel, the Union Hotel, opened to booming business. Fred Swan opened another bar and Romero Mauvais established a general merchandise store. Ben Rapp opened a brewery, a success from its first day. The first two tons of copper ore went on their way to a San Francisco smelter on September 19, 1863.

Earlier that year, in July, stock was sold in the amount of $80,000 to finance the Welch Quicksilver and Mining Company. That mine, under changing ownerships, continued producing quicksilver until 1950.

By January 1864 Mount Zion showed holes on all sides. The Keokuk drilled a tunnel, as did the Great Republic. The Pioneer, the Summit of Zion, the Unexpected, the Horseshoe, the Alpine, are the names of only a few. The Mount Zion tunnel drove more than one thousand feet into the mountain that same year. The Mt. Zion Copper Company drilled on the easterly slope of Mount Zion, from where the miners looked down on the village. On the opposite side, overlooking the Diablo Valley, miners looked out over that plain. The Mt. Zion brought out the richest ore. When Antioch citizens financed a smelter there, the Mt. Zion ore was hauled by four-horse and sometimes six-horse teams to that smelter.

All at once the bubble burst. The millionaires-for-a-day left their camps or hotels and often, with ragged breeches and boots out at the toes, trudged away.

In February 1864, a fire nearly wiped out the entire town. Both the Clayton Hotel and the Union Hotel went up in flames. So did Charles Rhine's store. Some owners rebuilt, the Eagle Saloon & Ice Cream Parlor for one; it still caters to the thirsty as the Clayton Club. Judge Morris built his residence, "Park Cottage," and operated possibly the best livery stable Claytonites ever saw. Opposite Jim Swan's hotel stood the new Palace Brewery. The brewery, one correspondent once wrote, " . . . is being kept in first-class order . . . good management, cleanliness and mechanical industry, an ornament to the village." One can't help but wonder if the reward for such journalistic reporting might have been the product brewed on the premises.

Joel Clayton divided his attention between his town and Antioch in 1865. His successful subdivision encouraged him to attempt to repeat his earlier achievements. This time he went to Antioch, where he filed a subdivision map on July 14, 1865, of 122 square blocks, the first filed in that community.

Back nearer his home, on his 1,200-acre homestead, Clayton raised hay and cattle. One winter day in 1872 he carried a sick calf across the field to his barn. The exertion was too much for him; he came down with a fever and passed away soon after from pneumonia.

The mine failures and the fire came in the same year, and the village never quite recovered. The area around Clayton produced heavy harvests of wine grapes, and two wineries opened: the Glen Terry Winery, with a 40,000-gallon capacity, and K. Erath's Mt. Diablo Winery. Several new businesses were built along Main Street: Margaret Larsen's bar; the shop of C. H. Trette, the veteran village blacksmith; John Condie's hotel and saloon; James Curry's livery stable; Lander and Keller's butcher shop; and Rhine's Clayton store.

Both the Congregationalists and Methodists built churches. The community hall was built by the Clayton Hall Association.

Jack Atchinson speaks of delivering the mail in the

Clayton Valley in 1918. The Gamble home is in the vineyard. Contra Costa County Historical Society

1890s: "In the fall of 1888 I got the job driving twenty-six days per month, every day but Sunday. . . . I drove four horses . . . carrying passengers and mail on the Martinez, Pacheco, Concord, Clayton run. My brother drove the Clayton mining district and Antioch run for mail and errands only. George wore rubber clothes some times in winter, with mail sacks strapped down. The mail bags were leather and padlocked. It was the law [to carry] a .45 caliber gun at all times.

"My new stage had three seat rows and could carry eight passengers. It had a top and I furnished carriage robes. It also had a baggage rack at the back of the stage to carry passengers' luggage. We charged from Martinez to Pacheco twenty-five cents; Martinez to Concord fifty cents; Martinez to Clayton seventy-five cents.

"We had to get the horses and carriage through the Martinez run even when Pacheco Creek flooded over. I had the body of the stage built extra high because in the winter I had to swim the horses many times."

Not many old-timers' names appear in the 1898 voters' register. However, their offspring kept up the enrollment in the two-room school house built on the two acres contributed by Joel Clayton. In 1899 sixty-one students were taught by two school teachers, Miss Lander and W. A. Kirkwood.

Both the Mt. Diablo Winery and the De Martini were closed by 1900 and soon Paul de Martini and his partner, A. Cherogino, were just names on cemetery headstones. And even though he sold his beer for only thirty cents a gallon (in quantity), Joseph Ruscher, the second owner of the Clayton Brewery, left his mark the same way, as a name on a tombstone.

In more recent years, John Hink, a Berkeley department store owner, bought forty acres near the Welch Quicksilver Mine and built two homes there. William H. Easley bought the Mt. Diablo Winery and did likewise. George Cardinet, a candy manufacturer, bought De Martini's Winery and converted it into a residence.

Clayton had two music teachers in its history, Professor Zack and Professor Zeck. Remembered best for the tobacco he chewed while he taught is the dancing teacher, Mr. Collins.

In the 1950s, Clayton residents lived in homes built long before. Each had his own well, and his sewage system remained as it had been for a hundred years. Subdividers were held at bay by the county health department's refusal to allow septic tanks and wells on the same lot.

In the ensuing years, until 1979, developers offered homesites for sale in fifty-five subdivisions. In 1979 Concord's Sewer District applied a moratorium and halted all new sewer connections, which stopped subdividing for four years. In 1983 the district lifted the ban; developers were ready and once again began turning grazing land into homesites.

Clayton Hotel, 1937. Contra Costa County Historical Society

Clayton Road at Treat Boulevard in 1940. Contra Costa County Historical Society

26

CONCORD

If incessant winter rains hadn't flooded the busy town of Pacheco year after year, there may never have been any reason for the town of Concord. Just as vital as were the torrential downpours, the generosity of a native Californian was the key to the town's creation.

Don Salvio Pacheco, owner of the 17,921-acre Rancho Monte del Diablo, gave lots away to anyone wishing to move from the waterlogged commercial and shipping center of Pacheco. In 1869 he divided twenty acres into nineteen one-acre plots and a one-acre plaza.

A merchant who came first, in 1869, built a store on the land bounded by the four streets, Bonifacio, East, Contra Costa and Galindo. A machine-shop owner arrived a month or two later, erecting his shop across the street from the store. In the same summer two men each built a house, and a month later an entrepreneur constructed a hotel. Before year's end, a livery stable and two or three saloons were doing business. The following year enough people were living nearby that their children filled a one-room school house.

Three years later construction started on a Catholic church. A butcher shop, a bakery, and a notions store opened. Farmers from Ygnacio, Clayton, and Diablo valleys came to trade in Concord.

When the town was only ten years old, the *Concord Sun*, a weekly newspaper, commenced publishing. Soon afterward a second newspaper appeared. Eventually it became the *Concord Transcript*, and it served the community for 100 years.

In summer, residents seeking relief from the heat walked in the shade of the tall eucalyptus trees in the plaza. Long summer evenings gave them time to visit with their neighbors in the cool of the park.

Over the years after he founded Concord, Don Salvio Pacheco gave land to his son, Fernando, and his daughter's husband, Francisco Galindo. When he died in 1876, Don Salvio owned only 425 acres. However, Fernando held title to 1,500 acres at the time of his father's death. In addition to the land given to him, Galindo had purchased more from his father-in-law until he ultimately owned nearly 5,000 acres. Early on, he had built himself a frame house across the road, facing his father-in-law's adobe (on today's Adobe Street). Fernando built his adobe north of his father's near what is now the intersection of Grant and Oliveira Road.

The principal commercial activities in town in the 1870s and 1880s were selling and repairing farm machinery and harness and furnishing farm families with groceries and other provisions.

Out on the farms wheat was being harvested in all the valleys. By 1880 a few progressive farmers were planting fruit orchards, and then years later nearly half the suitable land yielded fruit. In a number of areas farmers established vineyards. For the next thirty years more and more of them grew both table and wine grapes.

Prior to 1891 horse-drawn wagons moved freight in and out of Concord to the railroad station at Martinez. In that year the railroad completed its San Ramon branch, bringing passenger and freight serv-

Above, the adobe home of the grantee of Rancho El Diablo, Salvio Pacheco, facing Adobe Street, Concord. It became the Adobe Restaurant in the late 1940s. In 1980 the Associates National Bank occupied the adobe. Courtesy Ruth Galindo

Below, Fernando Pacheco's adobe before restoration. It faces Grant Street northwest of Highway 24. The Contra Costa County Horseman's Association has leased the adobe for many years. Ca. 1980. Contra Costa County Historical Society/Stein Collection

ice to Concord for the first time. Now passengers reached San Francisco in two hours; previously a once-a-day stage took five and a half hours just to reach Oakland.

The Southern Pacific station received the first telephone used in Concord, in 1891. Residents had lived their lives without the instrument and none but business users added to the number. Only six telephones served Concord in 1899, eight years after their introduction.

No public secondary education was offered anywhere in Contra Costa County at the turn of the century. Boys and girls usually finished their schooling at graduation from grammar school. Only those with families wealthy enough to board them in a city went on to high school. That situation was ended in 1901, when Mt. Diablo Union High School opened in Concord. Many youths from distant ranches rode horses to school. As customary as the outhouse which adjoined most elementary schools at the turn of the century was the shelter for pupils' horses. The three-walled, shed-roofed structure gave shade to the animals in summer and kept them out of the rain in winter.

Mt. Diablo High's first graduating class (1903) graduated two girls. In 1901 some parents still expected their boys to work on the family farm or in their shop instead of going on to high school.

The largest employer of its time in the Diablo Valley came to Concord three years after it incorporated, in 1905. The Cowell Lime and Cement Company built its town of Cowell that year and put men to work quarrying rock from the ridge on the east side of Ygnacio Valley. They carried the rock in the company's narrow gauge railroad's dump cars to the crusher from where it went into the roasting kiln and became cement.

Carloads of sacked cement left Cowell daily on the company's standard gauge Bay Point and Clayton Railroad. At Bay Point, nine miles from the plant, the cars went on their way to customers over the Southern Pacific, Western Pacific, or Santa Fe railroads.

As early as 1910 farmers threatened to sue over the

Concord's Salvio Street, looking east in 1908. The January Block is on the right corner. Contra Costa County Historical Society

The Mt. Diablo Union High School opened at 2450 Grant Street in 1901 and was torn down in the 1960s. Contra Costa County Historical Society

air pollution which coated their vines and orchards with a fine cement dust. The cement company built a 235-foot-high smoke stack in 1934 in an effort to dissipate the dust into the atmosphere where it wouldn't fall on a populated area.

Labor negotiations in 1947, in which the company was requested to pay five or six dollars a day, closed the plant.

Fire was no stranger to Concord, but the blaze of April 26, 1917, was the largest before or since. A lady living in an apartment in the back of the January Block, on the south side of Salvio between Galindo and Mt. Diablo streets, gave the alarm. Smoke poured up from the basement of the Concord Inn as the chef ran through the halls shouting to rouse the occupants. The smoke kept firemen out of the building as the fire spread to the Meehan Hardware Store and the Concord Mercantile Company.

Concord wasn't equipped for the raging blaze. Calls went out to Antioch, Pittsburg, Cowell, Walnut Creek, and Martinez. Martinez's new engine with 1,100 feet of hose came first. By that time oil and gasoline in the basement of the hardware store fed the flames. Firemen gave up trying to quench the fire in the January Block and concentrated on keeping the flames from burning other buildings.

Owners of the Concord Inn lost the most, over $100,000, with only a small amount covered by insurance. Concord Mercantile's loss exceeded $25,000, and the $40,000 loss of the Bank of Concord was only

partially covered. The Neustaedter Building was a total loss, as was the post office and all the equipment in it.

Although Concord didn't have a hospital until well into the 1920s, two physicians served the town from 1900 to 1923. Dr. George McKenzie came first. Dr. F. F. Neff came soon after, about 1900, serving until the day in the early 1920s when he drove his coupe in front of a speeding electric train at the Oak Grove and Meinert crossing. The Cowell cement plant's first physician assumed some of Dr. Neff's practice. Cowell's Dr. W. E. Bixby was followed by Dr. F. B. Cone and later by Dr. C. C. Fitzgibbon.

At that time patients needing hospitalization were driven over the Tunnel Road to Oakland. Two nurses ended that practice in 1928. Mrs. Viola Haywood and a twenty-seven-year-old registered nurse from Montana, Edna Gallagher, opened Concord's first hospital in 1928 in a residence on Concord Boulevard. It had four beds.

Concord's Plaza, ca. 1915.
Contra Costa County Historical Society

Concord's Elementary School on Willow Pass, one and a half blocks east of East Street. It was built in 1892 and razed in 1923.
Contra Costa County Historical Society

Concord's First National Bank, ca. 1917. It later became the American Trust Company. The site is the northeast corner of Salvio and Galindo streets. The first store in Concord, Samuel Bacon's general merchandise store, first occupied this site.
Contra Costa County Historical Society

A year later, Miss Gallagher assumed full ownership and with a $7,500 loan from a new father-in-law, bought a brick house on East Street. She and her husband, Jim Haywood, a mail carrier, without money enough for a home of their own, slept in the basement. They would wait for the patients to fall asleep and then wash and iron the sheets, pillow slips, and towels needed the next day.

The brick house had six beds and a surgery next to the kitchen. The surgery was soon moved to the second story of a tank house in the back yard. (The Haywoods kept their Buick on the ground floor.) The only heat came from a kerosene heater. In 1930 surgical patients were wheeled up a long outdoor ramp to the second story. Convalescing patients often sat in easy chairs in front of the house's fireplace.

The Haywoods completed a two-story wing in 1936. It included a delivery room, a six-bed obstetrics ward, an office, twelve private rooms, and the first elevator in Concord.

By 1941 Edna Haywood had a license for thirty-eight beds. A sincere, loving, caring person, she served as the hospital's administrator, business manager, dietician, director of nursing and head surgical nurse for seventeen years. In 1947 Edna sold her hospital to a doctor who later sold it to a non-profit organization that expanded it a number of times. Today the hospital is owned by the Concord Hospital District, which bought it in 1952.

Three air fields have served Concord over the years. The first was a 1,200-foot-long dirt strip called Mahoney Field, 100 yards west of the Concord station of the San Francisco-Sacramento Railway, approximately where the BART station is in 1986. Mahoney Field was leased by the Concord Chamber of Commerce and dedicated on April 25, 1920.

The California Aerial Transport Company flew the only plane it owned from Stockton to Concord, where passengers from San Francisco arrived in a limousine from the Palace Hotel. The plane went on

The northeast corner of Mount Diablo and Salvio, Concord, with the Majestic Theater on Mount Diablo. Ca. 1920s. Contra Costa County Historical Society

The Bank of Concord, established in 1901, ca. 1914. It occupied the southwest corner of Salvio and Mount Diablo streets. The Concord Mercantile Company was owned and operated by Frederick C. Galindo. Contra Costa County Historical Society

Southern Pacific's San Ramon Branch train at Concord, ca. 1910. The train is made up of two baggage and three passenger cars. Contra Costa County Historical Society

to Fresno, Bakersfield and Los Angeles. It was a Curtiss Eagle which carried seven passengers and was powered by three 150-horsepower engines. The interior furnishings included silk curtains, a carpeted floor, cut glass flower vases, gray whipcord upholstery, and recessed ceiling lighting.

The plane made three flights a week, taking four hours and forty-five minutes if it was on time. Its maximum speed was 107 miles per hour and it had a 475-mile range. It made its maiden flight on May 17, 1920 and its final landing six weeks later, when it crash landed on June 26. Mahoney Field was never heard of again.

The second air field was on 160 acres at the northeast corner of West Street and Clayton Road. Repair shops and service facilities were maintained there for the air mail planes flying in to San Francisco's Crissy Field, on the San Francisco Presidio. Fog is an ever-present hazard near the Golden Gate, and when air mail service commenced in 1924 an alternate landing to fog-bound Crissy Field was a necessity. The Concord Field was an obvious solution and planes flew in and out of there as the weather at Crissy Field dictated.

After the Boeing Air Transport Company started flying the mail in 1927, it established service to and

33

from San Francisco at Mills Field near San Bruno, San Mateo County. That left the Concord field open to private flyers, who used it in the mid-1930s until the Pleasant Hill airport, offering fuel and repair service, attracted them to Sherman Field.

Buchanan Field is so well known only its genesis will be reviewed here. It began when the county bought 407 acres of farm land for an air field in 1942. The federal government put up $542,626 toward its purchase, and in June 1943 the United States Military Command took it over. At once a squadron of P-39 fighter planes on alert for a possible Japanese attack made its home at the field. A support group of C-46 aircraft also was based there.

As time showed an attack by the Japanese to be less likely than had been feared, the field became an advanced training base for P-39 pilots. The Military Command added another 122 acres to the field, con-

structed new runways, and paved additional taxiways. Altogether the United States government spent $12,683,372 and the county $500,000 on the field.

When the war in the Pacific ended in 1945, the War Assets Administration took over the field. In 1946 the Military Command declared the facility surplus and turned it over to the county. The board of supervisors named the air field for the much-admired veteran of that group, William Buchanan of Pittsburg.

Civilian flyers flocked to Buchanan Field as Pleasant Hill's Sherman Field prepared to close so that its buyers might subdivide the site into the Sherman Oaks subdivision.

The War Assets Administration flew surplus planes from Arizona to Buchanan Field where they went on sale. Darrell Jensen, a long time resident of the county, managed their disposal for the government.

Buchanan Field in November 1946. It had been open to civilian pilots only a few months. Darrell Jensen was the first airport manager. The popular Pacheco Speedway, in the lower left corner, staged weekend evening auto races. Solano Way is delineated by the line of houses across the center of the picture, right to left. William Larkins Collection

Sparked by his fondness of jazz, enthusiastic Concord automobile dealer Carl Jefferson persuaded a handful of friends to help him create the Concord Jazz Festival. The city matched his and their contributions, and the eager group held its first festival on an undeveloped field adjoining the high school.

At that 1969 turnout of more than 17,000, Jefferson knew he was correct—the public is hungry for musical dishes when top quality artists serve them. While extremely happy over the initial success, he envisioned a facility where those in jeans would feel as welcome as those in more formal attire. What he brought into realization, in May 1975, is the Concord Pavilion, built at a cost of $4.5 million. The pavilion sits on the eastern edge of Concord, without the outside walls of a building. Thirty-five hundred listeners may sit under a roof, and forty-five hundred more may lounge on the lawn, picnicking or reclining while they enjoy some of the country's greatest performers.

No theater for the exclusive use of the elite, the Concord Pavilion offers a varied fare. Presenting ballet, symphony, rock, and traditional jazz, this Concord facility draws its audience from all over the Bay Area. Attendance remains high and makes it a money-maker for the City of Concord. It is unique in Northern California, and its creator is a public-spirited dynamo with an affection for all music for music's sake.

Concord's Buchanan Field in 1985. Ygnacio Valley is in the upper right corner; Clayton Valley is in the upper left corner. Courtesy of Ted Schroder

Bay Point & Clayton Railroad's 1907 Baldwin approaches Concord in 1940. Its destination is the cement plant near Cowell and Ygnacio Valley roads. J. E. Boynton Collection

Concord's high-rises in April 1986. Courtesy of Ted Schroder

Residence of B. F. Beebe, Concord.
From Smith & Elliott's "Illustrations of Contra Costa Co."

Residence and farm of J. E. Durham, Ygnacio Valley.
From Smith & Elliott's "Illustrations of Contra Costa Co."

PACHECO

In the days before any village existed at Pacheco, Walnut Creek, or Concord, prospector Frank Such found the limestone laden hills in Ygnacio Valley. With a partner, he burned the stone, making cement, which was bagged and then carted to a landing on the stream, Walnut Creek.

The landing was on the east side and was the first structure in the immediate vicinity of what would become Pacheco. The year was 1850.

On the west side of the creek all the land belonged to the Widow Welch, whose husband, William Welch, had been granted Welch Rancho in 1832. In 1853, G. W. Walrath bought a tract from the widow for his home, the first structure erected on the west side of the creek. At that time the widow was selling twenty-five acre lots a few miles south for $75.00 each. It may be safely assumed that Walrath bought his for that amount. Walrath went into business with two others building a warehouse between the two creeks, Grayson Creek and Walnut Creek.

Three years later (1856), before a dozen people lived near the landing, George P. Loucks bought out Walrath and his friends. Loucks, a native of New York, had been mining in Tuolumne County for a short time but had moved to San Francisco, where he went into the business of selling ships' stores and acting as a commission agent. With Diablo, Alhambra, and Ygnacio valleys growing heavy crops of grain, Loucks found his opportunity, buying and selling grain, mostly wheat. He first built a 150-foot-long warehouse and within a year lengthened it by another

125 feet. Like Walrath, Loucks erected his buildings between the two creeks. Five years later Walnut Creek had silted up so much that the ships coming for his shipments ran aground before they reached his warehouses. Loucks moved his buildings three-quarters of a mile downstream to deeper water in 1862.

For the first few years Loucks lived in Contra Costa County, the small community around his home was called Loucksville. The first child born in the village was his daughter Annie, born in 1858.

The first recorded store in Loucksville is the saloon, with a few shelves of groceries, operated by Pablo Moraga.

A newcomer, W. K. Hendrick, bought some acreage from Loucks on which he built a home and a flour mill. Milling grain was an enterprise which lasted longer than any other in the community except operating a bar.

In 1858, Dr. J. H. Carothers, who had come to Martinez three years earlier, bought land between the two creeks and laid out the town he named Pacheco. Soon tradesmen and merchants bought lots from Carothers, each looking to the many farmers in the neighboring valleys for their trade. Pacheco was ideally located. Farmers found a market at Hendricks' mill for their grain, which they brought in wagons with four- and six-horse teams. The miller shipped flour to market on boats which sailed up to his dock. Captain Gus Henderson brought his *C. E. Long* first. Captain Ludwig Anderson was next, sailing his flat-bottomed scow, *Ida*, which he soon re-

An artist's conception of Hale and Brother in 1858.
Contra Costa County Historical Society

placed with the larger and faster scow, the *Annie Carolyn*.

The first business building erected after Dr. Carothers laid out the streets was Hale and Fossett's "Long Store." Elijah Hook built the first two-story commercial building, which housed a general merchandise store on the ground floor and the *Contra Costa Gazette* upstairs.

Residents laid out gardens and planted family orchards. New businesses flocked to Pacheco: Anderson's Lumber Yard, Blum's Brickyard, Excelsior Soda Works, Standard Pacheco Plow Works, Bartnett Harness Factory, Jason Smith's Leather Shop, Pacheco Tobacco Company, French Hotel, Eagle Hotel, Thomas Simpson's saddle and harness store, and the largest blacksmith shop in all of California, G. F. Betts, Blacksmith. Two iron foundries and a wagon manufacturing plant were operating in Pacheco by 1860.

The town bought the first fire engine in all of Contra Costa County when it purchased Engine #1 in 1860 for $1,200. It came down river to Pacheco from Stockton.

The original stagecoach operator first ran his stages from Martinez into Oakland, but in 1860 Pacheco became his terminal. J. W. Morris ran a four-horse stage once a day to Oakland. The west bound trip took five and a half hours; the return took only four hours.

No other town in Contra Costa County could boast of as much trade as could Pacheco. Walnut Creek had a few stores, and Concord didn't exist in 1860. Alamo had a good trade but did no manufacturing and had nothing like the boats coming up the creek from the Sacramento River. Members of four lodges met regularly in Pacheco. Its French Hotel run by Monsieur Bateau served superb French dinners

Central Pacheco as one artist saw it in 1866.
Contra Costa County Historical Society

and travelers from Sacramento or San Jose praised the excellent service.

Weekly mail delivery from Oakland and the lack of telephones for another two decades made communication difficult. However, swift transfer of messages began when the Western Union Telegraph Company strung its line out Telegraph Road in Oakland, over the Fish Ranch Road to Antioch by way of Pacheco.

As in most communities in its day, fire plagued Pacheco too. The first, on August 11, 1860, destroyed the store, Farmers Block, the concrete building of Dr. Carothers and several others. Seven years later, on August 15, 1867, flames consumed the Pacheco Flour Mill. The most devastating broke out on September 5, 1871 and totally leveled three buildings belonging to Elijah Hook, and their inventory, the Contra Costa Gazette, the Odd Fellows Hall and four more stores.

But even more destructive were the floods Pacheco experienced. One writer speaking first of the fences wrote, "The fences . . . always were a rusty appearance [*sic*] because of the heavy freshets. Within a few years the good people have seen the sheer folly of living on the damp unhealthy mud banks between the [Walnut and Grayson] creeks, and have removed to a gently sloping hill to the west. Nearly all the better class of dwellings are now on the hill."

Indeed, when in the course of heavy rains the shallow creeks plugged up by brush, floating trees and dead farm animals, the overflow ran into wells and the alluvion in cesspools backed up in kitchen drainage. In light of present day comfortable indoor bathrooms, the discomfort is difficult to imagine when realizing Pacheco residents in the 1870s relied wholly on outhouses.

While the houses were built on higher ground, the commercial buildings remained on the lower ground between the creeks. Before the heavy rains of 1868

Pacheco Elementary School, ca. 1903. Contra Costa County Historical Society

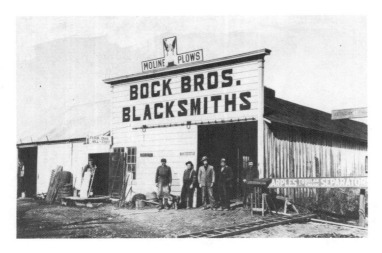

Bock Brothers, Blacksmiths. Contra Costa County Historical Society

saturated the community, the earthquake of October 21 cracked the walls of many of the town's buildings and shook some down. Hook's two-story brick building lost its rear wall, and Dr. Carothers' concrete building was badly shattered. The front and rear walls of Morgan's two-story brick and concrete structure broke free of the sides from top to bottom. Then came the floods.

During the next spring, as Pacheco dried itself off and repaired some of the earthquake damage, some proprietors questioned the wisdom of staying there. Apathy and short memories did nothing to hasten any removal to another location, but when torrential rains darkened the winter skies of 1868-69, minds were quickly made up when an offer of free land two miles to the east was made.

There, near his own adobe, the grantee of Rancho Monte Diablo, Don Salvio Pacheco, instructed surveyors to plot a town of twenty acres into nineteen blocks and a town square. Pacheco's merchants gradually moved to the new town, first named Todas Santos and later Concord. In their first year there the residents established an elementary school, a hotel, a Catholic church, a livery stable and two saloons.

Pacheco hadn't given up altogether. Some residents stayed, but the fire of September 1871 shook the resolve of a few of them. Standish's "Plow Works" moved to West Oakland. After bucking the trend for almost three years, the *Contra Costa Gazette* relocated back to Martinez.

Over the years following, almost all the merchants but the hotel keeper and the bar operator moved away. The Loucks family remained, as did the owner of the saddlery shop, Thomas Simpson. Anderson's lumber yard stayed in business into the twentieth century.

Another business which successfully defied the trend was the flour mill. It too operated into the twentieth century under the ownership of Russi and Sonners. The mill shipped its last load of flour out of Pacheco in 1926 in a sailing scow which picked up the load at the mill's dock.

After the big relocation of the early 1870s, Pacheco remained as a crossroads to pass by. Then, eighty years later, with the founding of the Diablo Valley College and the Sun Valley Shopping Center and the widening of the two creeks by the Contra Costa County Flood Control District, a wave of contemporary establishments came, making Pacheco a modern city.

Above: Pacheco flooded in 1914. Contra Costa County Historical Society
Below: A traveling photo studio, ca. 1870s. Contra Costa County Historical Society

Russi and Sonners Flour Mill, Pacheco.

Pacheco Cash Store. Contra Costa County Historical Society

PLEASANT HILL

Of all the major cities in Contra Costa County, Pleasant Hill is certain to have earned the title "Latest Bloomer."

Only five families lived within the present limits of Pleasant Hill in 1855. The stream, Walnut Creek, remains for practical purposes its eastern boundary. Sometimes Geary Road and sometimes Oak Park are its southern limits, and Diablo Valley College and the Contra Costa Country Club are its approximate northern perimeter.

When in 1866 the new school district counted noses, it tallied thirty-three children between the ages of five and fifteen, and three of them came from native Indian families. However, only a very few attended the original session, which lasted only two months and was held in one of the farm families' homes. Sixteen years later, in 1882, the seasoned school graduated only four eighth graders.

The farmers, the Hooks, Bosses, Clarks, Dukes, and Hollaways, harvested hay and grain. The men, constantly in close contact with their horses, livestock and fowl, rarely wore any clothing but their work clothes, their overalls. They farmed bare land from a few hundred acres in extent to as many as two thousand (William Hook's).

By 1890 there were nineteen farmers in Pleasant Hill; the smallest farm was seventy acres. Over the years Pleasant Hill farmers slowly copied what farmers in neighboring communities had found to be more profitable crops; here and there they planted a few fruit orchards on the hay and grain land. After the Southern Pacific Railroad came to the community in 1891 and the Hookston Winery began buying grapes at Hookston station (at the junction of today's Bancroft and Hookston roads) from Ygnacio Valley vineyardists, Pleasant Hill farmers also planted wine grapes.

As recently as 1898, 2,000 acres of Pleasant Hill land grew a crop in a single parcel. That year the California Beet Sugar Company (CBSC) grew beets on the flats between Hookston and Pacheco, hiring 600 Japanese laboreres to farm that alluvial soil.

Orchards and vineyards covered Pleasant Hill's undulating landscape in 1900. Ida Dukes Kutz Collection

Left to right: Lucy Dukes, her husband, Pleasant Hills pioneer William Dukes, Nettie Boss and May Dukes Hall, ca. 1914. Ida Dukes Kutz Collection

Pleasant Hill pioneer Edward Rodgers, his wife Letitia, daughter and granddaughter at their farm on the west side of Pleasant Hill Road. Rodgers came in 1870. Ca. 1890. Pleasant Hill Historical Society

Pleasant Hill's Farmer's Market was the first retail store not located on a farm. Ca. 1921. The market was located at the intersection of Boyd Road and Contra Costa Boulevard, where the monument is in 1986. Pleasant Hill Historical Society

Such heavy crops of beets grew on this land the CBSC delivered as many as twenty carloads a day to its loading platform at Hookston.

The CSBC gave up farming the land after the disastrous floods of 1899. February storms that year washed out the seed as well as roads all over the county.

The ranch manager, Robert N. Burgess, wrote in his memoirs about farming for the company:

"There was one picture [he wished he had saved] of 40 four-horse teams working in one field—160 head of fine horses and their equipment.

"We built levees to contain flood waters in a one-hundred foot wide channel. The flats many years ago were marshes, but the farms up the valley suffered much erosion over the years and the soil washed down by flood waters deposited in the Pacheco marshes until they were built up to the extent that in places we found three fences, one built on top of the other. It was fine alluvial soil . . . We had about 2,000 acres to plow and seed.

" . . . did not turn out as well as expected as there were large deposits of salt and alkali . . . in places."

But the pressure of increased population prevailed.

Robert N. Burgess bought his employer's land and subdivided it, and between 1900 and 1902 people eagerly bought his five- to ten-acre parcels. In the 1910 census tabulators tallied 330 persons—men, women, and children—living in Pleasant Hill.

By 1912 the only county-maintained roads were Pleasant Hill, Paso Nogal, Boyd and Hookston. Nevertheless, thirty-four students found their way across the fields and attended the grammar school built that year on Vessing property on Murderous Creek.

While guns were booming on European battlefields in 1917, many local men died there. Sheriff R. R. Veale conceived the idea of erecting a monument to honor them. By war's end a total of seventy-seven Contra Costa County men and women had lost their lives fighting for their country. The monument, designed by Clifford White and sculpted by Wallace Snelgrove, cost $35,000. To raise the necessary funds, Sheriff Veale stumped the county for donations. He succeeded, and a group of citizens chose the intersection of two prominent roads for the monument's site: Redwood Road (first Pacheco Road and now Contra Costa Boulevard) and Victory Road (now Monument Boulevard). The monument was dedicated on December 17, 1927. Some years later, when automobile traffic required an intersection free of obstructions, movers brought the memorial to its present location, one block south of its original site.

In the 1930s Pleasant Hill consisted of six farms between fifty and ninety acres and five that were over one hundred acres.

But down along Pacheco Road the first glimmer of businesses came to light. Probably the first retail store opened in September 1921, the open-air Pleasant Hill Farmer's Market, opposite the monument. The next business, a lumber yard, was opened by the E. K. Wood Lumber Company one mile north of Geary Road. The third was a garage which sold gasoline from a square tank on wheels. The buggy, as these dispensing vehicles were known, consisted of a tank, about a three-foot cube, with a hand pump on top.

For the next twenty years little change took place in Pleasant Hill. However, the first airport in the central county open to private flyers opened in Pleasant Hill in 1934.

In that year Dr. Samuel Sherman, a San Francisco surgeon and a private operator, financed Sherman Field on land which is now the Sherman Oaks Subdivision. Its boundaries are State Route 24, Monument Boulevard, and Cleopatra Drive. Because our military resources were being readied in 1941, the war department stepped in then, taking over the field for use in instructing fledgling pilots in both instrument and flight operations. Sherman Field closed on December 31, 1950, to become a subdivision.

Subdividers targeted in on Pleasant Hill farms when a deluge of World War II veterans and workers in the closing defense plants came looking for homes. The price for the farm land was so attractive to developers that one after another opened subdivisions. The homes they built sold for as little as $7,500 with only a $250 down payment required. By 1950 the demand had raised the price of the average home to $9,000.

The developers of the Gregory Gardens tract built 1,261 houses between 1949 and 1959. A total of 8,000 people lived in 2,000 homes in the new subdivisions, including Sherman Oaks and Fair Oaks. They began their shopping in the Gregory Gardens shopping center, the central county's second shopping center, when it opened with the P-X Market as its centerpiece of eleven stores in November 1949.

Across the street from the P-X Market, Pleasant Hill's first post office, a branch of the Concord office, opened its doors in 1953.

In 1951 the voters committed themselves to a park, recreation and parkway district, and a three-pool swimming facility opened on a ten-acre site on Gregory Lane in 1956.

Continuing heavy rains in April 1958 flooded Walnut Creek and areas along the creek's lower course. Row boats navigated many city streets, and at one time four-foot-high waves washed against some exposed walls in Gregory Gardens. Officials evacuated 1,000 residents from their homes, and, fortunately, no lives were lost. At that time the population total for all of Pleasant Hill came to about thirty thousand people.

Meantime the Pleasant Hill High School had opened in 1953 with Arthur Blake as its first principal. At the opening his faculty totaled sixty-nine.

In 1961, 5,407 Pleasant Hill voters cast their ballots in favor of incorporation, and the act became effective on November 14, 1961. Leland M. Watson became the new city's first city manager.

Pleasant Hill became the home of three institutions which affected many Contra Costa residents in one way or another. The first appealed to golfers, the second to student pilots and the third to many thousands of World War II veterans and high school students.

The first formed in 1925, two years before Charles Lindberg flew solo to Paris from North America and five years before the Great Depression. In that year a small group of California-Hawaiian Sugar refinery workers and a few Martinez businessmen formed what they called the Contra Costa Golf Club and laid out a golf course on thin soil over hard pan on a Pleasant Hill farm.

They divided the approximately one hundred-acre farm into homesites which surrounded the course, and space for nine additional holes they hoped one day to build. By promoting the future value of a membership, the early members sold 150 more. However, the special assessments made to improve the course and the hard times of the early 1930s swiftly cut the number of paid-up golfers to forty. Even fifteen years later, in 1945, only fifty-seven families made up the club's roster. They managed to put a second nine holes into play on July 4, 1950, and now in 1986 the membership list totals 517.

Thirty years after founding the golf club, the members built a 5,200-square-foot clubhouse. Now closed to new members, all the building sites are in the hands of the family memberships. The non-profit organization, built by volunteers, operates very much as its members planned over thirty years ago.

The Japanese military command surrendered aboard the *U.S.S. Missouri* in 1945, and our soldiers

The Pleasant Hill School, 1910. The site was on the east side of Pleasant Hill Road, south of Oak Park, on what is now Vessing Drive. Note the four horses being ridden in the school yard. Ida Dukes Kutz Collection

Every Pleasant Hill dweller depended on his windmill, in the early days, for pumping water, and on his elevated tank (inside the tankhouse) for pressure. Pictured is the facility on Cherry Lane, just off Geary Road, Ca. 1975. Henry Greenfield Collection

The boys are on the site of the future Pleasant Hill Park. This view looks north from Gregory Lane. Ca. 1956. Henry Greenfield Collection

In the 1920s virtually every teenager yearned to imitate the famous race car driver Barney Oldfield and to impress his female friends with his own cut-down. Here Hiram Hall of Pleasant Hill sits in his after he has removed the running boards, fenders, windshield and rear half of a Ford Model T touring car, ca. 1923. Ida Dukes Kutz Collection

and sailors returned home, some to take up their unfinished educations. To aid them, Congress had passed the GI Bill. Under its terms the federal government agreed to pay a man or woman a stipend for seeking higher education. However, for those in Contra Costa County there was no college to attend.

In December 1948 the voters approved the establishment of the Contra Costa Community College District. The district purchased a 100-acre site in Pleasant Hill and commenced construction in the spring of 1949. Contractors completed the buildings in 1951, and that year the Diablo Valley College (DVC) opened its doors to students.

In addition to the customary liberal arts program which characterizes most colleges, the DVC campus of the Contra Costa College District offers subjects which lead to early employment. Examples are hotel and restaurant management, dental lab technology, construction technology, apparel design, air conditioning and refrigeration, and the administration of justice.

DVC, with its two-year curriculum, is a statewide leader in transferring students to the University of California campuses, especially to Berkeley.

Now, thirty-five years after its founding, this Pleasant Hill college facility has approximately seventeen thousand students in its daytime and evening classes.

Bayshore Properties, a San Francisco commercial developer, opened the first shopping mall in Contra Costa County, in Pleasant Hill. On a 160-acre site between Contra Costa Boulevard and U.S. Highway I-680, the developer built the Sun Valley Shopping

Pleasant Hill's travelers first boarded the Southern Pacific trains at this station in 1891. Hookston station was at the intersection of Bancroft Road and Hookston Road. Beginning in 1911, when the Oakland & Antioch Railway connected with the Santa Fe at McAvoy, Pleasant Hill's San Francisco-bound passengers boarded the electric line at Las Juntas, the crossing of the electric and steam trains. Louis L. Stein, Jr. Collection

Above, this is the 360-acre Patrick Roche farm in North Pleasant Hill in 1979, looking south. Walnut Creek may be seen slightly left of center, in the distance. Henry Greenfield Collection
Below, Gregory Village, 1950. Note the orchard across Contra Costa Boulevard. Pleasant Hill Historical Society

Sherman Field's hangars faced Contra Costa Boulevard a quarter mile north of Monument Boulevard. This Pleasant Hill field opened in 1934 and closed at the end of World War II. Note the absence of commercial activity, except for the drive-in movie at the extreme right, on Contra Costa Boulevard. Vallie Jo Whitfield Collection

Center with 1.5 million square feet of floor space in 1967.

Tragedy struck Concord two evenings before Christmas in 1985. On the foggy night of December 23, a twin engine plane fell out of the sky, crashing through the roof of the Sun Valley Mall, through the upper level of stores down to the lower shopping floor. Thousands were doing their last minute shopping at the time. The three occupants of the Beechcraft died on impact, and four shoppers died soon after. Seventy-six persons suffered burns from the flaming fuel as it spewed out of the ruptured tank.

Majors and Dorman's Ranch. From Smith & Elliott's "Illustrations of Contra Costa Co."

WALNUT CREEK

Disappointed gold seekers, successful farmers from eastern states, and even sailors tired of voyages sometimes lasting more than six months, all flocked like homing pigeons to California's rich farm land soon after Congress declared statehood in 1850.

Known as The Corners until early in the 1860s, at the intersection of an east-west wagon road on the stagecoach route from Martinez to San Jose, the area now known as Walnut Creek lay in the shadow of bustling Alamo and the shipping point, Pacheco.

Farmers bought the fertile soil all along the west side of the creek, Arroyo de las Nueces (Walnut Creek), from Pacheco to The Corners. Seventy-five dollars bought twenty-five acres of the best land from the widow, Mrs. Welch. On the other side of the stream, a grandson of the grantee of all of Ygnacio Valley raised his price in the mid-1850s to ten dollars an acre and sold away his heritage.

The single store at The Corners didn't draw the trade the two at Alamo did. At first the Martinez to San Jose road followed the creek bank, and only after twenty years (in 1870) did the owner of the farm land which lay to the north of the road to Lafayette subdivide what became North Main Street. From 1870 to 1880 he sold only two or three lots a year, so little did the few townsmen think of them. In 1878 the Chinaman who established the first laundry in the village paid only thirty-five dollars for his North Main Street lot.

Until the 1880s, on land surrounding the town, farmers grew grain to sell and hay to feed their ani-

Looking south on Main Street from Botelho, ca. 1883. Courtesy Louis L. Stein, Jr.

mals. By the 1890s almost half the farmers had planted fruit orchards in order to earn more money than they were earning from their grain. As farmers spent more money more merchants established themselves in town. By 1890 a still more profitable crop, grapes, grew on nearly a third of the best land. Wineries competed for the wine grapes, and farmers with table grapes sold them in cities around the Bay Area. Again, slowly but surely, more merchants moved in. Then in the early 1900s farmers began to plant walnut groves. When the Volstead Act became law in 1920, prohibiting the manufacture of alcoholic beverages, most of the farmers who still had wine grapes pulled out their vines and they too established walnut groves.

For the first twenty years of the community, 1850-1870, inhabitants illuminated their homes with tallow or wax candles. Then from about 1870 to 1910 they burned coal oil (kerosene). In 1910 electricity came

Oak Grove Grammar School, Walnut Creek's first, was founded in 1854. This one-room school was built on the northeast corner of Oak Grove Road and Ygnacio Valley Road. After sixty years a two-room building with indoor toilets replaced this original structure. Ca. 1890. Contra Costa County Historical Society

down from power houses in the Sierra. Now, at night, people could see to read without straining their eyes. No street lights went up for a number of years, but porch lights on most town houses meant a person could stroll around at night and see where he was going.

Household water came from windmill pumps before electricity, and in some cases from hand-pumped wells, but now electric pumps slowly replaced some of the old systems. Many people kept their old windmills and pumps; they cost virtually nothing to oper-

ate, and electric motors and their power could be a financial burden.

An electric train came to town in 1911. For two years it ran from Walnut Creek to a connection with the Santa Fe at McAvoy. In 1913 swift, clean, fast trains carried local residents to San Francisco in just an hour and a quarter, including a twenty-minute ferry boat ride. Previously, ever since 1891, the Southern Pacific steam train had taken as long as two and a half hours to deliver its passengers to San Francisco's Ferry Building.

Even in 1915 Walnut Creek used no street lights and of course had no "Stop" signs. Not even a service station existed here. All the town streets were either dirt or gravel-surfaced. In 1914 residents had incorporated their village. At the time, automobiles were slowly replacing horses. After all, residents and farmers alike had been raised in families who knew no other means of locomotion than horse-drawn carriages and wagons. Not even when the city paved Main Street in 1921 did those vehicles disappear.

During the two decades between 1920 and 1940, Walnut Creek gained an air of sophistication. In a way, radio broadcasting helped. Station KGO, the first broadcaster in the Bay Area, brought news of the world before newspapers and magazines reached some areas of the rural community. One enterprising citizen who worked for a moving picture theater in Oakland showed movies here once a week in the Town Hall. These films often displayed wealthy glamorous lives which local farmers and merchants otherwise saw only in magazines.

All through the twenties and thirties families moved out to the area surrounding Walnut Creek. Farmers stung by losses in income during the Great Depression willingly sold off parts of their farms to buyers who offered what they needed: money. Again the population in the area grew some more and so did the number of merchants. Though it grew slowly, it grew steadily, and the increased population created problems. The 1920 count in Walnut Creek came to 528 citizens; the 1940 tally was 1,587. The city sewer system couldn't handle the increase and neither could the municipal water supply. Then in 1937 the Caldecott Tunnel opened, and more new residents poured through to take up living in the already-crowded community. Somehow everyone survived. The town merchants prospered. And then, suddenly, "Pearl Harbor."

Long before that tragic 1941 event the walnut crops in the area accounted for a big part of the community's prosperity. The Walnut Growers Association operated a large processing plant which covered both sides of Civic Drive, all the way north from and including the Civic Arts Theater (the walnut ware-

The west side of North Main Street, looking north from Mount Diablo Boulevard. Ca. 1872.

Main Street at Mount Diablo Boulevard, looking north, 1986. Courtesy Fred Emanuels

house) to the middle of the Grower's Square complex.

But what happened to Walnut Creek because of Pearl Harbor is best illustrated by pointing to the more than one hundred Greyhound buses which daily carried army trainees to Camp Stoneman at Pittsburg. From Greyhound buses and army convoys young men and women from all over America saw the walnut groves, the green hills six months of the year, and the golden grassy slopes the remaining months, and fell in love with Walnut Creek and its surroundings.

North Main Street looking north from Mount Diablo Boulevard. Two horse drawn buggies pass on a quiet day in 1918. Duncan Street comes in at the right with the San Ramon Valley Bank on the corner. Across Duncan is Rogers Hotel. Contra Costa County Historical Society/Stein Collection

North Main Street looking south from Bonanza. The town hall is on the corner of North Main and Bonanza, at extreme right. Walnut Creek Meat Company's windmill is over the tree tops at extreme left. Ca. 1901. Louis L. Stein, Jr. Collection

When World War II ended, many of the discharged veterans came back to Walnut Creek to make homes for themselves. But before they could occupy new houses, two fundamental services needed expansion: water and sewer services. Before Pearl Harbor, Walnut Creek's water supply faced periods of drought. The town's sewer farm (large septic tanks) threatened public health even before World War I. Central Contra Costa County Sanitary District expanded its service area, hooking up to Walnut Creek in September 1948, and gradually subdividers connected to the district's lines.

Walnut Creek City Attorney John Nejedly led the drive to bring first class water to the city. As a result of a 1951 Act sponsored by State Senator George Miller, East Bay Municipal District began supplying clean, pure mountain water to the city in December 1952.

Little more than Main Street stores existed before 1950. The solution was to enclose both creeks in large box-like concrete culverts. The city enclosed Las Trampas Creek from where it ran under Main Street over to where it joined San Ramon Creek, under the present Bank of America parking lot. This permitted construction of Broadway Plaza, and in 1951 J. C. Penney and Sears Roebuck moved into twin stores at the corner of South Main Street and Broadway Plaza.

At the south end of the shopping center H. C. Capwell began construction of its store in early 1953 and moved into it in March 1954.

The city did the same with San Ramon Creek from where it flows under Newell Avenue, underground to its junction with Las Trampas Creek to become Walnut Creek, where it flowed north as an open stream, keeping Broadway from being a through avenue. In 1971-72 the Contra Costa County Public Works Department enclosed Walnut Creek as far as the eastern edge of Broadway, permitting the city to pave Broadway and create the thoroughfare it is today.

Developers built scores of apartment houses in the decade between 1965 and 1975 as the city improved streets such as Creekside Drive and Civic Drive. The

Looking north on Locust Street before 1900. Louis L. Stein, Jr. Collection

rush to live in Walnut Creek mushroomed in this decade. BART trains, which commenced running in May 1973, brought more residents to fill all existing vacancies and continued bringing them as fast as contractors built new residential space.

Old time residents (anyone who came before you did) cringed at the increase in population. Twenty-four hundred and twenty inhabitants in 1950 grew to 10,000 in 1960, 40,000 in 1970, and 60,000 fifteen years later. Where formerly heads of families went to work over the hills to the Bay cities, the reverse became a new trend by the mid-1980s. Workers came to work *from* San Francisco to occupy new high-rise office buildings here.

The 1975-1985 decade earned the label, "The Age of High-Rise Offices in Walnut Creek." The three-story H. C. Capwell building held the honor as Walnut Creek's tallest building until the Security Pacific Bank built its eight-story high-rise at the corner of South Main and Newell Avenue in 1969. When California Drive, from Newell to North Main Street, became a thoroughfare upon completion of the pav-

ing in 1970, it permitted the construction of the Fidelity Savings headquarters at 1990 California Drive. Fidelity occupied this ten-story structure in 1971. Two years later Broadway became a thoroughfare when work on the street all the way from Newell on the south to Pine on the north was completed. For a decade residents lived with the two high-rises and with the two thoroughfares which eased the heavy traffic burden on North Main Street.

At the time the city incorporated in 1914, the closest semblance to sophistication of a member of the community appeared when someone drove a *matched* team in silver-decorated harness down Main Street. In 1985 that same man's grandson may be driving his imported sports car down the same street, now paved.

On any morning in those early days almost every man walking down Main Street wore either overalls or work shirt and pants. Now, these clothes are as scarce as a Model T Ford.

For Walnut Creek, coming of age means a high-rise building standing shoulder to shoulder with another, casting a shadow on virtually every down-

This Sacramento Northern train is between downtown Walnut Creek and Saranap (Tice Valley Boulevard) on today's Olympic Boulevard. Ca. 1937. Moraga Historical Society

Dick and Alta Lommel's creamery and bus station was at the northeast corner of North Main Street and Civic from 1939 to 1974.
Courtesy Dick Lommel

town street. No city in Contra Costa County has achieved the preponderance of office space Walnut Creek had built by 1985. Now, in the final fifteen years of the twentieth century, Walnut Creek is not suburban, it is a center. Separated from San Francisco Bay communities by a range of hills, Walnut Creek is now the hub of a developed financial and residential society.

Builders constructed more than a million square feet of office space in just two years, 1984 and 1985. And, a five-story building, costing an estimated $55 million, with 165 rooms and a 600-car parking garage, is under construction as this is written. Also, the $150 million Town Center project, estimated in 1985, is gaining approval from several of the city committees reviewing the plans. But, as large as it is, it is only one more immense block of concrete dimming the memory of The Corners.

Looking south on North Main Street from Civic Drive, ca. 1940. The El Rey Theater and the El Rey Market were torn down in 1984 for the construction of this Civic Plaza Building. Walnut Creek Historical Society

Looking south on North Main Street from Civic Drive, ca. 1986. Courtesy Fred Emanuels

Above, Walnut Creek's North Main Street on the afternoon of April 2, 1958. Walnut Creek Historical Society
Below, on April 2, 1958, the creeks in the Walnut Creek area ran over their banks. This view of the south side of Broadway Plaza was taken at half past three in the afternoon. Walnut Creek Historical Society

Above, downtown Walnut Creek in 1986. Fred Emanuels Photo
Below, Walnut Creek highrises from North Main Street, ca. 1986.
Courtesy Fred Emanuels

Arthur Williams came to Walnut Creek in 1877 and started the Walnut Creek Meat Company. When he sold out to Foskett, Ellworthy and Keller just after the turn of the century, he became the town constable. Here he is patrolling Lafayette Road, as Mount Diablo Boulevard was known then, on a winter day. Williams died in 1915. Contra Costa County Historical Society/Stein Collection

Residence of Antonio Silva De Botello, Walnut Creek.
From Smith & Elliott's "Illustrations of Contra Costa Co."

Residence of James T. Walker, Ygnacio Valley.
From Smith & Elliott's "Illustrations of Contra Costa Co."

Residence of William C. Prince, Ygnacio Valley.
From Smith & Elliott's "Illustrations of Contra Costa Co."

ALAMO

Aunt Polly Mitchell, at a camp meeting at "the ol' swimmin' hole," just up the creek from the Mitchell farm, watched as a cattle rustler was being led into the creek for a spiritual bath. Just at the solemn moment, doubting his conversion, she let her true feelings get the better of her. She shrieked, "Take him below the falls, boys. Take him below the falls. I don't want his sins washin' down into the water my cattle have to drink!"

In November 1851, Aunt Polly and her husband, William, came to the valley now filled by the community of Alamo. With another family, they moved into a two-story adobe house on a knoll in what is now the center of the town.

The John M. Jones family, who shared the adobe, established the first postoffice between Martinez and Mission San Jose. In later years, Mrs. Jones recalled handling the mail in the early years, beginning in 1852: "We had no stamps then, nor envelopes. We wrote our letters, folded and sealed them with sealing wax, and then paid ten cents for delivery." A mail carrier rode his horse from Martinez to Pueblo San Jose twice a week.

Two adobes, only a mile and a half apart, were the first structures of any consequence in Alamo. Francisco Garcia built the one occupied by the Mitchell and Jones families in 1848. The same year Jose Miguel Garcia built the other. It was on Austin Lane just north of Stone Valley Road, about a mile and a half east of the village. Sixty-one-year-old Silas Stone moved there in 1853. Stone sent his cattle, which he had driven across the plains, out onto his 800 acres.

Even before Silas Stone came, families settled down and established themselves on farms of all sizes. Merchants put up stores. The first was Henry Hoffman's and the second, established the same year, was George Englemire's.

Hoffman is better remembered for his "Henry's Hotel." He constructed a store abutting the south side of his hotel. His buildings faced the Danville Road on the southeast corner of Stone Valley Road. Across Danville Road, his competitor, George Englemire, opened his general merchandise store.

Henry Hoffman built the Alamo landmark, Henry's Hotel, in 1853 on the east side of Danville Boulevard at the corner of Stone Valley Road. Wreckers tore it down in 1953.

Original Stone Valley Road Bridge near Alamo Square, ca. 1900. San Ramon Valley Historical Society

The hotel was a man's establishment, although women stayed there too, staying to themselves in their second floor rooms. The bar, kitchen and dining room were on the lower floor. The bar, the busiest room in the hotel, was big enough to house a billiard table. Brass cuspidors, at least four of them, were conveniently placed around the room. Patrons of the hotel used out-houses, there being no toilets inside the building.

One of Alamo's most generous citizens was farmer August Hemme. Born in Prussia, he came to New York two years before the gold rush. He came to California in 1848 and found his way to the Feather River in May 1849. He found gold and kept it long enough to come to Alamo in 1852 and buy 3,000 acres. He farmed there for eleven years and then formed a firm in San Francisco, Reihn Hemme and Company, Assayers.

August contributed to a number of religious groups without regard for their denominations. Among his contributions, one stands out—he gave three acres of land on the west side of Danville Road, a mile south of the village, for a school of higher learning.

In March 1859, a number of concerned citizens formed the Contra Costa Educational Association, and this group built the three-story Union Academy. The Reverend David McClure headed the faculty of

this day school and boarding school. Thus Alamo holds the distinction of having the first school with classes beyond the eighth grade in both the Diablo Valley and San Ramon Valley.

Residents of Alamo were also the first to appeal for a tunnel through the Oakland hills. The initial meeting came in 1860 to stir up interest in the route from Alamo to Moraga and thence through the hills. Virtually every ten years thereafter a new group agitated for the same purpose, to no avail until 1901, when Alameda County and the Merchant's Exchange of Oakland began drilling the old high-level tunnel.

An organization founded in Alamo in January 1858 and still active today is the Alamo Masonic Lodge. Fifty-five members rented the upper floor of Cohen's Store, which was in a two-story brick building, the first brick structure in the town. The 1868 earthquake destroyed the building, and the lodge moved to Danville. Five years later it moved again, to the second floor of James Stow's new building in Walnut Creek.

Once loggers stopped cutting redwoods in the canyon area and moved away, Alamo became a prominent village in the county, second only to Martinez. All through the 1850s and 1860s it remained a commercially busy community. Socially prominent people maintained homes nearby, including Squire Silas

Alamo Post Office at the northeast corner of Danville Boulevard and Las Trampas Road.
San Ramon Valley Historical Society

The first elementary school in Alamo. Contra Costa County Historical Society/Stein Collection

Stone, alcalde for the district prior to statehood; John M. Jones, a postmaster, county superintendent of schools and an early county assessor; James West, another county assessor; and August Hemme, philanthropist and San Francisco businessman.

During the 1860s Pacheco, because of its warehouses and docks, newspaper, flour mill, race track, and farm machinery plant, grew in importance, overshadowing Alamo.

Alamo maintained some prominence in the 1870s. Its citizens held meetings, circulated petitions, and collected donations for a narrow gauge railway to connect them with Martinez. Again they renewed their drive for the county to build a road to Oakland

via Moraga and a tunnel through the Berkeley hills. They collected money and turned in petitions but to no avail.

One Alamo farmer may have earned the right to be named the father of Contra Costa County's walnut industry. All through recorded time, black walnut trees had grown along stream banks in the central county. However, the shells of their nuts were so hard to crack and the meat so difficult to extract that the nuts had little or no commercial value.

In 1873, Myron Ward Hall grafted a cutting of the soft-shell Persian variety to a native black walnut trunk. In time the resulting harvest was so abundant

Ladies in fancy hats gathered at Hemme Park, Alamo, on
the east side of Danville Highway near Deodora Lane.
San Ramon Valley Historical Society

that farmers came from miles around to see Hall's successful soft-shell walnut tree.

He gave away scions to scores of farmers who called on him, and their resulting successes ultimately gave birth to the walnut industry in the county.

Farmers planted the hardy black walnut rootstock, and when seedlings had attained several years' growth, they grafted an English soft-shell variety to them.

Alamo's fertile soil furnished its farmers with heavy orchard and row crops. Stock raisers of Portuguese descent bought the principally hilly land in the area up Livorna Road and across Miranda to Stone Valley, and farther out that road. The Ventura, Macedo, Gaspar, and Botelho families were just a few. This general area became known as "Portugee Gulch."

The site of the Round Hill Golf and Country Club was once grazing land, some of it owned by the Mello family. In 1957, realtor Harlan S. Geldermann and Lou Spott envisioned a country club to be the drawing card for a subdivision which would include 100 lots and a three par golf course. Geldermann sold lots to local contractors, many of whom built homes on speculation.

Over the years since, thanks to foresight and quality planning, Round Hill has attracted affluent buyers. Its golf course has been expanded to tournament size acceptable to the Professional Golf Association. Over four hundred quality homes have been built on the former grazing land. The club membership includes over one thousand families.

70

DANVILLE

Pioneers who rode the trail all the way from San Ramon to Walnut Creek followed the west bank of San Ramon Creek. First trod only by Indians, later packed with ox carts and stagecoaches, this winding road became the nucleus of each village along its path.

But the earliest arrivals in the San Ramon Valley were farmers, who sought the open expanse of large fields for grazing stock and sowing grain. Those who came first located out in the valleys, Green, Sycamore and Tassajara.

Messrs. Boyd and Field probably came before any others. Both settled in Green Valley in 1850.

Leonard Eddy, who also came in 1850, selected a site in Sycamore Valley. The cabin he built the year he arrived survived wind, rain and earthquake, and is still standing after 135 years.

Over in Tassajara, Daniel R. McPherson established his farm in 1851. Several of his descendants still live in the area.

Not until 1852 did the first settlers come to the future site of Danville. They were brothers Daniel,

Sycamore Valley home of Leonard Eddy, built in 1852, is still standing. Photo 1960.
Contra Costa County Historical Society/Roy Bloss Collection

Hartz Avenue, Danville, ca. 1880. San Ramon Valley Historical Society

for whom the town was named, and Andrew Inman. When Daniel settled along the creek, his neighboring farmers called the place Inmanville. He declined the honor and they called it Danville instead.

Though he arrived in 1852, he didn't buy the land he settled on until 1857. It included the acreage facing the road which wound its way along San Ramon Creek's west bank. On it, Inman built a shop for a blacksmith, as sorely needed then as a service station is today. The site of the shop would be on Front Street near the corner of Diablo Road today.

Daniel Inman raised sheep and cattle beside accommodating merchants wanting to establish their businesses near the blacksmith. In 1858 the first Danville Hotel was built across Diablo Road from Inman's, where a Mobil service station is today. A grocer came and built himself a home, only the second dwelling in the village. He sold groceries from his home.

Within a few years the crooked path of Front Street, the only thoroughfare through the village, became the home of a post office, a temporary school, the Odd Fellows Hall and a Grange Hall.

When the first grammar school was built it was put up on Front Street where #279 is today, around the corner from Tiger Alley, where houses of dubious virtue were clustered. Tiger Alley is now known as East Prospect Avenue.

For the next few years Danville hugged Front Street. It was a muddy road in winter and a dusty one in summer. In the countryside and in the village everyone depended on candles for light, a wood-burning kitchen stove for heat, and their horses for transportation.

The Grange Hall, the farmers' cooperative meeting place, became the social center. Only after Danville's first church was built in 1876 did the Grange Hall share its importance as the town's meeting place. That year the Presbyterian Church opened its doors.

John Hartz became the area's first subdivider. He capitalized on the Southern Pacific Railroad's construction of its San Ramon Valley branch. The line branched off the main line at Avon, four miles east of Martinez, running south through Concord, Walnut Creek, and Danville, to its terminus at Limerick (later named San Ramon).

Hartz plotted six blocks incorporating Railroad Avenue, Hartz Avenue, Prospect Avenue, Church Street and School Street. With the station and the new Danville Hotel (the first burned down in 1873) both on Railroad Avenue, the trains started bringing passengers from Oakland and San Francisco, and this street became the main thoroughfare.

By the turn of the century coal oil lamps had replaced candles, but wood-burning kitchen stoves supplied all the heat, and horses were still the only

Front Street was a busy Danville street in the 1860s.
San Ramon Valley Historical Society

The Danville Livery Stable. San Ramon Valley Historical
Society

source of transportation. Out in the valleys peach, pear, plum and prune orchards were yielding heavy crops. Besides carrying fresh and dried fruit to market, the railroad also loaded grain and hay, both in great demand by San Franciscans for their horses.

In the first decade of the 1900s, in balmy weather Danville's Ramona Park attracted revelers and picnickers to its twelve-acre grove of buckeyes and maples. Its dance platform and tables welcomed customers on April 19, 1906, just one day after San Francisco's earthquake and fire.

Girls and young ladies defied tradition when they dressed for an outing at Ramona Park. Black or gray had been their mothers' colors, but now, in 1906, they rode over the dusty roads in pink, lavender, or blue dresses. They had ruffles on their skirts and parasols.

The usual evening dances usually concluded with a supper spread out on picnic tables.

Boys and girls had no high school to attend when they finished the eighth grade in the Danville Grammar School. Boys went to work on their father's farm or in his store or shop after finishing the eight classes. Girls shared full responsibility with their mothers until they attracted a suitor and married. All that changed in Danville in 1910, when Harvey Eddy's cottage became the first San Ramon High School. The first year it attracted thirty-eight pupils who were instructed by two teachers. About a dozen of them rode on benches in a farmer's wagon from Walnut Creek. Although Concord's Mount Diablo High School had opened in 1901, no public transportation existed from Walnut Creek. But when the Oakland

The Danville Emporium. San Ramon Valley Historical Society

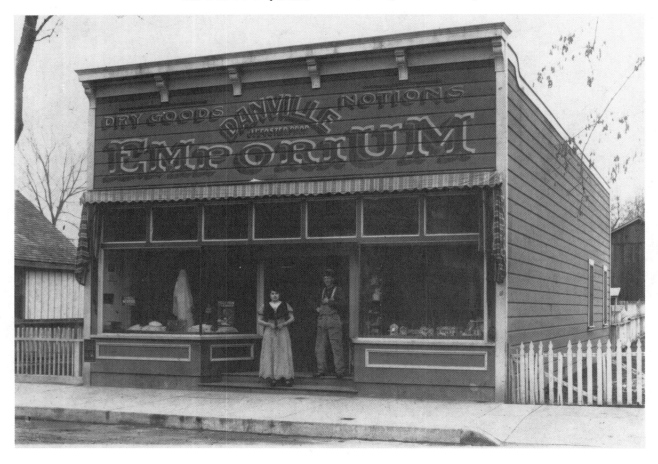

A Southern Pacific freight train backing up to pick up empty box-cars at Danville's warehouses, ca. 1900. San Ramon Valley Historical Society

and Antioch electric line started running to Concord in 1911, Walnut Creek students began going there.

In 1912, only twenty-six students enrolled. During the years 1914-1916 the high school held classes in the Odd Fellows Hall, still on Front Street.

In its first sixty years Danville advanced from a typical country village without a river or port, with no mineral resources, and of no political importance, to a maturing town. It had telephone service as far back as 1882, but no electricity for thirty more years.

Danville's first library was started by Lillian Close in her home in 1913. Street lights were installed in 1915, when the streets were still unpaved.

Until June 1914, visitors to or from San Francisco boarded the Southern Pacific steam train for the two-and-a-half-hour ride. In that month the Oakland, Antioch and Eastern Railway, an electric line, started running trains from Danville to Walnut Creek, where after transferring to a main line train, the passengers arrived in San Francisco one hour and fifty-five minutes later—a schedule not conducive to commuting. It is no wonder that ten years later the electric line ceased running on the Danville branch.

Danville supported its merchants. The Sunset Nursery started doing business in 1906 and closed seventy-eight years later. Some later merchants which old-timers will recall are: the Danville Emporium, the Wiester Hay Warehouse Company; and the news-papers, first the *Danville Sentinel* and later the *Danville Journal.*

The earliest super market was Acree's at Prospect and Hartz. Acree was a grocer who carried charge accounts. The store became Varsity Market in 1951. Over at Danville Square, developed by Harold Root and Maury Marott, the P-X Market opened in November 1945. It is now a liquor store. Manual telephones came to Danville in 1882 and dial phones reached town in 1952.

The community has had excellent citizen involvement over the years, and two women's clubs should be mentioned. The Danville Women's Club was founded back in 1911 and remained without its own building until 1955, when the members moved into the present clubhouse on Linda Mesa.

The Danville-Alamo Garden Club, organized in 1973, serves both communities. Its members supply fresh flowers to rest homes and donate plants and trees to the town's parks.

The San Francisco-Oakland Bay Bridge opened in 1936 and the Caldecott Tunnel a year later. The expected rush of homeseekers into the San Ramon Valley turned out to be only a trickle. During the intervening four years before World War II only a few hundred home buyers came to Danville.

At the war's end Danville had only 2,000 residents. However, principally because of the improved water service brought to the valley in the 1950s by the East Bay Municipal Utility District, and the service of the Central Contra Costa County Sanitary District at the same time, the valley did grow. The 1985 census of the town revealed a fourteen-fold increase from 1945, to 28,000 persons.

Danville's Southern Pacific Station, ca. 1910. San Ramon Valley Historical Society

The Oakland, Antioch and Eastern's Toonerville Trolley *returning from Diablo to Saranap along Hartz Avenue, Danville. This branch operated from March 12, 1914 until March 1, 1924. Ca. 1923.* Contra Costa County Historical Society/Stein Collection

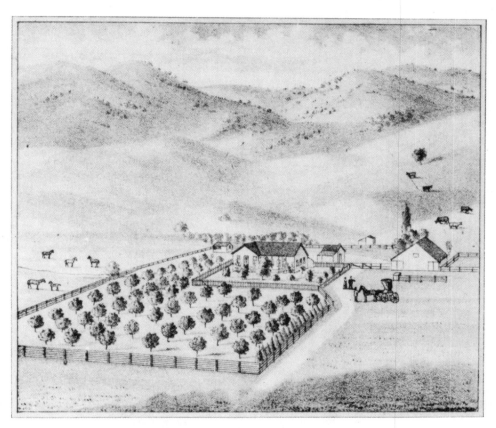

Residence of M. M. Fairfield, Sycamore Valley.
From Smith & Elliott's "Illustrations of Contra Costa Co."

Residence of Francis E. Matteson, Sycamore Valley.
From Smith & Elliott's "Illustrations of Contra Costa Co."

DIABLO

Anyone looking down from the top of Mount Diablo in the direction of Danville on a day in 1875 would have been distracted by the sight of a group of larger than ordinary farm buildings a few miles short of that village. A turret-capped five-story barn, immaculate in its white paint and green trim, stood apart from a two-story house, a classic structure which contained nine bedrooms besides the usual sitting room, dining room, office and kitchen. Oaks surrounded the house as if planted there to enhance its grandeur.

Numerous small buildings, sheds, barns, and a stable dotted the grounds. A "Billiard Hall" stood several hundred feet uphill from the house, with a bowling alley in its basement.

Riding down the dirt road the rider's horse would pick up its ears as it heard the neighing of stallions in their corrals. Roaming the ranch's fields were mares in foal with thoroughbred colts that would one day be trained for trotting races. A closer look would show one hundred horses sharing the pastures with nearly three hundred pedigreed cattle. Wheat, barley and hay grew on 2,400 acres, and 200 acres of orchard yielded pears, apricots, peaches and other fruits.

The "Big Four" of railroad fame owned the 10,000 acres in 1876, and successive owners cared for the property with fondness and money. Sometime after 1889 the owners named the property "Oakwood Park Stock Farm."

Several owners occupied the farm before 1913, but that year Robert N. Burgess, a young farm manager turned real estate speculator and developer, headed a group which bought it for $150,000. The young man, Danville-raised, had a grandiose idea for the property. He would tempt the rich among the hundreds of thousands coming to see the Panama-Pacific International Exposition that would open in San Francisco in eighteen months.

The view of Danville from the summit of Mount Diablo had fired his imagination ever since he'd walked the trail to that summit as a boy. He would drive his prospects for building sites at "Diablo," as he called his subdivision, to the mountain top, stirring their imaginations too, especially those of the flat-landers from the Ohio Valley and the plains states.

Burgess bought the land abutting the northeasterly border of his Oakwood Park Stock Farm all the way to the top of Mount Diablo. He already owned some of its northwesterly flank, starting from Ygnacio Valley.

He bought a steam-shovel and had its operator grade a road suitable for auto travel to the top of the mountain. That road completed, he had the machine's operator grade another down the mountain to Diablo.

He needed better transportation to get his prospects out from Oakland and San Francisco. At his urging, friends on the board of the new Oakland, Antioch and Eastern Railway extended its line to Diablo in 1914. He persuaded another friend, the president of the Pacific Telephone and Telegraph

Company, to string his company's line to the club-house he had made of the Billiard Hall and to the homesites he was offering for sale. The Pacific Gas and Electric Company also extended its 4,000-volt line the three miles from Danville.

Burgess made an inn of the old mansion. He offered memberships in his Mount Diablo Park Club at sixty dollars each, all of it refunded if the member bought a lot. He charged annual dues of twenty dollars. His building sites sold for $600 each and by 1916 fourteen homes were being lived in. That year the United States Post Office granted his request for a post office, making official the name he had chosen, "Diablo."

The following year the developer built the "Red Horse Tavern" and the "Chalet." The latter, an imposing three-story white wooden building, stood on a hill behind the inn and across from the clubhouse. It contained fourteen apartments. A long arched brick colonnade connected the Chalet with the inn. The golf course opened in 1916 with nine holes; a year later members and guests played the full eighteen.

Burgess's company debt grew and he worked hard to sell William Randolph Hearst a share of his acreage. Hearst obligated himself to advertise the Diablo lots in all of his newspapers but reneged on the understanding the two had worked out that he would put money into the property.

The Oakland, Antioch and Eastern ran its finest cars every weekend right up to Diablo, showing off the fine buildings, swimming lake and "tank," the tennis courts and stables. Among the railroad's crews and some of the press these special trains became known as the "Millionaire Specials."

Hearst's nationwide advertising and the deluxe trains notwithstanding, the building sites didn't sell. With restrictions put on the public when the United States declared war on Germany in 1917, the Burgess company's ability to pay its bills ended. It filed a petition of involuntary bankruptcy in 1919.

Over the next twenty years a succession of owners acquired the land. First the Mount Diablo Country Club operated the built-up area. The State of California took over the largest part, establishing the Mount Diablo State Park in April 1931.

Vehicles stopped to pay the toll collector at Diablo when entering the state park. San Ramon Valley Historical Society

Diablo Country Club, ca. 1917. San Ramon Valley Historical Society

This was the era of the Great Depression, and Diablo suffered from its effects too. Club membership dropped from 400 to 160. A small group of bondholders whose money had financed recent utility improvements foreclosed and became the new owners of the club. By 1938 they were operating in the black and the membership returned to its former high.

Three years later, after Pearl Harbor, gasoline rationing curtailed the number of visitors and part-time residents coming out to Diablo, and again the club ran deficits too big to survive. The solution came when two members bought out all the others and acquired the club and all its acreage. They sold forty-two acres at an average of $300 an acre but found no buyers for the rest of the property.

Lawrence Curtola stepped into the scene in 1948 and bought out the two owners. He operated the Diablo Country Club in the traditional style of such clubs until 1961. In the effort to stay out of the red he attracted large outside groups to hold their balls, dances, company parties, and regular luncheons at his facility. Horsemen's groups rented stable space from him and rode the nearby trails of the state park.

In 1961 the club members bought the club back from Curtola for $440,000 with funds raised from a mortgage. In 1974 they paid off this indebtedness. Still unincorporated, the community is self-sufficient. It has grown from a fashionable summer resort to an enclave of suburban homes showing permanence, their gardens matured by years of loving care, and their family club reeking with tradition.

Christian Wiedeman's Norris Canyon home, built in the 1850s and occupied by his great-granddaughter in 1986. Contra Costa County Historical Society/Roy Bloss Collection

SAN RAMON

The history of San Ramon has to be a recounting of the most abrupt change in any community in Contra Costa County. Within the last quarter of a century, farmers and their workers, probably fewer than two hundred in all of the area, have given way to as many as twenty-five thousand people who are employed in offices and stores.

Irish names identify many of the farmers who came to San Ramon between 1849 and 1860. These early arrivals acquired immense tracts of land. The first, Leo Norris, bought 4,450 acres in 1849 from Señor José Amador. He built a two-story house which eventually contained thirteen rooms.

In 1857, Joel Harlan, who at age twenty-eight bought 1,000 acres from Norris, built on the county line. He sold 718 acres to David Glass, who built a house on San Ramon Valley Boulevard in 1857 which still stands today, in 1986.

Also coming to the south end of the county in the early 1850s was another Irishman, James Dougherty. Altogether he bought 17,000 acres, some of it in Alameda County.

A mile to the north of Glass's site, Major Samuel Russell acquired 600 acres in 1852. Still farther north, across San Ramon Creek (Crow Canyon Road), William Meese purchased 320 acres. He and twenty-four-year-old Robert Baldwin ultimately accumulated 900 acres. Meese made news with his 1853 crop of onions. He is reported to have harvested 14,000 pounds from one acre of virgin soil.

Christian Wiedemann started his farm in the Nor-

H. C. Hurst operated this store from the mid-1890s until 1924. William C. Ferreira owned the store for the next forty years and for thirty-four years was San Ramon's postmaster. His son, William J. Ferreira, ran the San Ramon garage, next door to the store, from 1945 to 1963. He was appointed chief of the San Ramon Fire Protection District when it was formed in 1963 and retained that post until his retirement in 1978. San Ramon Valley Historical Society

ris Canyon hills. The house he built in 1865 is still occupied by his descendants in 1986. He gradually added to his acreage and at one time bought 1,000 acres from Leo Norris. Wiedemann sold meat from a butcher wagon he drove around to his neighbors.

Others moved in; carpenter John White, blacksmith Eli Brewin, Leo Lynch the merchant and postmaster, Reuben Harris the hotelkeeper, three saloonkeepers, and even a Chinese laundryman moved into the village.

While some large families hired a teacher who taught their children and boarded with the family, the community built its first school in 1856. Four years later, on the west side of San Ramon Valley Boulevard a few hundred yards north of Crow Canyon Road, the predominantly Protestant population built the one and only church in the village. The Methodist Episcopal worshippers outnumbered those of other faiths, who had to seek their spiritual strength in Danville churches.

Originally the village took the name Brevensville, a quaint twist of the blacksmith's name, Brewin. In 1860 the name became Lynchville, and sometime before the Southern Pacific Railroad ran its trains to the community in 1891, it was changed to Limerick.

Before the coming of the railroad, a stagecoach line ran to the village from Martinez. Farmers had little need for the stages, but commerical travelers relied on them.

In their homes, farmers' wives wore long black dresses, usually under an apron. When going to the local store or further afield, they wore a corset under the dress. On their heads they wore either a sunbonnet or if they were going to a social affair, a wide-brimmed straw hat. They dressed their young daugh-

San Ramon Town Hall on San Ramon Valley Boulevard just north of Old Crow Canyon Road, July 1959.
Contra Costa County Historical Society/Roy Bloss Collection

ters in plain dresses made at home. When dressing up, the girls usually wore a plain hat with a ribbon or two hanging down the back.

At social events most men, but not all, forsook their customary overalls for the one black suit almost every man owned.

It is alleged that Leo Norris was a confirmed gambler, who, to pay his debts, needed to sell 1,000-acre pieces, at different times, to Harlan and Wiedemann. Apparently he further indebted himself to a San Francisco attorney, Thomas Bishop. When he failed to meet the terms of his obligation in 1906, Bishop took over Norris's remaining 1,850 acres.

What happened to Thomas Bishop's ranch may not be a carbon copy of what occurred to his neighbors, but it will shed some light on what took place in some of the area. Bishop, a lawyer and never a farmer, formed the Thomas Bishop Company to include both his San Ramon property and a large ranch he owned near Goleta, California. At San Ramon he hired Frank Rutherford for his manager.

The ranch buildings Rutherford built included a bunk house for about sixty men, a mess hall, stables for the mules and horses, and an immense barn for storing hay and equipment. At Chicago livestock fairs Bishop's prize sheep regularly won honors, but back at the ranch coyotes frequently killed lambs. Rutherford kept a pack of six greyhounds and at the sighting of a coyote by the driver of the steam-driven tractor, he would blow the whistle. On hearing the alert the man closest to the kennel immediately released the dogs, who would outrun the coyotes, keeping down their raids on the lambs.

Deer were once plentiful in the hills, but in Rutherford's time they were rarely sighted. Commercial hunters had killed venison for the San Francisco market for years until so few remained it made their hunting unprofitable.

Rutherford's most notable achievement was the planting of tree crops. He first planted walnuts in 1905 and put large acreage where grain had been raised into pears. He had a walnut huller and drying racks constructed, then a pear packing shed and a large silo for storing barley or wheat.

When Frank Rutherford died, the lawyers for the Thomas Bishop Company chose his son-in-law, Vern Andreasen, to manage the property, as there were no male heirs of suitable age in the Bishop family.

In 1955 Robert Livermore succeeded Andreasen as foreman of the Bishop Ranch, still at 1,859 acres. He was a University of California graduate and had been trained as a manager at the Davis campus. A year after his arrival the property reached its highest productivity, with 500 acres in walnuts and 300 in pears.

Between eighty and one hundred harvest hands picked pears and walnuts, cut and baled hay, and harvested barley and wheat. They received six and a half dollars a day plus room and board, a significantly higher wage than was customary at the time.

Dividends from the Bishop Ranch were unsatisfactory to the four female heirs of Thomas Bishop, and in 1960 they agreed to sell the property to Henry Crown. Unfortunately for the buyer, that year signaled the decline in both walnut and pear production. A virus hit the pear trees and a disease, black-line, started killing the walnuts at the graft. The taxes had been about $20,000 in 1955; in 1965 they exceeded ten times that amount.

The Western Electric Company, anticipating the need of a new factory, which never materialized, bought the ranch from Crown in 1970. Livermore remained as manager for about two years and then left to go into business.

In 1977 Masud Mehran bought out Western Electric. In 1980 his Sunset Development Company started developing its Bishop Ranch Business Park, which will cover 585 acres.

Four major corporations have bought parts of the acreage: Chevron USA, 143 acres; PacBell, 100 acres; Toyota, 30 acres; and Beckman Instruments, 33 acres.

Even with all the change, there are those still around who remember San Ramon's Town Hall, near the school and Methodist Church. They recall the dances which brought them together with their neighbors and the plays they acted in there. The building is gone now.

No one is left who can remember the two ladies who in 1899 owned the triangular piece of land

San Ramon School with Methodist Church behind to the right. Ca. 1940. San Ramon Valley Historical Society

Southern Pacific's San Ramon Station, ca. 1910. San Ramon Valley Historical Society

bounded by the creek, Crow Canyon Road and San Ramon Valley Boulevard, now covered by the Shell station and the Chevron station. Mrs. M. A. Barrett and Mrs. M. E. Redmond each owned an acre; one in between those two they owned together.

Who can recall the steam train ending its run from Oakland at Limerick? Many will remember the freight trains when Southern Pacific extended the line through to Pleasanton in 1903. A few will recall the picnickers getting off the train at San Ramon to visit Cox's Hill or Meese's Grove. But not for long. Soon all the old landmarks will be obliterated and then a newer account will have to be written.

This view looks down on San Ramon village in the 1960s. Crow Canyon Road cuts across the upper left corner while Old Crow Canyon Road winds from the top (right of center) down to the town hall, general merchandise store, elementary school and the Methodist Church. Contra Costa County Historical Society

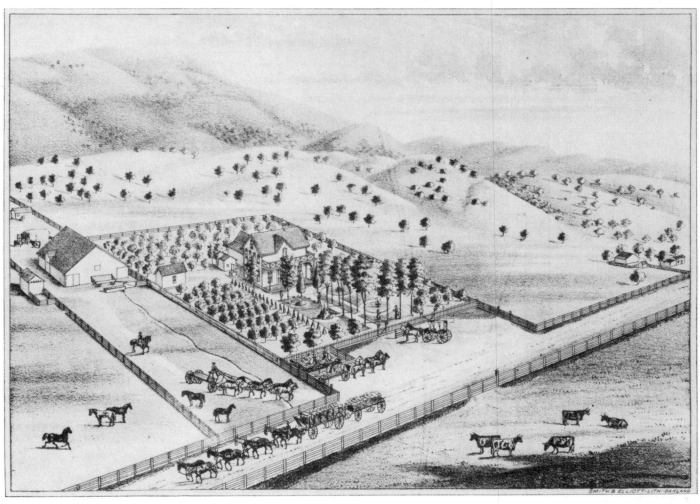

Residence of Mrs. Minerva J. Harlan, San Ramon Valley.
From Smith & Elliott's "Illustrations of Contra Costa Co."

Residence of David Glass, San Ramon Valley. From Smith & Elliott's "Illustrations of Contra Costa Co."

David Glass built this home in 1859 about three miles south of San Ramon. He raised seven children there. The house still stands (1986). A grandson, Claude Glass, lived for eighty-four years in the San Ramon Valley. Lucille Glass Mauzy of Walnut Creek is his daughter. San Ramon Valley Historical Society

LAFAYETTE

The first few pioneers who came to each area of California in the early days usually stayed there only long enough to hear news of another area, to which they moved in hopes it might be their El Dorado.

Not so Lafayette's first two citizens. Not even the news of the discovery of gold at Coloma moved them.

In 1846 Elam Brown, a widower with four children, and Nathaniel Jones, a married man who later became Contra Costa County's first sheriff, crossed the plains in the same wagon train. After a short stay at Sutter's Fort, they rolled their wagons through the Livermore Valley to Mission Santa Clara.

Along the way Brown married Margaret Allen, a member of their wagon train whose husband had died on the trek west. She had eleven children.

In the spring following their arrival, Brown and Jones hired out in Contra Costa County's redwood logging district. This area, in the valleys southwest of today's Moraga, consisted of three stands of very large trees: Moraga Redwoods, Peralta Redwoods and San Antonio Redwoods. The two pioneers whipsawed lumber at the San Antonio Redwoods, hauled it by ox team to the Oakland Estuary and transported it across the bay to San Francisco.

While delivering lumber, Brown heard of 3,300 acres being offered for sale within easy riding distance of where he was working. Though Brown had no money of his own, his new wife had $900 she had hidden in a crock among the things she brought west. The seller, William Leidesdorff, a San Francisco trader, accepted Brown's offer of $900 and the land

was his. From Oakland to his acreage Brown crossed hilly country. The trail across, unnamed in 1847, became known successively as Summit Road, Telegraph Road, and in 1903 Tunnel Road. He passed through almost impenetrable groves of a variety of oaks and finally, on his own property, crossed the trail of oxen pulling loads of lumber from the lumber camps to Martinez.

Elam Brown sold his friend Nathaniel Jones 372 acres for $100, glad to have a good friend for his only neighbor. Grain grew profusely all over Contra Costa County in the days of virgin soil. Brown and Jones harvested heavy crops of wheat and hauled it in wagons pulled by oxen to the nearest flour mill at San Jose, but valuable time was wasted in the trips back and forth. So, in the spring of 1853, Brown bought a second-hand horse-powered grist mill at Benicia and installed it on what is today Plaza Way near First Street.

Soon disappointed miners and tradesmen looking for an opportunity to establish themselves in the new state stopped at Lafayette and some settled down. Among the first was Milo Hough, who built a hotel with a bar. Teamsters walking behind their oxen, hauling lumber from Canyon to Martinez, rested their teams and partook of Hough's hospitality.

Jack Elston opened a blacksmith shop in 1853 in what became the center of the community, the area between Brown's mill and Lafayette Creek, at approximately the site of La Fiesta Square.

Benjamin Shreve, a disappointed gold-seeker,

Above, Mount Diablo Boulevard in 1869, now Highway 24, looking east toward Lafayette. The covered wagon by the fence served as the photographer's dark room in which he processed his glass negatives. Undoubtedly the horse missing from the picture carried the heavy camera and plates up the hill behind where the Cape Cod House is in 1986. Contra Costa County Historical Society

stopped in the village in 1853 and taught the first school there. In 1855 he closed the school and began operating a general store. He supplied the needs of the villagers and of some of the lumber mill workers in the redwoods. Later, Shreve applied to the United States Post Office Department for permission to open a branch at what he named "Centerville." Because of a conflict with another town of the same name in California, Shreve changed the name on his application to "Lafayette."

Shreve also farmed 250 acres which he bought from Brown. He lived a full life in the town he named, dying in 1890.

Elam Brown capitalized on his acreage, not only by raising heavy crops of grain but also by selling off small farms to people seeking a home in Contra Costa County. Brown hired eleven employees to help his wife keep house for the large family. He listed them in the 1860 census: eight servants, two inside servants, and one butcher.

When lumbering in the redwoods stopped in the mid-1850s, traffic through the village also stopped. Growth halted, and by the 1870s, Martinez, Walnut Creek and Concord were the trading centers. A railroad served the latter two towns beginning in 1891, but a trip to Lafayette was either by stagecoach or horseback. The slow ride over Telegraph Road remained a deterrent to the single horse-drawn vehicle until 1903. In that year Alameda County drilled a tunnel through the Berkeley Hills, cutting down the grade to be surmounted by an elevation of 300 feet.

Left, New Lafayette Hotel, looking west on Mount Diablo Boulevard. Moraga Road crosses the picture this side of the hotel. Elam Brown's gift to the village, the Plaza, is in the foreground. Pioneer Store is on the left border, Ca. 1913. Moraga Historical Society

Central Lafayette, looking east, ca. 1912. Lafayette Hotel, built in 1900 at Mount Diablo Boulevard and Moraga Road, is in center with the Lafayette Plaza immediately to left of the hotel. The Good Templars Hall, also known as "The Church on the Hill," is left of center. In 1986 a service station is on the church site. The hotel burned down in 1925 when the cook left food cooking in an open pan while he napped. The rest of Lafayette survived, thanks to Walnut Creek's fire department. Lafayette Historical Society

The Lafayette Plaza in 1986.
Fred Emanuels photograph

This was Lafayette's school house in 1900. The Methodist Church moved into this building in 1927. Lafayette Historical Society

The merchants association of Alameda paid more than 50 percent of the cost. This first tunnel, some 200 feet above Caldecott Tunnel, was sufficient for slowly moving horse-drawn vehicles. When automobiles started going through at speeds faster than a walk, drivers needed to look through the bore to see if their way was clear. If it was not, the second vehicle waited for the first to exit before entering.

In the early days of autos not every vehicle came equipped with a top. Water always dripped from the ceiling of this "high-level" tunnel, and many were the passengers to emerge from it with mud-spattered clothes.

At the time of the tunnel's opening, two hotels were operating in Lafayette. The original school (Shreve's) had been on Second Street and now, in 1903, the second school was built on Mount Diablo Boulevard. Today it is a bar. The Methodist Episcopal Church, the only house of worship, was known simply as "the Church on the Hill."

Social life in summer pivoted around the Pioneer Store and the park across from it, given to the community by Elam Brown. Known as the "Historic Triangle," in 1986 three historic buildings still face it. They are the Pioneer Store (1854), Geil's Building (1880s), and Wayside Inn (1894). Today one may find a plaque identifying the park with one of Brown's grinding wheels embedded in concrete. In the old days, on balmy evenings, impromptu foot races and even wrestling matches took place in the park. Boys played marbles and their fathers talked over the news in San Francisco's daily papers. When riders raced their horses around the park they raised so much dust that William McNeil, owner of the Pioneer Store, fenced off the area to halt racing.

In 1902 the Berkeley Oil Company, which had been selling stock since it leased farmer Edward Flood's property in 1900, began drilling for oil. The drillers came up empty-handed and left Flood with a derrick as a reminder of their venture. By this year the population of Lafayette had grown to 150 persons.

Twenty years later another company sold stock to develop the same land for the same purpose. In 1921 the Central California Oil Company sold shares, but despite their optimistic geologic assurances, failed to produce any crude oil.

In the meantime, the electric railway progressed. Its coming would change the area from a valley of farms to one of suburban homes. The Oakland and Antioch Railway first built the line from Bay Point (Port Chicago) to Lafayette, beginning service in 1911. In 1913, as the Oakland, Antioch and Eastern, the railroad started running through to Oakland and San Francisco. Ten trains a day each way brought families making their homes in the country. A score or more brought their children out when school closed for the summer vacation, to newly-built summer cottages. The men who commuted to work from Lafayette reached 40th and Shafter streets in Oakland in forty minutes. Commuting to San Francisco's Ferry Building required an hour and ten minutes. Both times were very nearly the same as the time it took commuters to go to the same places from North Berkeley. As a result new families moved to the country, and many of Lafayette's farms were divided into two- and three-acre homesites.

When Lafayette was still a community of small farms, dances and town meetings were held in one of the town's large barns. In 1911 a group of public-spirited citizens assembled at the Pioneer Store the

Peter Thomson's blacksmith shop stood, until the 1950s, where Lafayette's Bank of America is in 1986. Contra Costa County Historical Society/Stein Collection

Right, Otto E. Brown is caught waiting for the postoffice to open in this 1910 shot. The building stood on the north side of Mount Diablo Boulevard across the street from Moraga Road. Lafayette Historical Society. *Left, Lafayette's Good Templars Hall, ca. 1890s, also served as the Methodist Church. Elam Brown gave the land. In 1937 the church was torn down to make room for a Union Oil service station.* Contra Costa County Historical Society

Lafayette's Town Hall was built in 1914. Frank and Rose Ghiglione gave the land and $200 toward its construction. The Lafayette Improvement Club was organized in 1911 for the purpose of erecting the town's first social and entertainment center. The hall has served many uses, a few of which are theater, library, church, and nursery school. Lafayette Historical Society

evening of November 11 and formed the Lafayette Improvement Association (LIA). Their goal was to finance the building of a Town Hall. Eventually they succeeded in their aim, and on May 2, 1914 staged their Grand Opening Ball. Dances were held in the Town Hall into the late 1920s. About that time they devoted their efforts to solving local problems as a quasi government and were less interested in the social life of the community.

The owner of a 100-acre farm in Happy Valley, Colonel M. M. Garrett, when interviewed by a reporter at a later date, described the town: " . . . first came to Lafayette in 1920. At that time Lafayette was a dimunitive little village of about five hundred to eight hundred people, a couple of grocery stores, a blacksmith shop, a hot dog stand, a service station, a hardware store, a barber shop, a rickety little post

office (about six by six in dimension), a volunteer fire department with a Model T truck, a little church on a hill, and a couple of frame school houses."

Electricity came in 1920, and telephone service arrived two years later. In 1927 the town still didn't have any street lighting. The East Bay Municipal Utility District completed building the Lafayette Reservoir in 1929 and began serving Lafayette with water in 1931. The fire department continued using the Model T truck until 1933.

While families were moving to Lafayette throughout the 1920s and the early 1930s, the increase seems small compared to the growth of the community after the Caldecott Tunnel opened in 1937. With its two bores of two lanes each, people went through in time they hadn't thought possible. The name of the road changed once again. Originally the route over the

Lafayette's Wayside Inn, erected as a hotel and tavern about 1894, still stands at 3521 Golden Gate Way in 1986. It was designated a California Point of Historical Interest on June 13, 1970. Lafayette Historical Society

Fred Emanuels photograph

hills was called Summit Road. Then in the late 1850s, when the telegraph line to Antioch was strung from poles along the way, it was called Telegraph Road. When John Olive raised fish and his wife served delicious meals at his farm near today's Gateway Boulevard overpass, people started calling the thoroughfare Fish Ranch Road. When the first tunnel invited traffic the road became known as the Tunnel Road, and still later it became State Route 24. At this time (1937) 4,000 people populated Lafayette. Fifteen years later over 10,000 lived in the community.

Lafayette had its troubles with fire. Over a period of years three different hotels, all built on the corner of Moraga Road and Mt. Diablo Boulevard, went up in flames. One of the most destructive fires to strike the town started about four o'clock in the morning on March 17, 1969, virtually across the street from the fire department. Flames consumed seven stores, in-

cluding La Fiesta Market in La Fiesta Square.

All through the years until July 1968, Lafayette operated as an unincorporated community. Volunteer groups acted to improve the quality of life within the town. The Lafayette Improvement Association was the earliest and the most active. But others whose efforts have made impressions on the community include the Lafayette Chamber of Commerce, the Fiesta de Lafayette committees and the Lafayette Design Project Committee. Many others accomplished their goals, often with little recognition for their efforts.

On July 9, 1968, the citizens voted to incorporate, and in the fall of 1985 the city council moved its meeting place from the Veteran's Hall, where it had met since incorporation, to the new Community Center, the former Burton School on St. Mary's Road.

Lafayette Reservoir (looking northeast) was completed in 1928.
The Bancroft Library

Home of Elam Brown at the Rancho Acalanes, Lafayette.
From Smith & Elliott's "Illustrations of Contra Costa Co."

"Locust Farm," residence of Nathaniel Jones, Rancho Acalanes near Lafayette.
From Smith & Elliott's "Illustrations of Contra Costa Co."

MORAGA

Squeezing Mexican grantees out of their land and heirs to the land out of their heritage occurred regularly in California between 1850 and 1870. The eventual owner of Rancho Laguna de Los Palos Colorados (the Lake of the Redwoods) appears to have turned that practice into a fine art.

Joaquin Moraga and his cousin, Juan Bernal, received the grant from their government in 1835, but only Moraga lived on the land. His cousin predeceased him. Moraga built his adobe along the road to Orinda, about four miles south of the Crossroads. It is on a knoll above the Del Rey School.

Squatters moved onto his land in the early 1850s, ignoring his claim of ownership to half of the 13,314-acre grant. Not understanding the legal process of proving the validity of his title, Moraga turned to a lawyer, William Carey Jones, to represent him before the United States Land Commission. A point in the middle of the lake on the Campolindo High School campus was the center of Moraga's lawyer's claim.

Moraga died on June 7, 1855, two months before his claim went on automatic appeal to the United States District Court. The final decree confirming the claim was dated April 8, 1858.

Meanwhile both Bernal and Moraga's heirs had bartered land in order to pay lawyers' fees and past due taxes. They borrowed on their respective half-interests and committed themselves to interest rates as high as 5 to 7 percent *per month.* Consequently they had to forfeit more land when such loans became due.

By 1857 squatters had bought 1,808 acres in the valley. A single store, built in 1854, served their needs. John Courter's emporium/saloon was the first frame structure in the area.

A land-grabbing lawyer, Horace W. Carpentier, having bought up the Bernal family mortgage papers, filed a claim for an undivided half-interest in the grant. Of twelve ranchers who were farming in the Moraga area, by the 1880s only two retained ownership. One was Michael Carroll, who had made an outright purchase in 1865 from Carpentier. The other was Jesse Williams, who stood the lawyers' onslaughts and made good his claim to ownership in court. Members of the Carroll family lived on part of this original farm as recently as 1984.

In 1883 Carpentier's niece, Maria Hall, probably urged by her uncle, filed an action for all the unsettled titles. Four years later, in 1887, the court did confirm ownership of 12,259 acres to Maria Hall and Horace W. Carpentier.

When Gabriel Moraga, grandson of the grantee, was evicted from the family adobe in 1886, he and his wife, Ella, and their children went to live at the Fish Ranch.

A partnership of experienced railway construction contractors, Angus A. Grant and James A. Williamson, the husband of Carpentier's niece, formed the Moraga Land Association and the Moraga Valley Railroad in 1889 to capitalize on the possible routing of the California and Nevada Railroad to Walnut Creek through the Moraga Valley. This narrow gauge

Moraga is yet to be built in the valley seen behind the last car. No shopping center or sub-division is in this picture, only the pear orchard they replaced. The route of Camino Pablo crosses the picture horizontally on the left, barely above the roof of the last car, and on the right it skirts the lower edge of the distant pear orchard. Train #27 left Concord daily at 4:05 p.m., with its passengers scheduled to reach San Francisco's Ferry Building at 5:35 p.m. Ca. 1937. Moraga Historical Society

line, then running from Emeryville to San Pablo, had received promise of land for a station in Walnut Creek from the Botelho family. The construction was well on its way to Orinda and construction beyond there appeared to be in the offing.

The Moraga Land Association bought all of Carpentier's land in 1889 for $435,000, to be paid in $50,000 installments. The California and Nevada never did lay any track beyond the Orinda Crossroads, and the directors of the land association gave up and moved to Southern California. The county

attached their purchase for non-payment of taxes, and Carpentier bought it back for $43,000.

The first graded road from Moraga to Orinda came about as the result of the Moraga Valley Railroad's expecting to get the contract to lay ties and rails beyond Orinda. It graded about four miles south to the site of the Moraga Shopping Center today, leaving an excellent dirt road when the principals moved away.

Between 1893 and 1918 Carpentier made his home in New York. With lessening interest in the land he

Looking east from Moraga along the Oakland, Antioch and Eastern right-of-way in 1917. Five people died in the automobile which drove onto the crossing in front of a speeding train. Note the wood spoke wheel in the wreckage. Saint Mary's Road roughly followed the railroad right-of-way. Here Canyon Road turns to become Moraga Way (today it is Munster Drive for a few blocks). Contra Costa County Historical Society/Stein Collection

Looking north from where Canyon Road turned to become Moraga Way. The two-story building was built in 1914 as the Moraga Hotel, later became the Moraga Mercantile General Store, and today is Moraga's only saloon, the Moraga Barn. The cottages in the distance served the Moraga Company administrative staff. Later the railroad's depot was built across the street from the hotel. Ca. 1917. Contra Costa County Historical Society

had coveted for more than fifty years, in 1912 he sold all the remaining rancho land to the C. A. Hooper Company, owner of large tracts of land on the Sacramento River from Bay Point to Pittsburg.

Sensing an opportunity to sell a large number of homesites in the Moraga Valley, James Irvine, president of a new corporation, the Moraga Company, bought 10,000 acres in a number of separate parcels at thirty dollars an acre from the Hooper Company between 1912 and 1919.

The company's Moraga Townsite subdivision built the Moraga Hotel in 1914 on Viader Drive, known as Railroad Avenue at the time. Across the street from the hotel, the company replaced the frame shelter at Moraga Road with a substantial stucco-finished station. It paved the street in front of the hotel (The Barn today), installed concrete curbs and sidewalks and a divider strip with very large concrete urns down the center of Moraga Way. One of the urns survives today as a planter in front of the Moraga Library. The new hotel and all the amenities gave the scene a touch of affluence, suitable for the buyers of homesites who would come to the subdivision.

Actually the Moraga Townsite sales agent found only one buyer, and except for one store on Country Club Drive and the Moraga Company's ranch headquarters east of it, the land continued being farmed. "Bill" Barnes, who managed the ranch for the Irvine interests, was said to be despotic, firing and hiring at his pleasure. He continued the planting of a large acreage in Bartlett pears and English walnuts and raised beef cattle on some of the less productive acreage.

Outwardly the Moraga Valley changed very little during the years 1920-1955. In 1916, the Moraga Company donated land at the south end of School Street for an elementary school. At the time the district was known as the Willow Spring School District and the school itself as Willow Spring School #2. A much earlier school, located behind today's Moraga Hardware and Safeway's store, had fifty-six pupils enrolled in 1908. Today the Willow Spring School #2 is the Valley Church of Moraga.

The scene did change in part when the Christian Brothers moved Saint Mary's College to a 400-acre site at the east end of Moraga Valley. The school had opened in San Francisco during the Civil War (July 9, 1863) on Old Mission Road at a spot now called Saint Mary's Park. In 1889 the brothers built a brick building at Broadway and Thirtieth Street on the outskirts of Oakland. A fire damaged the school in 1894, and it returned to San Francisco for one year. In 1918 fire gutted the two uppermost floors, which were rebuilt when the athletic field's grandstands were torn down for the reconstruction.

In 1928, seeking a site where young men would find an atmosphere more conducive to study, the Christian Brothers accepted James Irvine's tentative offer of 103 acres in the Moraga Valley and bought 300 more adjoining Irvine's gift. They built the college in Spanish Revival style among the rolling hills of Rancho Laguna de Los Palos Colorados.

When the Japanese bombed Pearl Harbor the United States Navy immediately enlisted hundreds of pre-flight recruits. In need of schools, the navy lost no time in accepting the Christian Brothers' offer of their campus early in 1942. Though three navy pre-flight schools were training future pilots in the East, Saint Mary's campus was the only such facility on the West Coast. From June 1942 to June 1946, the school turned out 14,000 graduates for the navy.

From before the Great Depression until after World War II, almost all the few homesites sold by the Moraga Company were between Glorietta and the northern boundary of Moraga. Finally, after more than forty years of ownership, the Moraga Company sold out. In 1953 the Utah Construction Company bought the remaining 5,000 acres. For most of these later years Manuel Neves served the company as ranch foreman.

One of the early subdivisions which failed to attract buyers was the Oakland Sunland, which went on sale in 1926. About the time it failed, in 1934, industrialist Donald Rheem bought a nearby house on a ten-acre site. He soon started expanding the building, twice making second-story additions. Rheem built stables, a track for exercising his horses, and a carriage house with servants' quarters. After installing a very large swimming pool, he had his gardener plant a series of formal gardens around the pool terrace.

The swimming pool area reeked of elegance. To one side Rheem built a sumptuous bathhouse, not just a cabaña. At the far end and set back from the pool some distance, he built another red-tile-roofed building. Approaching it, one passed through columns supporting a roof which extended out from the entrance. Once inside, the visitor saw a comfortable lounge, naugahyde-covered chairs welcoming him. The room was two floors high. To the right was a wall with a projectionist's aperture some ten feet off the floor. A large moving picture screen, rolled up on its reel, was ready to make a theater of the lounge. To the left of the entrance was a bar, the ceiling over it reduced to an eight-foot height. Rheem often showed first-run films for his guests, bringing them from his Orinda Theater.

Rheem sold his home in 1961 to the Christian Brothers. The Moraga Park and Recreation Authority bought it from them in 1973 and the Town of Moraga assumed control of it in 1977.

Back in 1950 Donald Rheem had started his Moraga Center, later named Rheem Center. Among the initial stores were Clark's Market, the hardware store and a service station. Rheem built a residential subdivision on one side of his own ten-acre site, and later, in order to create more business for the center, he added more homes to the north on Rheem Boulevard. He built the handsome Rheem Theater in 1957, undoubtedly influenced by his love for movies.

Ownership of the Rheem Center changed hands in 1972 when Gordon H. Doheman bought it. No development occurred for the next six or seven years due to a recently-passed state law requiring an approved city-wide master plan. Moraga, newly incorporated, didn't have one until March 1979, and as a consequence only about half the developable land has been improved.

Now, in 1986, the shopping center Donald Rheem planned has grown far beyond what he must have expected. More than fifty merchants cater to Moraga's residents. Rheem Center is now called "The Park in Rheem Valley." Some of its better known

Above, built as the Moraga Hotel in 1914, in 1986 this is the Moraga Barn, on Viader Drive at Munster (formerly Country Club Drive). Fred Emanuels photograph *Below, first motorized public transportation to serve Moraga Valley, ca. 1950.* Moraga Historical Society

tenants are Longs Drugs, Petrini's, Homestate Savings and Loan Association, and Bank of America.

In 1960, Russell Bruzzone bought a parcel of land of more than two thousand acres from the Utah Construction Company. On a corner of it he built Moraga's second shopping center. His first tenant, Safeway Stores, opened its doors in 1965. Twenty years later, in 1986, forty stores occupy the Moraga Shopping Center.

Nearby, standing in front of The Moraga Barn and looking down the street, one needs the keenest memory to see the cars of the old electric line go speeding down the tracks parallel to the one-block-long Viader Drive.

The Christian Brothers established Saint Mary's College in Moraga in 1928. This view looks north. Across the center of the picture the Sacramento Northern tracks and electric poles may be seen. Saint Mary's Station is the small white building near the middle of the picture. Contra Costa County Historical Society

Saint Mary's College Chapel at Moraga. Saint Mary's began as an elementary school in San Francisco's Saint Mary's Cathedral in China-town about 1860. In 1863 it became a boarding school for elementary and high school students. The Christian Brothers arrived in 1868 and added the college department to the school's curricula. Moraga Historical Society

CANYON

In the early 1840s, when grizzlies and black bears roamed the forests at the very west end of Moraga Valley, sailors who jumped ship at Yerba Buena found employment in the forests felling redwoods as thick as thirty-two feet and as high as three hundred feet. Lumberjacks astride the fallen logs pulled up a long saw blade, and another pulled it back down from below. They were whipsawing the logs into rough lumber.

After only two years the sawing stopped. At this time condors flew over the trees, as many as fifty in a flock. Mountain lions and bobcats hunted their prey through the forests. Two pockets of redwoods hung from the east side of the hills, coming together along what is called Pinehurst Road today. The more easterly grove took the name "Moraga redwoods," and in a pocket higher up the east side of the Oakland hills was another grove called the "Middle redwoods." Over the summit, facing Oakland in a valley now called Dimond Canyon, was the "San Antonio redwood grove," three and a half miles long.

Evidence exists that even before 1840, those building Mission San Jose felled trees in the San Antonio grove for the long beams needed for the church.

After about four years of hushed sounds, the whirl of steam-driven saws began in 1850.

By that year trees fell every hour of the day. About one hundred lumberjacks toiled in each mill; one mill ran by water power, and the saws of nine were driven by steam. So many men worked in the three groves, Contra Costa County established a voting precinct there for the state's first election, in 1850. The votes cast in the three groves exceeded the total of all other precincts in that election.

Teamsters hauled lumber to Martinez via Moraga and Old Jonas Hill road through Lafayette. Here drivers of loads headed for the port rested their oxen and refreshed themselves at the Lafayette bar.

Over in Oakland the teamsters from the San Antonio woods were an unwelcome lot. They were considered a rough element and earned the name "Redwood Boys," a name synonomous with violence. What happened is unrecorded when 250 of them marched down from the hills one day to teach D. C. Porter, the deputy poundmaster, a lesson. Undoubtedly he had criticized their treatment of their oxen while carrying out the duties of his office. It is hoped he escaped their wrath, yet the Redwood Boys were credited with four hangings and never brought to justice.

By 1850 loggers, speculators and gamblers dominated the community called Sequoia (the Post Office Department changed the name to Canyon in 1927). Two "hotels" catered to the men employed in the groves. Joseph P. Lamson ran one, a lodging house with a liquor and grocery store attached. He located it about two hundred yards up the canyon from where the Redwood Inn would one day be located. The other, owned by Harry Bird, stood halfway between the inn site and the Canyon School. Bird later

Resting after a ride down Pinehurst Road to Canyon, ca. 1900. Contra Costa County Historical Society

became postmaster at Moraga and in 1889 shot and killed a man, for which he served a life sentence in San Quentin Prison.

By 1856 all three groves had been stripped of their large trees, and by 1860 only a sea of stumps remained. Several families stayed on in Canyon, relishing the freedom and solitude they found there.

Residents trapped for furs, burned charcoal, and in season sold blackberries and huckleberries. Some kept small herds of cattle and still others raised and sold vegetables.

For the next sixty years a few residents lived out their lives amid the stumps and second growth. They frequently heard draymen urging their teams, as they hauled hay, grain, or fresh fruits or grapes over Canyon Road to the summit, on their way to markets in Oakland and Berkeley.

Life in the redwoods remained quiet and undisturbed until after 1910; then an occasional automobile wound its way up the dirt road, heading for the East Bay communities. Without any water supply except what they developed themselves, and without electricity or telephones, the few living along Canyon Road (now Pinehurst Road) lived contentedly enough, little knowing what was in store for them.

In 1911 Austrian tunnel diggers began boring an electric train tunnel through the hills three miles west, above the Canyon Store. The Oakland and Antioch Railway was grading its line, which would ultimately connect Oakland to Sacramento by electric trains. Five Austrians died during the construction of the 3,400-foot-long bore. Many of the construction crew made Canyon their home for the sixteen months it took to complete the job.

In anticipation of the opportunity to live in the country and ride to work in only fifteen minutes, many Oakland citizens bought property in the Moraga Redwoods and built homes. The first was Judge John J. Allen. The Saturday before the line opened (March 2, 1913), at Judge Allen's request, the railway spotted a flat car loaded with lumber for new homes, on the main line opposite his building site. Early on March 2, a locomotive arrived and pulled the empty car back to Oakland.

Judge Allen's homesite was one of several in Redwood Heights. Others built summer homes, and only a handful lived there the year round. Redwood Inn, a bar and post office, dated from the first of the railway construction days.

To promote weekend traffic on the line, the Oakland, Antioch and Eastern leased land from East Bay Municipal Utility District for picnic and amusement parks. Pinehurst Park, with a dance floor built over the creek, sat at the intersection of today's Pinehurst Road and Moraga Road. A quarter mile uphill stood Canyon Park with its picnic site and merry-go-round. Another quarter mile uphill was Madrone Park, across the road from the train's Pinehurst Station.

Many summer weekends saw large groups patronize Canyon's sites. Most fraternal organizations met there once each summer. Pacific Gas and Electric

The Canyon Store, formerly the Red-wood Inn. Both were run by George and Con Williamson. Contra Costa County Historical Society

Canyon Store. Entrance to Canyon Park at extreme right. Ca. 1925. Moraga Historical Society

Company held a picnic there on its fiftieth anniversary, in 1916, bringing in eight cars of passengers on a single train. Judge Allen's two sons, Don and Liston, ran a jitney service, five cents a ride, between the three parks on weekends. One drove a Ford Model T touring car and the other a slightly larger motorcar. George and Con Williamson ran the Canyon Store, formerly Redwood Inn. The beauty of the area brought in more prospects for summer homes and by 1917 almost one hundred sites had been sold in subdivisions named Alden Dell, Canyon City, Moraga Redwood Heights, Moraga Redwood Heights Extension, and last, in 1925, Hillside Vista Acres.

Al McCosker became the first graduate of the Canyon School, which opened in 1918 as the Valle Vista School (changed to Canyon School in 1920). The only eighth grader in the class of 1922, Al delivered the *Oakland Tribune* throughout the area while still in grammar school. He also collected fares on the merry-go-round on weekends while his chum, the "engineer," ran the machinery. The operators fired both boys one day when they discovered Al had allowed too many of his relatives to ride free.

With only the affluent driving automobiles before 1920, Canyon's amusement attractions and the picnic areas remained a desirable and accessible place for city dwellers to enjoy their weekends.

Although only sixteen students were enrolled in Canyon's school in 1937, their Boy Scout and Girl Scout troops were organized before Moraga's.

After World War II, population declined further, and it continued to decline as EBMUD bought up as many vacant properties as it could in order to protect the watershed of its San Leandro Reservoir.

Don and Liston Allen ran these two autos between Redwood Canyon's train stations and the three amusement parks. Contra Costa County Historical Society

A typical scene along Pinehurst Road, headed for the Canyon Store, in 1900 and today.

The persistent rains of 1958 flooded homes and washed out sections of the road through Canyon, cutting off food supplies to the store. Dairy deliveries stopped, but Moraga horsemen came to the rescue, riding through rain and mud every day to deliver milk to families with infants.

In the 1960s antagonists of the establishment began moving into vacant homes. Some non-conformists lived in trailers without approved connections. Representations by the few permanent residents brought out the county health authorities. Numerous violations of sewage disposal and building codes came to light and strict enforcement eventually induced many of the violators to move on. Hippies made an effort to use the old Canyon Store but their makeshift repairs failed to satisfy the authorities, and when a dynamite explosion razed the old

building in 1967 very few residents regretted the loss.

From 1969 to 1979 a trailer served as the United States Post Office. Now a modern, roomy, well-lighted building serves about 250 people. No more than ten houses may be seen from Pinehurst Road. The new post office building abuts the foundation of the old store. A modern school serves the community. Train whistles no longer alert residents to their passing.

Today privacy and freedom from inquisitive neighbors are again the attractions of living in Canyon. Gone are the amusement parks, the picnic sites and the fields where weekenders played their games. Homes meet high standards. The few dozen families living near Canyon live in a redwood forest only a few minutes drive over the hill to Oakland or down the road even fewer miles to a Moraga shopping center.

Canyon School, 1986. Fred Emanuels photograph

Canyon Postoffice, 1986. Fred Emanuels photograph

ORINDA

Soon after the United States surveyor general issued his 1878 survey, a land rush materialized in the Orinda area. Even before the final survey was issued, two enterprising men each claimed a parcel along Telegraph Road, later State Route 24.

The first was William H. Buckley, who came about 1875 and homesteaded 320 acres. He built a home and lived in it for almost sixty years. Highway construction workers tore it down in 1935, to make way for the east portal of the Caldecott Tunnel.

The second was John Olive. He arrived in California in 1854 but drove stages and farmed in the Stockton and Sacramento area before filing claim for his Contra Costa homestead in 1879. His claim fronted on Telegraph Road west of today's Gateway Boulevard. For a time his location was described as just below Rocky Point. His property abutted Buckley's to the east.

Olive and his wife made their new home a stage stop for the daily Oakland to Martinez stage. He operated a small saloon, and Mrs. Olive, said to be an excellent cook, served meals. Olive built some fish ponds and raised both fish and frogs. Mrs. Olive probably served the freshest fish in Contra Costa County and may have been the only restaurateur to offer frog legs.

Olive knew his horseflesh and besides pasturing horses for Oakland owners, he also bought and sold them. He provided corrals for stockmen driving cattle or sheep over the road to slaughterhouses in West Berkeley and Emeryville. His reputation for honesty and square dealings earned him a good trade in dealing in horses. Originally known as Oakland Trout Farm, his Fish Ranch became a popular eating place.

On down the road toward the bottom of the hill on the lefthand side was the fifty-six-lot subdivision called Maple Grove Homestead. The map, filed in October 1878, divided what is today approximately the northwest corner of the Orinda Crossroads. The BART western parking lot is about in the center of the subdivision. An ex-mayor of San Francisco, A. J. Bryant, and six friends owned the parcel at the time it was put on the market.

Farther on, up the hill going toward Lafayette, lay the 600-acre parcel owned at one time by Augustus Charles but in 1879 in possession of Henry Pierce. Now known as the Charles Hill area, it passed through many hands, eventually being subdivided in 1935 by Vernon Hardy.

In 1882 General Theodore Wagner came to Orinda and spent about $140,000 building a home and improving the 241 acres which he named Oak View Park, near today's intersection of San Pablo Dam Road and Wildcat Canyon Road.

Wagner was the first, and for some time the only, owner of a telephone in the community, having a direct line to Berkeley. The year he built his home he gave land for the Orinda Park School. He built his house of bricks manufactured in his own brick kilns. He planted a pear orchard, operated a dairy, had a conservatory, a mushroom cellar, and a carbide gas plant.

John Oliver's Fish Ranch was founded in 1879 on Telegraph Road, two miles west of Orinda, as a bar and restaurant. About 1898 Max Seeger began operating it as The Ideal Summer Resort. Contra Costa County Historical Society

When Wagner's house was only five years old, fire ignited from a defective kitchen flue burned it to the ground. When Wagner rebuilt a smaller house, he also constructed a hotel on the south end of his property, nearer the road to Martinez. Called the Orinda Park Hotel, it was leased to a couple who attracted dinner guests from Berkeley and Oakland. Boarders included fishermen and hunters seasonally, as well as farm hands during harvest. Workmen tore down the hotel in 1913.

The name Orinda Park was shortened to Orinda in about 1900. Originally the name Orinda was given the area by the daughter of John Marsh, the first settler in Contra Costa County.

Alice Marsh married William Camron, a land speculator. He bought 2,937 acres of Orinda land from Miller and Lux in 1875, paying twenty dollars an acre for most of it. That land lies north of State Route 24.

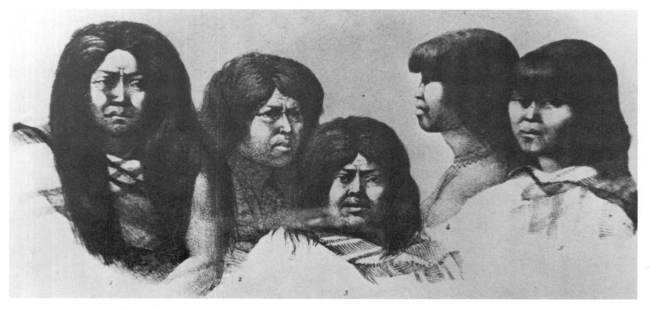

L. Choris sketched these natives of the Bay Area in 1816. He identifies the two on the right as being Saklan (a Miwok group living in the Orinda-Walnut Creek area). The one on the left and in the center are Guymen (a coast Miwok tribelet in Marin County). The second Indian from the left he calls a "Utschuin" (i.e. Huchium or Chochenyo, an Alameda County group). San Pablo Historical and Museum Society

Among the stations on this California and Nevada timetable are three in the Orinda area: Orinda Park, De Laveaga, and Bryant, called Orinda today. Moraga Historical Society

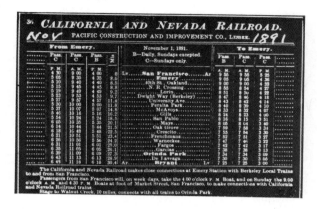

A California and Nevada Railway train approaching Orinda in the early 1890s. Moraga Historical Society

C & N train at De Laveaga station, ca. 1892. Contra Costa County Historical Society

Mrs. Camron was very interested in the classics and early English poets. One of them, Katherine Fowler Philips, had adopted the name "Orinda" within her circle of friends. The name appealed to Mrs. Camron, and she and her husband used it as the name for their 1876 subdivision, Orinda Park.

Camron spent his wife's inheritance, received from the sale of what was left of John Marsh's Los Meganos grant. He overextended himself with other purchases and ultimately forfeited his interests for non-payment of loans.

Camron deserted his wife and they were divorced in 1895. Mrs. Camron and her daughter moved to San Francisco, where she ran a boarding house.

Orinda pioneers rode the train to Orinda Park years before there was service for ranchers in the Diablo Valley, or from Walnut Creek to the San Ramon Valley.

The narrow gauge California and Nevada Railroad started operating trains from Emeryville as far as Berkeley in 1885 and two years later as far as El Sobrante. A wood-burning engine pulled a passenger and freight car as far as General Wagner's property beginning in 1890. Executives of the railroad project-

ed the line to Lafayette, Walnut Creek, Livermore, San Joaquin, Stanislaus and Tuolumne counties, and even on to "the rich mining camp" at Bodie in Mono County, and in another direction dug a tunnel a short way under Charles Hill.

Farmers at Orinda and along the way did ship hay and some farm produce. Passengers came to Orinda, some riding the stage to Walnut Creet, and others making the connection with another stage line to Alamo, Danville, and the San Ramon Valley. That service lasted only until 1891, when the Southern Pacific started running its trains from the Oakland ferry terminal to Martinez and thence on to Limerick, today's San Ramon.

Heavy rains created frequent wash-outs on the California and Nevada, and in winter service was frequently interrupted. On weekends, in times of good weather, picnickers filled the coaches, necessitating twice-daily service. The end of the line was at Bryant Station, the site of the future Crossroads.

In 1899 the railroad went into receivership. The Santa Fe Railroad acquired the line's right-of-way from Richmond to Emeryville and for over sixty years ran its trains over the California and Nevada

Canary Cottage at the east end of the high-level tunnel, ca. 1920. Contra Costa County Historical Society/Stein Collection

Orinda Country Club, ca. 1927. Contra Costa County Historical Society

route. In the 1970s the Bay Area Rapid Transit District acquired the right-of-way from Richmond to El Cerrito, and their trains use that route today.

The name de Laveaga goes back to 1887 in Orinda, when the brothers Jose and Miguel bought 1,178 acres for $50,000. Miguel's grandson Edward has been prominent in the twentieth century development of the community. In 1921 he graded roads on the hill west of San Pablo Dam Road and bulldozed a small lake named Lake Orinda and later Orinda Park Pool. He named the subdivision of the property Orinda Park Terrace. In 1923 de Laveaga laid out what would one day be developed into Orinda Village.

In 1922 Edward de Laveaga bought land on the east side of San Pablo Dam Road and constructed a dam to form Lake Cascade. He organized Hacienda Homes, Inc. to develop his east side subdivisions. It affiliated with the Orinda Improvement Association for twenty-five years, 1941–1966.

He started construction of the Orinda Country Club in 1924, building a clubhouse and an eighteen hole golf course which opened the next year. Lake Cascade became the jewel in the 159-acre club setting. In subsequent years the club added a swimming pool and tennis courts for its members.

De Laveaga went on developing Orinda subdivisions, although he lost his personal fortune during the Great Depression. In time he returned to his banker, the American Trust Company, the full amount of every loan. During the depression, occasionally a lot in one of his subdivisions was sold, but not until 1937, when the Caldecott Tunnel gave quick access to the community, did Orinda see new residents in appreciable numbers start buying homesites once again.

The Crossroads, the intersection of San Pablo Dam Road and Tunnel Road, became the focal point of Orinda for all but the residents of the de Laveaga

115

subdivision down at Orinda Village. On the south side of Tunnel Road, about two hundred yards before the intersection with San Pablo Dam Road, there stood for many years a restaurant known from the 1930s to the 1950s as The Willows. An open-air dance platform adjoined the restaurant, and inside a large tree reached through the floor and out the roof.

Orinda supported a hotel in 1858. Conklin's Hotel stood near the present site of Casa Orinda. Like every hotel of its day, as differentiated from a boarding house, it contained a bar with a billiard table, a separate dining room, a few bedrooms and of course outside toilets. In the years after 1880 the establishment became known as Conklin's Tavern.

In the late 1890s the tavern offered a picnic area to travelers over Tunnel Road and visitors on the railroad coming to the end of the line. In more recent years, in the 1940s and 1950s, the establishment relied on banquets and diners in private parties.

Businesses clustered around the Crossroads as automobile traffic brought increasing numbers of people past the intersection. Gus Reuter opened a Standard Oil gas station and the Crossroads Restaurant in the 1920s.

Henry Craviotto opened a market next to the restaurant in 1936. In 1943 he sold it and it became Bradley's Cash Market.

Ruth and Don Thompson bought the Crossroads Restaurant in 1945 and operated it until forced to relocate because of the highway widening project of the 1950s. The Thompsons moved to Lafayette and opened a new eating place, The Curve.

The first traffic light was installed in Orinda at the Crossroads in 1941. This was the same year Donald Rheem opened his Orinda Theater just in time for Christmas.

The East Bay Municipal Utility District started serving Orinda with Mokolumne River water from the Sierra mountains in 1934.

In 1943 the widening project turned Tunnel Road from a two-lane road into a four-lane highway.

The first Orinda fire house was built in the town in 1924; in 1935 it was expanded to house a second

These signs face Moraga Way and are between the present Casa Orinda restaurant and the Grubb and Ellis real estate office. Ca. 1937. Contra Costa County Historical Society/Stein Collection

engine and at the same time a library was constructed next to it.

The first post office in Orinda was in a blacksmith shop in 1888. A year later it moved to a more becoming location, the Orinda Park Hotel. Beginning in 1903 and continuing until November 1945, Orinda received its mail as a rural free delivery route from Berkeley.

Orinda students of high school age have only since 1962 traveled a reasonable distance to attend school. The first high school open to them was the two-room Richmond High School, which opened its doors for the first time in 1906. A horse drawn farm wagon supplied them their transportation to Richmond for several years. At that time the San Pablo Dam Road was a dirt road, and for at least forty years the route curved back and forth with hardly ten yards of straight road on the entire route. Remnants of the winding road may still be seen at a lower level than the 1986 fast highway.

Ultimately the county paved the road. Students attended the Richmond school until 1940. Then Orinda joined the new Acalanes Union High School District and until 1955 they studied at the Lafayette campus. That year the Acalanes Union High School

Looking north along Orinda Way, ca. 1926. Contra Costa County Historical Society/Stein Collection

District established Orinda's first high school, Miramonte. In 1962 the district opened the Campolinda campus, and today Orinda's students are divided between the two schools.

With the university in Berkeley and Diablo Valley College in Pleasant Hill, some may question the need of another school of higher learning in Orinda. But when the John F. Kennedy University opened in 1965, the founders had established a university for older adults who did not fit into the traditional setting because of job or family commitments. Acceptance of the school came slowly.

The original enrollment consisted of sixty students but has grown to 1,600 in 1985. The university offers a juris doctor (doctor of law) degree and a broad range of upper division bachelor and master's degree programs in business administration, clinical psy-

chology, clinical holistic health education and museum studies. It is the only university in the nation to grant an academic degree in parapsychology and one of the few to establish a graduate school of consciousness studies.

JFKU boasts schools of law, management, professional psychology and liberal and professional arts. Besides its university headquarters, library and classrooms in Orinda, it conducts classes in Walnut Creek, Oakland, San Francisco and Concord.

After operating under the umbrella of County Government Services all the years of its growth, the citizens voted to incorporate and thereby choose the level of services they wanted, in June 1985. Orindans hired the former El Cerrito city administrator, Tom Sinclair, to become their first city manager, selecting him from a field of 130 candidates.

Looking east at the Orinda Crossroads. Camino Pablo (left) and Moraga Way (right) are under Highway 24 in this 1986 photo. Fred Emanuels photograph

WEST COUNTY

Kensington • El Cerrito   Richmond • San Pablo
El Sobrante • Pinole • Hercules
Rodeo • Selby • Crockett • Port Costa

KENSINGTON

What would one day become the village of Kensington was a 900-acre tract of land clinging to the west side of the Berkeley hills, jutting just over the top and looking down into Wildcat Canyon. The lowest corner dropped 750 feet down from the crest. Despite its steepness, the site had something which would draw newcomers as long as a vacant lot remained: an unsurpassed view of San Francisco Bay and the Golden Gate.

In 1896 a sawmill and dry kiln readied eucalyptus logs for market on the present site of the Lutheran Church. But the wood proved unsuitable for its intended use, and the mill shut down.

Buyers came slowly to the remote area. A few wealthy persons came by auto, others only by horseback or horse and buggy. Very few homes were constructed before 1911. That year the Oakland Traction Company extended its streetcar line from downtown Berkeley, out Grove Street to the Alameda, up Marin to the Circle and along Arlington Avenue to the county line.

Without any employment available in the area,

Looking down Amherst Avenue (right) from Oberlin Avenue, Kensington, 1912. Louis L. Stein, Jr. Collection

Looking north on Arlington Avenue in 1914 with Amherst Avenue on the right. This intersection is now the site of the Kensington Shopping District. Louis L. Stein, Jr. Collection

Kensington's growth came because of visionary real estate developers. Dodge, Van Mehr and Company ran advertisements offering lots for sale in "Kensington Park" featuring "the residence tract that will make Berkeley famous!" That theme, the view, and the street car combined to draw buyers.

In 1911 Berkeley Park, down by Colusa Circle, went on the market, and in 1913, Berkeley Highlands opened up the hill. In 1914, lots in Berkeley Highland Terrace were offered for sale. That ended subdividing until the end of World War I.

The first subdivision to open after the war was Arlington Acres. Though many lots were sold, only a few houses could be seen. In 1920 the Kensington census totaled 226 men, women, and children.

Nevertheless, more subdivisions came on the market—Berkeley Woods in 1920 and the Maybeck Development the same year. All of this time Kensington was dark at night; the first street lights were installed in 1922. At that time the village had neither a public school nor a shopping center.

What would change all that happened on September 17, 1923. That afternoon a small lick of flame from a brush fire in Wildcat Canyon crossed Grizzly Peak Boulevard near the head of Marin Avenue. With a north wind blowing at the time, a wood-shingled house caught fire, unobserved at first by neighbors. By the time the alarm sounded the entire house was engulfed in flames which spewed embers onto its neighboring homes. Before morning virtually all of Berkeley north of the university campus was a desolate, stark, naked scene, only chimneys standing where just hours before handsome homes had lined each street.

Even though firemen and equipment responded from as far away as San Francisco (by ferry), the small water mains of the East Bay Water Company (not EBMUD) prevented an adequate supply from reaching the hydrants. To reduce even further the small supply, almost every garden hose in North Berkeley was turned on as residents wet down one home after another ahead of the advancing flames.

Street cars from downtown Berkeley served Kensington by coming out Grove Street, going up Hopkins to Marin Circle, and then following Arlington Avenue out to the county line. Ca. 1914.

Kensington's original service station and grocery shop, ca. 1930. Later the building at the left became the fire house. Louis L. Stein, Jr. Collection

Following the Berkeley fire, many displaced home-owners located in Kensington. Vacant lots disappeared and the need for schools and stores became more pressing.

In three successive years the community enhanced its image. In 1926, the George Friend Company opened a subdivision featuring the exclusive Arlington Estates. At a time when an adequate two-bedroom home could be built for $4,000, Friend's advertisements featured "... homes not costing less than $5000."

In 1927, the community finally received its own elementary school. Two portable buildings were moved up from Richmond for that use.

In 1928, the Arlington Avenue Shopping Center opened. Its cornerstone store was the Arlington Pharmacy at the corner of Arlington and Amherst. Louis L. Stein, Jr. was a popular merchant at this store for five decades. The shopping center stores included two groceries, a real estate office, a meat market and a barber shop. Early additions were a shoemaker, service station, beauty shop, dry cleaner and variety store. In 1955, Stein built a three-office medical building, occupied by a dentist and two physicians.

Before 1935 Kensington had no police service. The Berkeley Police Department patrolled up to the line but not in the village. Contra Costa County would respond in due time from Martinez, but not soon enough to protect Kensington in an emergency. So the community hired one man, a Mr. Norton, to patrol the area. Each household contributed one dollar a month for his salary.

A year before Pearl Harbor, Young's Market and the Variety Store came to town. That same year a nursery school opened.

At the end of World War II the community formed a Police Protection Unit and hired patrolmen, who cruised in their own cars. In 1949, the district bought its own patrol cars.

Until 1959 Berkeley handled Kensington's mail. That year Louis Stein's pharmacy was appointed a branch post office, and at long last local residents had one within walking distance.

In 1960, the Kensington Community Council incorporated and elected John Chittenden its first president.

Kensington Shopping District before widening. Ca. 1950. Louis L. Stein, Jr. Collection

EL CERRITO

A talented Frenchman, a score of Chinese boys, a future United States Supreme Court chief justice, several quarry operators, and the promoters of a greyhound racing track, all made their influence felt in El Cerrito in the twentieth century.

In the late 1840s, Victor Castro, ninth son of the San Pablo Rancho grantee, built his two-story U-shaped adobe home on what is today the site of El Cerrito Plaza. Victor's father had received from the Mexican government all of today's El Cerrito, Richmond and San Pablo. Indian men worked Victor's cattle, slaughtered them, readied the hides for market and rendered the tallow into hide bags. The women on the rancho kept the house and did the cooking under the supervision of Victor's wife, Luisa.

Like so many Californians, Victor fell prey to wily Americans, some of them unscrupulous lawyers. In the 1850s, a few settlers moved onto his land to farm.

El Cerrito was first called "Rust" after William Rust, blacksmith and pioneer citizen. Contra Costa County Historical Society

By 1860 he had sold much of his land for insignificant amounts. One of the sales was to John Davis, who acquired 320 acres. Davis ultimately became one of the area's most prominent farmers. By 1900 Castro retained little more than his adobe and a few acres surrounding it.

Before the turn of the century the community was called "Rust." William Rust came to the area in 1884 and established himself as a blacksmith, serving the few farmers in the vicinity. One journalist of the day described what he saw about this time: " . . . only an orchard or two greets the eye along the plains; its great bayfront lies dull and unimproved."

Although the Northern Railway ran its trains through Rust in 1868, little changed before 1890. Then a young Berkeley realtor, George Schmidt, with his partner, Berkeley veteran Anson Blake, began cutting up large farms and selling off smaller ones and small residential lots. In 1898 the two opened Schmidt Village. They offered five acres for $750 with $100 down and $10 a month. They sold homesites for $75 cash or $10 down and $5 a month.

These favorable terms attracted new residents, among them Louis Navellier, who set up a laundry; Edward Minor, who opened a grocery store; and William Huber, who established a law practice.

The dirt road, San Pablo Avenue, saw only horse-back riders or horse-drawn vehicles along its muddy or dusty trail. The town was called El Cerrito by its neighbors, non-industrial Berkeley and newly-industrialized Richmond. They hemmed it in, making it a bedroom community for both beginning in 1904.

The East Shore & Suburban Railway ran heavy, fast streetcars from the new Santa Fe station in Richmond to the county line, where after a transfer to Oakland Transit they went on to downtown Oakland along San Pablo Avenue.

The community was still mostly farms, several of them large. Until 1908, residents walked along the avenue only if they had no choice, wading through mud in the winter and dust in the summer. That year the community, still unincorporated, built a 400-foot-long wooden sidewalk on the east side of the street all the way from the county line to Fairmount Avenue.

As early as 1912 an airplane flew from an El Cerrito field. A skilled Frenchman, Pierre Allinio, startled his neighbors when he built his own plane and flew it, only nine years after the Wright brothers had made their historic first flight. At the time only a few East Bay residents had ever seen an airplane.

Beginning in 1903, quarry operators became the backbone of such industry as existed then. In 1903 the Bates and Borland Quarry started operating and employed scores of men, buoying the economy of El Cerrito. From the 1930s until 1943, Tallentyne Hut-

San Pablo Avenue on the right looking north from Portrero Avenue, ca. 1914.
El Cerrito Historical Society

San Pablo Avenue, El Cerrito, in the immediate foreground, with street car tracks for the cars running from Oakland to Richmond. Schmidt Lane runs from the store at the left up to Hutchinson and Brown's quarry. Bates and Borland quarry is at the extreme right of the picture. A tram line of buckets carried gravel from the quarry at Arlington, on the summit (left of center) to the Bates and Borland stockpile, near right border of picture. El Cerrito Historical Society

chinson quarried on 130 acres between Moeser Lane and Manila Avenue, loaded rock into railroad cars and sent them on their way.

Local cattle men herded their fat stock down San Pablo Avenue to the Echman family's slaughterhouse at Scott and Navellier Street. Even Marin County ranchers sometimes ferried their cattle to market. They brought them on the Richmond-San Rafael auto ferry to Point Richmond and then drove them out Cutting Boulevard on their way to Echman's.

At this time saloons and taverns dominated the avenue. With the passage of the Volstead Act in 1919 the sale of alcoholic beverages was prohibited beginning in January 1920. The avenue saw the saloons gradually replaced by garages, service stations, auto courts and eventually motels.

Chinese orphan boys were displaced from their home when the Heinz Company built its plant at

Ashby Avenue and San Pablo Avenue in Berkeley. They came to what was the old Chung Mei home in El Cerrito. Following the directions of their leaders, they built a new home for themselves called the Armstrong Preparatory School. Records don't show if it was the boys or their fathers who worked at the Vigorite Powder Company at neighboring Point Isabel, but in 1901 only Chinese were employed there and at the California Cap Works at Stege.

The community incorporated in 1917. Underlining the Standard Oil Refinery's importance to the new city were the results of the first election for a board of trustees. Three Standard employees won seats in that election.

Most Bay Area residents who had never thought twice about El Cerrito before 1932 learned about it then. Dog racing at El Cerrito became the East Bay's biggest drawing card. Legalized gambling went on at the greyhound track. Along San Pablo Avenue

1910 view of sparsely settled El Cerrito. The Bates and Borland quarry is to the left of the roof's peak. El Cerrito Historical Society

This is the twelve-room Fairmont School which burned down in 1924. A larger school was rebuilt on this site in 1927. El Cerrito Historical Society

nightclubs sprang to life, centralizing near the Carlson-San Pablo Avenue intersection. Crowds came from all over, even from Los Angeles and Reno, to bet on the dogs, to drink smuggled liquor and dance and be merry at the many nightclubs, all operating illegally.

The El Cerrito Kennel Club, a front for the gambling interests, which took their percentage first, operated a quarter-mile track and built a 3,000-seat stadium. Among the first-rate casinos were the Cave, Yosemite Club, and Rancho San Pablo. The College

Inn, 333 Club, 90 Club, and The Wagon Wheel were operated by "Big Bill" Pechart. When The Wagon Wheel burned down the owner replaced it with the most elegant of all, the Kona Club.

"Big Bill" had a partner, "Bones" Renner. But Pechart was the front man. He was a rotund, jovial proprietor who lived in a sumptuous penthouse atop his well appointed offices, between Carlson and Lassen Avenue. He maintained a large elaborate establishment and hired top quality dance bands for the pleasure of his customers. It has been alleged that "Big Bill" maintained a slot machine repair shop to service the 5,000 slot machines said to be in the Bay Area.

In the early thirties, a hamburger stand operator from Emeryville regularly visited the 90 Club. Vic Bergeron later turned his White Spot stand into the first Trader Vic's restaurant, likely inspired by what he saw at the 90 Club in El Cerrito.

Contra Costa County's district attorney regularly closed most of the clubs for their gambling activities, and just as regularly they opened again. Prohibition was repealed in 1933, but gambling remained illegal. "El Cerrito, the wide open town; you can get anything you want there," the saying went. By 1939 the California state attorney general had had enough of the ineffective Contra Costa authorities. He stepped in. High-principled Earl Warren, later United States Supreme Court chief justice, decided to "clean up the town."

With easily gathered evidence in hand, Earl Warren gave "Big Bill" a choice: "Take your machines and get out of California, or stay here and have me destroy your equipment." Pechart quickly chose the former and lost no time in closing down, and El Cerrito soon lost its appellation, "The Wide-Open Town."

By 1940 the population had reached 6,000 persons, most of them living within five blocks of San Pablo Avenue between the county line and Potrero Avenue. A large percentage of them commuted to work outside the community.

One year later, with four Richmond shipyards in full operation and Albany and Berkeley reaching the peak of their growth, El Cerrito built to its limit as quickly as World War II restrictions allowed.

Nineteen forty-two saw El Cerrito's junior high school completed. In 1946 the community formed a police protection district and hired a force which used its own automobiles for patrol. In 1949 the district bought its own cars.

The charter revision of 1949 made the next significant change in the city government by establishing the office of city manager. Edwin Howell took over as the first to hold that post, succeeded in 1950 by Kenneth Smith, who remained as city manager until 1966. That year Richard Brown came up from San Fernando to fill the vacancy.

The most significant commercial development came in 1958, when the El Cerrito Plaza opened. By 1975 two more shopping centers were in business.

El Cerrito Fire Department. Note the two Model T Ford trucks. El Cerrito Historical Society

The official population figure for 1976 was 22,950; in 1984 it had dropped to 22,731.

El Cerrito's Dog Race Track and Sunset Mausoleum are prominent in this ca. 1933 view. The dog track became a drive-in movie during World War II. The intersection of Fairmount Avenue and San Pablo Avenue is close to the left edge of the picture. Contra Costa County Historical Society

STEGE

At one time Stege was a separate town and had a post office before Richmond had one. It had a Southern Pacific railroad station when Richmond was only a flag stop. Stege station was at Forty-seventh Street between what is now Hoffman and Carlson boulevards.

Richard Stege, a forty-niner, roamed the gold fields from Downieville to British Columbia and even Siberia. In 1870 he married a Contra Costa County widow with 600 acres and a large home near what later became Stege station. Besides farming he raised frogs, selling their legs to San Francisco's finer restaurants and hotels. His gardens included beds of roses, violets and carnations. He planted palms, other trees and a variety of flowers.

When Richmond was still a tent town (1900), Stege was home to industry. Among the plants in operation were the Metropolitan Match Factory, the California Cap Works, the Stauffer Chemical Company, and the Tonite Powder Works. The town had a hotel, a lumber yard and several stores.

In 1912 Richmond annexed the town of Stege.

Pierre Allinio bought this British World War I fighter plane, a "Bristol," and brought it to El Cerrito in the early 1920s. He lived at 609 Kearney Street. He made a five-passenger transport of the fighter by enclosing the open cockpit. Note the hatch cover. Ca. 1926. Courtesy Bancroft Library

RICHMOND

No community by the name of Richmond existed before 1900, but the history of some of the area's landowners prior to that time is worthy of note. Among a score of farmers who occupied the land were John Davis, who held over 300 acres, H. F. Emeric, who eventually owned over 700 acres, and George Barrett, with 457 acres. Two who have special significance are Captain George Ellis and Dr. Jacob Tewksbury.

Captain Ellis bought hundreds of acres of swamp and tidal lands before 1860. From the landing he established, where he built two warehouses, most of the hay and grain grown in the area and any passengers destined for San Francisco embarked on one of his sailing barges, the twenty-eight-ton schooner, *Sierra*, or the thirty-one-ton sloop, *Mystery*. The captain's land is now occupied by the Richmond Inner Harbor, the Ford Motor Company, the F & P Cannery, and others.

The high land in the Point Richmond area, Nicholl Knob, was originally an island, separated from the mainland by sloughs and marshland. At high tide the freight boats sailed through the channel from San Pablo Bay and through the site of the present Chevron refinery to Ellis Landing on San Francisco Bay. Soil washing down the hills and silt deposited by floods gradually began to fill this area.

Jacob M. Tewksbury, M.D., who had come to Contra Costa County in the 1860s, had retired from his profession. Of all the early arrivals, he accumulated more land than anyone else. His total holdings came to 2,214 acres, making his wife, Emily, a very wealthy woman when he died in 1878.

Owning contiguous tracts, Dr. Tewksbury constructed dikes, one at the mouth of San Pablo Bay, and the other starting at Ellis Landing. These dikes destroyed the usefulness of the channel, but the doctor succeeded in making Point Richmond a peninsula.

Standing on top of Nicholl Knob one day in 1895, real estate entrepreneur A. S. Macdonald gasped at the realization of what lay before him. The railroad carrying freight to San Francisco was pulling its cars twenty-four miles farther than necessary. It didn't need to go all the way to Oakland. It was wasting money every day, dozens of times a day. The point of land below him, if turned into a railroad terminal, would save the railroad an immense amount of money.

Macdonald presented his idea to Collis P. Huntington of the Southern Pacific. Huntington was embroiled in numerous lawsuits at the time and failed to act on Macdonald's suggestion. But in 1897, Macdonald turned to Robert Watt, a vice president of the San Francisco and San Joaquin Valley Railroad. On behalf of his company, which would soon become the Santa Fe Railroad, Watt paid John Nicholl $80,000 for fifty-seven acres on Point Richmond. Two and a half years later the Santa Fe started carrying passengers on its *Ocean Wave* on the forty-minute leisurely scenic ride across San Francisco Bay. Besides the ferry terminal, Point Richmond soon had a brick

The Cutting Boulevard land sale attracted this crowd. The Bancroft Library

factory and a recreation beach, Kozy Kove. Here railroad workers and later refinery employees sought diversion from their ten- and twelve-hour work days. Later additions at the beach were bath houses and a dance pavilion with a bandstand.

On the north side of the Knob, West Richmond Avenue and Washington Street became the center of activity of the boom town. First, Mr. and Mrs. Critchett built their hotel there. The Langs constructed their drug store, and soon the Bank of Richmond was established on the same corner.

Simultaneously the railroad moved its shops there from Stockton. Then the lack of housing became so

Forty-one years before Richmond was founded, George Ellis, a forty-niner who didn't strike it rich in the diggings, turned to the shipping business. In 1859 he built his wharf and house on the mud-flats near an Indian shellmound at the end of South Eighth Street. With two flat-bottom sailing scows he ferried passengers and farm produce to San Francisco. Richmond Museum Association, Inc.

132

Standard Oil Company's tankers at Point Orient in 1907. The square-rigged ships took on wooden cases of five-gallon kerosene-filled cans for delivery to the Orient. The box and can factory in the foreground packed two cans per case. Richmond Museum Association, Inc.

Right, here an addition is being made to The Hunters Home, a favorite watering spot in Point Richmond, built in 1898. Contra Costa County Historical Society

critical that A. S. Macdonald stepped in. With Santa Fe backing, he and his associates bought the 450-acre Barrett farm and subdivided it. Barrett's farm was bounded by what is now Barrett Avenue on the north, Ohio Street on the south, First Street on the west and Twenty-third Street on the east. Macdonald would see to it that this property would one day become central Richmond.

Meanwhile the Pacific Coast Oil Company left its Alameda refinery and moved to Richmond in 1901. It became part of the Standard Oil Company in July 1906. An industrial achievement at the time was the oil pipeline from Coalinga and Kern County, which started delivering oil to Richmond in July 1903. By August that year the line was carrying 3,000 barrels a day. The tank farm we see today had its beginning in 1904 when the oil company built twenty-five steel tanks on 165 acres known as Point Orient, two miles northwest of Richmond.

When the Santa Fe moved into the area, the company named the community at the base of the Point Richmond hills "Eastyard." This differentiated that village from the hamlet near the ferry landing south of the tunnel. Eastyard, by 1902, had become the center of the oil industry west of the Mississippi River.

The fledgling village got along very well without any school until the Santa Fe shop workers' families arrived in 1901. Then the lack of instruction could be ignored no longer. A two-room school opened that year on a site donated by the Tewksbury estate. This school was an elementary school for six years before it became Richmond's first high school. After only one year the town financed a new high school, which opened in August 1908. The growth of the community called for a second elementary school, and one opened on the second floor of a barn at Sixth and Ohio streets. The one room had such a low ceiling that when the superintendent came to visit he could not stand erect. For that reason and because on warm spring days the stench rising from the stable below became too strong, the school closed there after one year, reopening at Fifth and Maine streets. Students from as far away as Orinda came to this high school.

To better accommodate the children moving into the new subdivision around First and Second streets at Macdonald, a one-room school opened on the west side of Second a little north of Macdonald.

In a concerted move to consolidate the one- and two-room schools, two larger buildings were erected. For the west side youngsters, a six-room building opened on Standard Avenue, and for the east side

Chinese Shrimp Camp, Richmond, ca. 1907. The Bancroft Library

children, a four-room facility was erected on Tenth Street between Macdonald and Bissell.

In August 1905, Richmond's 2,115 citizens incorporated their town. The easterly city limit became Twenty-third Street. Before long John Nicholl built the first City Hall. The site was in Point Richmond, one door removed from the corner of Washington Avenue and West Richmond Boulevard.

A year before incorporation, in 1904, William S. Rheem, then head of the Standard Oil Company, and a group of his friends formed the East Shore and Suburban Railway. They planned this local street car line to serve the need for transportation to and from the Santa Fe passenger station. Service began, within Richmond only, on July 7, 1904. It ran out Ohio Street to Sixth, as Ohio appeared to be the main business thoroughfare. At Sixth Street the line turned north to Macdonald, on which it proceeded out to San Pablo Avenue. In 1905 the cars were running south along San Pablo Avenue to the county line. There passengers to or from Oakland and Berkeley changed cars to proceed further. No streets were paved in 1904; wading out through mud to board a car in winter was all too common an experience for men and women alike. Several branch lines served segments of the community. One ran from Macdonald and San Pablo Avenue out San Pablo to McBryde, where it turned east as far as Grand Canyon Park, an amusement and recreation park complete with bandstand and dance platform. Grand Canyon Park today is Alvarado Park.

In 1910, F. M. "Borax" Smith combined his Oakland Traction Company (Key System) with the East Shore and Suburban, permitting travelers to remain in one car when crossing the county line. In its final year of operation, 1910, the East Shore and Suburban carried 2.7 million fare-paying passengers.

By 1907 Richmond had enough industrial plants to give work to all who wanted it. A chemical plant, a shipyard, and the Richmond Manufacturing Company hired hundreds of men. The Berkeley Steel Company, the Richmond Pottery Company, and four large brick works required hundreds more. Around Point Molate, the California Wine Associa-

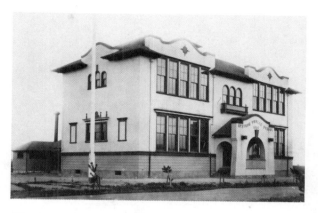

This Nystrom Public School was built on land given by John R. Nystrom, grandfather of Stanley Nystrom, in 1908 on South Thirteenth Street. Later it was moved to the intersection of South Harbor Way and Maine Avenue. Contra Costa County Historical Society

tion built "Winehaven," an immense brick winery and storage warehouse. They carved out the world's biggest vat in the rock formation under the building. Once the tank was formed, they faced it with glass-like cement two feet thick. Today it is a navy fuel depot. Around Point San Pablo a whaling station received whales which were towed in through the Golden Gate, cut them up and pressed the blubber. This plant continued in operation until 1957.

With all the industrialization of the community, Richmond was in dire need of hospital facilities. The nearest was in Berkeley until 1908. That year two brothers, Dr. C. L. Abbott and Dr. U. S. Abbott, opened Richmond's first hospital. They built the three-story Abbott Sanitarium.

In 1910 the Pullman Car Company opened its plant in Richmond and refurbished railroad and sleeping cars until the 1950s. Nineteen ten was also the year the *Richmond Independent* newspaper commenced publication.

The Southern Pacific at first offered only a wooden shelter to passengers at its Barrett Avenue crossing. In 1905 the railroad built a small station and in 1915

Indian statue tops the fountain at Washington Avenue and Park Place, Point Richmond. When it was unveiled on September 4, 1909, it filled a need for a public watering place for horses, dogs and humans. The Women's West Side Improvement Club installed it, ca. 1914. Contra Costa County Historical Society/Louis L. Stein Collection

replaced it with a more modern facility. A combined Amtrak and BART station accommodates passengers at the same crossing today.

The Mechanics Bank, organized in 1907 with its first office at Eighth and Macdonald, took over the assets of a family-owned independent bank, the Iverson Banking Company, founded in 1905.

In 1915 new stockholders joined the Mechanics Bank. One of them, E. M. Downer, was elected second vice president. In 1919 Downer purchased the controlling interest and became the bank's president. He was self-taught, having come to Richmond from Pinole, where his previous experience included being the Southern Pacific telegrapher, Pinole's city clerk and later its mayor. He also had published the town's weekly with the help of a partner.

Downer, always sensitive to the needs of both individuals and corporations, succeeded in making his bank a necessary part of the community. Under his guidance and that of two succeeding generations of Downers, the institution has prospered. Today it has ten branches, with its head office at Hilltop Mall Road.

In 1913, two men organized the Richmond-San Rafael Transportation Company. Proposed by Raymond Clarke and financed by Oliver Olson, the company first operated with only the 133-foot-long *Ellen*, making its first run on May 1, 1914. The little vessel carried automobiles and foot passengers, as well as livestock penned in corrals on deck. Three months later authorities condemned the *Ellen*. The *Charles Van Damme* replaced her, and in 1920 the *City of Richmond* was added to the service. By 1924 the company had added the larger ferry, *City of San Rafael*. It served the public until completion of the Richmond-San Rafael bridge in 1956.

The Richmond Municipal Natatorium, on Richmond Avenue at Garrard Boulevard, has been open to the public since 1926. The John Nicholl Company, a corporation administering the estate of John Nicholl, gave the community the land for the facility, and Richmond bonded itself to build one of the finer indoor swimming pools in the East Bay. The pool is 60 feet by 160 feet and uses a mixture of fresh and salt water.

A person important to Richmond formed the Parr Terminal Company to bring new industry to the waterfront, thereby increasing employment opportunities for the town's citizens. Fred Parr had both vision and energy when he founded the firm in 1927. Mainly through his efforts, the Ford Motor Company opened its assembly plant in 1931, building 400 cars a day. Between 1931 and 1941 Ford assembled 390,000 cars and trucks in Richmond and then built jeeps during World War II. Other industries followed Ford to the new port, among them the Felice and Perrelli Canning Company.

The year before Pearl Harbor, Henry J. Kaiser and S. D. Bechtel received a contract to build thirty freighters for Great Britain. Construction began in January 1941 on seven shipways. They opened Yard #2 in April 1941, building ships for the United States government. One month after Pearl Harbor they opened Yard #3, and later Yard #4, to build frigates, pint-sized Liberty ships and landing ships. Kaiser Shipyards hired and trained men and women to weld, rivet, and learn other shipbuilding skills.

What was to become known as Kaiser's speed and style was exemplified by its building the first ship in nine months. In that time twenty-four thousand piles had been driven in the marshy soil and 674,000 cubic yards of material moved in, thirty necessary buildings constructed and the first ship completed.

By the middle of 1944 the Richmond yards had turned out 519 cargo vessels, troop transports, frigates and LSTs. Then Kaiser started putting together the larger and faster Victory ships. The *Robert Peary*, built in record breaking time, was launched in four days, fifteen hours and twenty-six minutes after its keel was laid. By the end of the war, Kaiser's four Richmond yards had built 747 ships.

The City of Richmond faced an enormous problem when the yards brought in 90,000 workers during 1941 and 1942. Because of an extreme shortage of housing, the first arrivals slept in cars or parks, rooms in private homes and dormitories. The housing authority initiated the largest housing program in the country in January 1941 when they spent $35 million for 31,743 units.

At the end of World War II, Richmond's central district was still on Macdonald Avenue between Fourth and Twenty-third streets. The Central Valley Bank stood at Sixth Street. Richmond Hardware's large store commanded the corner at Seventh, Penney's was at Eighth, and the Mechanics Bank head office was on the corner of Ninth Street. The hand-

A popular picnic site, Grand Canyon Park is now Alvarado Park, at the top of McBryde Avenue. This area had been called Arroyo Cañada by the Castros and their neighbors since the 1830s. August Boquet's family, who served meals in the Chateau, thought Grand Canyon too pretentious and changed the name of the forty-three-acre site to Alvarado Park. San Pablo Historical and Museum Society

Oliver Wylie operated his cafe at 55 Washington Street, Point Richmond, in 1909. Contra Costa Historical Society

some Don Hotel and Macy's Department Store both operated a block away at Harbor Way and Nevin Avenue.

The start of an exodus of Richmond residents became obvious in 1948, and merchants in the core area counted decreasing sales each successive year thereafter. By 1955 some stores had gone out of business; in 1956 the city's progressive merchants paid for a survey to find out where they could expect the new business center to locate. The answer came clearly: outer Macdonald Avenue. Montgomery Ward moved into the area soon after, and ever since Macdonald Avenue east of Twenty-third Street has been the center of retail activity for Central Richmond. In 1975 Hilltop Mall opened, drawing customers from areas far beyond Richmond.

A number of other industrial and commercial activities thrive in Richmond's fifty-five square miles (San Francisco contains forty-nine square miles).

Among them are the Safeway Stores and United Grocers distribution centers; the United States Bulk Mail Distribution Center at Point Isabel; Chevron's refinery cracking unit completed in 1984 at a cost of over half a billion dollars; the Port of Richmond's new computerized container-handling facility; and on the site of the early California Cap Works, which made blasting caps, the University of California Field Research Station.

Encouraged by Richmond's excellent port and rail facilities, additional industries have come to take advantage of them: Black and Decker, Eastman Tag and Label Company, Gar Wood, General Chemical, Hall-Scott, Montgomery Ward, Pacific Vegetable Oil, and the Texas Company.

Richmond Harbor is busier, in terms of waterborne tonnage leaving its docks, than any other in San Francisco Bay.

The intersection of Macdonald Avenue and San Pablo Avenue (right) in 1912. The street car is headed for Oakland via San Pablo Avenue. The tracks on the right lead out San Pablo Avenue (north) to McBryde Avenue, where they turn right and end at Grand Canyon Park, now Alvarado Park. Contra Costa County Historical Society

Above, the Richmond-San Rafael Ferry and Transportation Company started operating on May 1, 1914. Raymond H. Clarke, the company founder, leased the North Pacific Coast Railroad Company's wharf at Point San Quentin, and their ferry, the side-wheeler Ellen. *The ferry landing on the Richmond side was at Point Castro.* Zuerner photo, George C. Collier Collection
Below, streetcars serving the Richmond-San Rafael Ferry enabled pedestrians from Oakland and Berkeley to reach Marin County with ease and at a minimum cost. Streetcar service to the ferry ended in 1933. The Bancroft Library

During World War II New York Elevated Railway's old wooden cars were brought to the East Bay where they carried shipyard workers from Oakland and Berkeley to Richmond's shipyards. At the war's end many cars were literally put out to pasture. They ended their lives in an El Sobrante graveyard on the north side of Dam Road just west of Valle Vista.
Richmond Museum Collection

NICHOLL KNOB—RICHMOND'S KITTY HAWK

Before anyone but their fellow townsfolk ever heard of the Wright brothers, R. H. Botts constructed a workshop atop Nicholl Knob in which to build an airplane. He went to work on his steam-powered machine in 1902. The lifting device was two horizontal propellers in the center of the ship. He attached a vertical driving propeller and a rudder to the stern. Botts prudently included a parachute, a gas bag, and a glider in the design.

In May 1902, a demonstration of the engine in the

Santa Fe yards, powered by compressed air, proved the motor would work.

In August 1902, Botts prepared to fly his machine. The evening before the initial takeoff he left the airplane outside the shop. That night a storm-velocity wind swept across Nicholl Knob, tumbling the airship down the steep slopes, where it broke apart on the rocks below.

Botts left Richmond in bitter disappointment and was soon forgotten by all.

SAN PABLO

About 1845 Jesus Maria Castro, a son of Rancho San Pablo grantee, Don Francisco Maria Castro, completed building a home for his widowed mother at what has become Church Lane and San Pablo Avenue.

He and his wife lived with his mother until 1849, when one of his sisters and her husband, Juan B. Alvarado, decided to move in; Castro and his wife moved out.

Juan B. Alvarado had been California's governor from 1835 to 1842 and collector of customs at Monterey, as well as colonel of militia forces until the American occupation in 1846.

When California's argonauts streamed down from the gold fields, weary from their search for the yellow metal, those who came through Rancho San Pablo saw some of the best quality fruit orchards, the largest variety of pears, and plums and cherries. Many immigrants squatted on land in the vicinity of Alvarado's adobe, making homes for themselves, wanted or not.

By 1852 a school, hotel, blacksmith shop, livery stable, saloon and store were all in operation. Fifty years before Richmond existed, San Pablo's first school sat on a knoll overlooking a lagoon on San Pablo Avenue. In 1852 this first school was moved to the corner of McBryde and San Pablo Avenue. Henry Dohrmann operated the San Pablo Hotel, a one-story adobe house.

In 1853 a large group of Portuguese moved onto the ranches around San Pablo, their coming coinciding with the establishment of Saint Paul's Catholic Church. For a long time they were the dominant element in San Pablo. They maintained strong fraternal activities, and their religious festival, the Holy Ghost parade, dance and banquet, held annually, became the best attended of all the social activities in the community.

In 1854 Tom Wright opened a general store which also held the post office. He had competition from Jacob and Levi's General Store. Jacob Romer ran a butcher shop, and Greenwood and Moran a clothing store. Boquet's Union Saloon adjoined his blacksmith shop. Dohrmann's San Pablo Hotel prospered and was named the town's finest building after the additions he made to his adobe house. Dohrmann bought 2,000 acres of farm land between today's Giant and Hercules, naming his place Rancho Encinalitas.

The Alvarado Adobe

141

Jesus Maria Castro built this adobe in 1845 on the open plain which is now San Pablo. He built it at what is now San Pablo Avenue and Church Lane. His brother-in-law, Juan B. Alvarado, the governor of California from 1835 to 1842, moved into it in 1848 and lived there until his death in 1882. The adobe was torn down in 1954 and has been replaced with a replica on the same site. San Pablo Historical and Museum Society

The earliest Protestant church in the growing town was the Baptist Church, erected in 1863.

The Northern Railway, later acquired by the Central Pacific Railway, ran its rails from Oakland, through San Pablo, to Martinez, beginning in 1868.

Ex-Governor Alvarado, a full-blooded Spaniard, described by his contemporaries as a "great and retiring man," while governor had advocated measures and helped pass laws for the public good, unlike some more selfish and greedy politicians of his day. He saw land-hungry invaders scheming to take the ranches from their rightful owners, heirs forced to sell land to defend titles which were never in doubt until the Americans came. Litigants fought over his own acreage. Alvarado even had to defend himself against his in-laws, who accused him of using undue influence on his wife's mother, Gabriella Castro.

In 1875 Alvarado was being asked for interviews by the historian H. H. Bancroft. Whether doubting that the historian would reveal that his compatriots had stolen the birthrights of so many of Alvarado's fellow Californians, or seething with frustration over their loss, Alvarado refused to meet with Bancroft. The historian made many efforts through second parties but was always refused. Finally, through the efforts of Alvarado's long-time compatriot, General Mariano G. Vallejo, Alvarado acceded. In 1876 he met with Bancroft's chief writer, Henry Cerruti, and over many months related his experiences and reminiscences about both civil and political events.

Alvarado died in the old Castro home on July 13, 1882. J. P. Munro-Fraser described the home at the time of Alvarado's death: " . . . directly opposite the old vine-covered house is the village saloon. The house is one-story in height, and is built of adobe. . . . Traces of former care and taste are visible in the arrangement of the yard, but now weeds and thistles are among the flowers, and a general appearance of ruin and neglect is about the entire place."

Munro-Fraser described what he saw in 1882: "San Pablo is a quiet little town . . . situated on the San Pablo Flat, about five miles from the bay. Around the railroad station are a few scattered houses and further east, nearer the ridge of hills is a small group of houses in the neighborhood of the Alvarado Place.

"The place and the vicinity is not in a very flourishing condition, owing chiefly to the unsettled condition of land titles."

In spite of the historian's views, San Pablo did grow in population and by the turn of the century had the largest school enrollment in the county. The San Pablo School District employed eight teachers in its three elementary schools.

At this time the area had three churches and besides the usual complement of storekeepers also had harnessmakers and shoemakers. Both the Western Union Telegraph Company and Wells Fargo served San Pablo. Some of the larger enterprises in the 1880s were a group of explosives manufacturers with plants along the shoreline of the bay: California Powder Company, Vulcan, California Cap Com-

Looking north on San Pablo Avenue, San Pablo, ca. 1890s. San Pablo Historical and Museum Society

The same scene as above from Church Lane in 1902, with the San Pablo Hotel on the right. Vic Batha Collection

The Union Saloon, later the Country Inn, on the northeast corner of San Pablo Avenue and Church Lane, San Pablo. The right-hand-drive auto has acetylene headlights, but no windshield. Note the absence of any structure on the south side of Church Lane. San Pablo Historical and Museum Society

pany, Granite Powder Company, Safety Nitro, and the Excelsior Powder Company.

While both the railroad station area and that around the ex-governor's adobe were important centers in the community before 1900, by that year the corner of San Pablo Avenue and Church Lane had definitely become the center of the town. William F. Belding had arrived in San Pablo in 1885. Shortly after his arrival he rented land next to Alvarado's adobe on which he constructed a store. His business prospered and, in need of larger quarters, he bought the land abutting the rear of the adobe. He built a huge general store and Belding's became the town's leading store.

Hay, grain, orchard crops and dairy products had been the backbone of San Pablo's economy until the arrival of the automobile. Change came in the 1920s and 1930s. Then the important additions to farming included sugar beets, rhubarb and potatoes. In recent times the favorable climate has made nursery plants and flowers commercially feasible.

In 1924 the epidemic of hoof-and-mouth disease in California cost Contra Costans dearly. San Pablo stockmen suffered along with the rest. Tens of thousands of head of cattle were lined up near deep trenches, driven in, and shot and killed. When the corpses were covered over the disease stopped spreading, but the loss to the ranchers was catastrophic.

San Pablo citizens incorporated in 1984. Before then policing was up to the county sheriff's department, not always beyond looking away when confronted with minor illegal activities. Back in the 1920s and 1930s, when a liberal sheriff cooperated, San Pablo, as well as El Cerrito, became a home of gamblers. Card rooms flourished unhindered, and slot machines whirled in many back rooms. San

At Saint Paul's Church in 1914, the faithful still came by horse and buggy. Vic Batha Collection

East Richmond Hotel, at Natalie Court and San Pablo Avenue, was established in 1860 by Charles Pedretti. The building is still there. The lady in the middle upstairs window is now Mrs. Mary Ginochio, a 1986 Rossmoor resident. Ca. 1917. Vic Batha Collection

Pablo even had its own dog track, where trackside betting drew thousands from all over the San Francisco Bay Area.

Until World War II San Pablo residents in need of hospital care went to Richmond's Cottage Hospital at Ninth and Nevin streets. This ten-bed facility served the community until after the war. The Kaiser Hospital in Richmond received its patients exclusively from the Richmond shipyards. After the war a group of local businessmen and physicians organized the effort which founded the West Contra Costa Hospital District. Richmond cooperated in the effort to build a facility, and a five-story 165-bed hospital opened on November 22, 1954. The Brookside Hospital in San Pablo was responsible for bridging Wildcat Creek, which links San Pablo's Vale Road with Richmond's Twenty-ninth Street.

The popularity of Brookside from its very beginning meant an addition before long. In the intervening years two more floors, new emergency and surgery facilities, and a burn center have been added.

Higher education came to west county in 1950. That year the Contra Costa College District (formed in 1948) offered its initial curriculum in one of the

145

San Pablo's airfield was on land now occupied by Kidd Manor and the El Portal Shopping Center, at Broadway and San Pablo Avenue. In the 1920s Dexter's Service Station served gasoline to airplanes. Note the long hose used to serve Pierre Allinio's five-passenger transport, with a water-cooled engine. Air meets with races and parachute jumping were features at this airfield in the 1920s. San Pablo Historical and Museum Society

This Standard J-1, a surplus World War I plane, flew from San Pablo's airfield. San Pablo Historical and Museum Society

vacant Kaiser shipyard buildings in Richmond. After six years of planning and construction, the district moved its west campus to its permanent home in San Pablo in 1956. In 1985 some seven thousand students study at a campus on a eucalyptus-lined knoll looking out over large green playing fields.

During World War II shipyard workers came from the southern states in large numbers. An influx of immigrants from Mexico in the 1970s and more recently from Central America and Southeast Asia has increased the numbers of people in the community.

San Pablo has recently built one of the most attractive city centers in Northern California. To accomplish this goal, architects designed an entire complex of early California style buildings for the corner of San Pablo Avenue and Church Lane. Alvarado's adobe had been torn down in 1954 but in 1978 was reconstructed on its original site and is today the focal point of Alvarado Square, the San Pablo city government complex.

The 1924 statewide epidemic of hoof and mouth disease hit San Pablo's McMahon Ranch. As with every stock raiser's herd, at the first outbreak of the disease, every animal was driven into a trench, shot and interred. Vic Batha Collection

Alvarado Square, San Pablo's Community Center, houses its city administrative offices, police department, chamber of commerce, Maple Hall (an auditorium seating 250), San Pablo Historical and Museum Society and the Alvarado Adobe, a replica of the home built for Dona Gabriela Berryessa de Castro, the widow of Francisco Castro, the Rancho San Pablo grantee. Alvarado Adobe is in the lower right corner. Courtesy Monte Hess, San Pablo Community Development Director

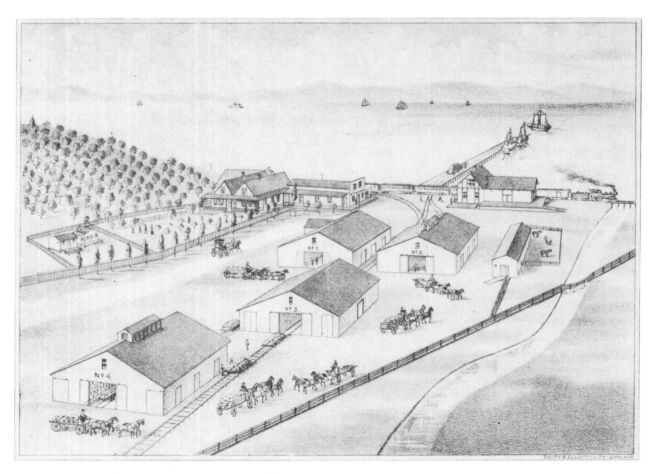

Residence, warehouses, wharf and vessels of Bernardo Fernandez, Pinole Landing.
From Smith & Elliott's "Illustrations of Contra Costa Co."

EL SOBRANTE

The alert sons of a Contra Costa grantee recognized that the boundaries of their father's land and those of his four neighbors left a large tract vacant between them. Thus, in 1841 they applied for and received from the Mexican governor title to what turned out to be 17,000 acres. They gave it the name Rancho El Sobrante, the Spanish "sobrante" meaning extra, vacant or remaining. The most recognizable feature of this grant became known as San Pablo Valley.

The west border of the grant started near the intersection of San Pablo Avenue and San Pablo Dam Road, stretching along the crest of the hills to Grizzly Peak. The southern line ran from Grizzly Peak down to Charles Hill in Orinda. The northeast line varied but averaged a mile and a half beyond San Pablo Creek from Orinda to a point within half a mile of San Pablo.

The brothers, Victor and Juan Jose Castro, sold the first part of their land in 1847 to Colonel Smith, the founder of Martinez. Before long claimants started living on parts of the grant, and squatters simply made their farms out of other parts, all of them taking the chance that the United States Land Commission would not confirm the Castros' title, hence allowing their claims. By 1873, Horace W. Carpentier, the Castro brothers' attorney, claimed a large part of the southern end of Rancho El Sobrante (Orinda and Bear Creek), which he sold in smaller parcels as fast as he could.

Fights broke out after squatters stole cattle and horses, trespassing on vacant land. Claims and coun-

Patricio Castro, the grandson of Rancho San Pablo's grantee, Don Francisco Maria Castro, who lived on San Pablo Dam Road at Castro Ranch Road. He moved to his 100-acre ranch there in 1868. In 1882 he claimed to be the oldest living person born in Contra Costa County. El Cerrito Historical Society

Richmond Oil Company's well at the south end of Clark Road, El Sobrante. Ca. 1910.
Contra Costa County Historical Society

ter claims led to gun fights so frequently in the 1870s that the decade became known locally as the "Bloody Seventies."

When in 1882 the land commission issued its final decree settling all claims, only several hundred acres of the original 17,000 were awarded the Castro heirs. Victor's son, Patricio, built a shack on the 500 acres awarded him, where he raised cattle and hogs. This parcel ran for about a mile along San Pablo Dam Road's north side, beginning about a half mile below the present dam.

The first subdivision in the modern sense divided 407 acres near the south end of the reservoir, near Orinda, in 1885. At the other end of Rancho El Sobrante, as late as 1889, farmers held parcels ranging from 80 acres to 160 acres in size. In 1899, the year the California and Nevada Railroad shut down, rain-bedeviled and plagued with washouts of its roadbed, three farmers owned all the frontage from Patricio's farm down to the end of the rancho. On the other side of San Pablo Dam Road, six farms faced the road.

The narrow-gauge line which failed had started running trains from Emeryville to Berkeley in 1885

and extended its line to San Pablo in 1887. It steamed through El Sobrante to Orinda in 1890. Its El Sobrante station stood east and a little north of where San Pablo Avenue and San Pablo Dam Road meet. By the time the line began serving Orinda, all thoughts of the original plan to lay rail to Walnut Creek, Modesto and Nevada had dissolved. The cars carried more picnickers than freight and more hay than lumber. The line suffered damage to its trestles and roadbed each winter.

An important source of revenue was the large number of weekend visitors and picnickers to El Sobrante's Oak Grove Park, near the intersection of May Road and San Pablo Dam Road, the site of a mobile home park today. Visitors came from as far away as Walnut Creek and Oakland. Fraternal organizations and church groups brought thousands each year to the grove. It was a happy time in the summer, when the railroad pressed into service every car it owned, passenger, freight and flat car, to carry the multitude of eager patrons to El Sobrante.

Throughout the years, from the days of 500- to 1,000-acre farms down to the 2- to 80-acre plots of 1915, each household depended on its vegetable garden, its chicken coop, milk cow, and for transportation, its horse or horses. In winter farmers started their chores before daylight and quit work after dark. Times for a change in their routine came rarely. Whenever anyone held a rodeo, a fiesta, a wedding celebration or a dance, only an emergency kept their friends away.

Patricio Castro made a living on his 500-acre farm raising cattle and hogs but really prospered the day in 1916 when the East Bay Municipal Utility District (EBMUD) broke ground with horse-drawn scrapers to build the dam which they completed in 1919, creating the San Pablo Reservoir. For the three years it took to build the dam, Castro supplied the large quantity of meat the camp kitchen needed to feed the hundreds of workers.

The creation of the reservoir fulfilled long standing dreams of engineers. As far back as the early 1890s, plans for the damming of San Pablo Creek were on their drawing boards. In those early days they pro-

Moraga Historical Society

In the 1890s the California and Nevada Railroad trains would stop at Laurel Glen Resort, a picnic area on the Castro Ranch. It had a dance platform and a recreation area, and was run by a Frenchman by the name of Chapeute, popularly known as Sharkey.

Contra Costa County Historical Society/Stein Collection

jected the area of the watershed draining into San Pablo Creek and Bear Creek to be 20,830 acres *above* the dam site, *thirty-two and a half square miles.*

At the time the dam construction began, San Pablo Dam Road was a single lane dirt road. The Skow family were operating a dairy farm, which is now covered by the lake. In 1918, during construction, they moved to a ranch off Clark Road and delivered milk from Point Richmond to Pinole, until they sold out in 1955.

A young physician who served El Sobrante, Dr. Clark Abbott, came in 1900, directly out of medical school in Chicago. Before ranchers in the area owned a telephone, word would somehow reach the doctor at his San Pablo boarding house that he was needed "out in the country." He would ride his horse up through Sobrante Canyon day and night, in both fair weather and foul. After he graduated to a horse and buggy, he enjoyed his travels in comfort. Though he eventually made his home in Point Richmond, the doctor always claimed his medical roots had sprouted in Sobrante Valley.

In the early 1900s mail came to El Sobrante from Berkeley, delivery starting when the post office department initiated rural free delivery. The route began at University Avenue and San Pablo Avenue in Berkeley, coming out the latter to San Pablo and then turning up San Pablo Dam Road. The first El Sobrante post office opened in 1956.

After EBMUD completed the dam in 1919, Contra Costa County improved the one-lane road to Orinda into a two-lane paved highway with a crown of asphalt down the center designed to cut down on head-on collisions by making it difficult to cross the center. At that time the road consisted of one sharp turn after the other, and drivers who wandered over the crown in the road found that it made return to their own lane difficult and often actually caused head-on accidents. Eventually, in 1952, the county rebuilt the highway, both straightening and widening it.

All through the years before World War II, El Sobrante remained a rural community, and even today it is unincorporated. It has no fixed boundaries except for those of neighboring incorporated cities which hem it in. When the first subdivision since the one of 1885 was approved in 1937, El Sobrante's population came to only 100 persons. At that time it had a library in Mrs. Blanche Burg's home, and not until ten years later, after the war ended in 1945, did the library get a building of its own, purchased by the El Sobrante Women's Club. The county built the present library in 1961, expanding it in 1975.

Volunteer firemen protected the fledgling community until 1944, when shipyard workers making their homes there numbered 1,800. That year the El Sobrante Fire District hired Charley Matteson as chief. He served unpaid until 1949 and then the district put him on the payroll and hired an assistant chief, Harold Huffman, also paid. The volunteers had relied on a Ford Model A truck, but in 1949 the district bought two used engines, modern at the time, an American La France and a GFC. The station on Appian Way went into use the same year.

The year 1948 was notable for three events. The war was over, subdividers were building homes by the score, and every house needed some furniture. Char-

Richmond High School's R.O.T.C. encampment on the Castro Ranch in El Sobrante, ca. 1922. Contra Costa County Historical Society

les Morales opened his furniture store that year on San Pablo Dam Road.

With all the veterans returning from war duty, the El Sobrante Veterans Club grew and took an active community role. In 1948 the club committed itself by sponsoring Boy Scout Troop #126.

And in 1948 the county, when the land thereabout was almost all grazing land and uncultivated fields, built a two-lane bridge across San Pablo Creek, connecting Road 20 with San Pablo Dam Road.

While all these events were taking place, the only public transportation available in El Sobrante was that supplied by the Beringer Brothers bus line. It operated from the Herald Building out to the Rollingwood subdivision.

The Herald Building housed Mr. and Mrs. Ed Galli's poultry business and newspaper office. As El Sobrante's population continued to increase, they discontinued their poultry line and devoted all their time to the newspaper. Ed Galli came from Oakland where he had worked on the *Post-Enquirer* and the *Oakland Tribune*. Besides publishing the *Herald*, the Gallis also printed the *Pinole Progress* and *San Pablo Democrat*.

In 1952 Appian Way was still unpaved. The grocery store, now Central 11 Market, was there. On San Pablo Dam Road, Oliver's Hardware and a small Fry's Market were both serving the public. A variety store, a service station, and a barber shop also operated on San Pablo Dam Road. In 1952 no traffic lights held up autos on the main thoroughfare.

La Honda Bowl served as the principal place of entertainment before the Park Theater opened. The Bowl, actually built in a ravine, consisted of a dance floor, a swimming pool and an aviary. The owner, a Mr. Smith, lived in two old railroad cars. During prohibition, 1920-1936, it is alleged dancers bought alcoholic beverages in a cave under the dance floor. Over the years many local organizations held money-raising parties at La Honda Bowl to benefit local causes. Fraternal groups held barbecues and dances there for many years.

In later years, the El Sobrante Improvement Club assumed the responsibility of a town government. Its

Looking south from the San Pablo Dam over the reservoir. Ca. 1950. The Bancroft Library

clubhouse, at the intersection of Valley View and Appian Way, served as a town hall and meeting place. It was not only a place to conduct the affairs of the village, but was also used for dances for groups young and old.

The East Bay Regional Park District developed Kennedy Grove as a recreational site near the San Pablo Dam, but in 1979 and 1980 they closed the area when EBMUD drained the reservoir and rebuilt the sixty-year-old dam to meet state earthquake standards, at a cost of $15 million.

153

*Bernardo Fernandez, born
in Oporto, Portugal, in 1830.*
Contra Costa County Historical Society

Bernardo Fernandez' Pinole Wharf in 1915.
Contra Costa County Historical Society

PINOLE

The first building in Pinole Valley was the adobe built in 1824 by the grantee of 17,000 acres, Don Ignacio Martinez. Around his house, about three miles north of San Pablo, Martinez planted a vineyard and a pear orchard. He constructed corrals for his horses, and his cattle roamed his twenty-six square miles of meadow. Martinez died in 1848, and later that year an Englishman who had stopped there earlier returned to visit his widow and her family.

Young Dr. Samuel Tennent had sailed from England to Hawaii, where he served King Kamehameha II as his personal physician. Upon hearing the news of the gold discovery in California Tennent embarked for San Francisco and, buying a horse there, he headed across the bay and rode off toward Sacramento. Night found him in heavily wooded Pinole Valley where, seeking shelter, he was welcomed by Don Ignacio Martinez. Martinez' daughter Rafaela served him breakfast. The doctor traveled no farther, sailing back to San Francisco instead.

Later that same year, when he heard the news of Don Ignacio's death, Tennent returned to Pinole Valley, wooed Rafaela and soon married her. He took his bride to San Francisco, where they lived for one year before returning to Pinole. Meanwhile Tennent had his house built there of surfaced lumber he had shipped out from Maine.

"Pinole" was a word used to describe a gruel made of dried acorn meal, a staple of the Indians. The land grant given to Ignacio Martinez was originally called Rancho El Pinole.

The most favorable landing place along the shoreline of San Pablo Bay in the early days was the beach at Pinole. With his small schooner, a Portuguese sailor started trading between there and San Francisco in 1854.

Bernardo Fernandez left his birthplace in Oporto, Portugal, in 1843 at age thirteen. He sailed first to Brazil and then spent the next ten years sailing to every continent in the world. He became master of a sailing ship before his twentieth birthday. In August 1853 he arrived in San Francisco Bay on the clipper *Staghound*. Late the next year he found the landing at Pinole. Before long he bought forty-three acres from the United States government and settled down.

The Bernardo Fernandez mansion, now owned by Dr. Joseph Mariotti. Contra Costa County Historical Society

Fernandez first built a storeroom and a warehouse. From here he traded, buying grain and local crops and selling them in San Francisco. But he wasn't the first to trade from Pinole. His competitor was one Manuel Sueyras, who had lived on Tennent's land since 1850 and traded with his five-ton sloop, *Citizen*.

In the 1862 flood Fernandez' first warehouse was washed away, but he soon replaced it with two larger ones. He bought so much grain that by 1876 he had to build two more warehouses and later he built a fifth one. At one time the enterprising ex-sailor was storing as many as 100,000 sacks of grain.

In 1859 Fernandez married Charlotte Cuadra, a Chilean, and the couple raised a family of six children. Fernandez ultimately owned over 3,000 acres of land and became one of the richest men in Contra Costa County.

Families of average means populated Pinole, and many of the children became important people in the community. One typical family was that of John Collins, who was born in Ireland. He arrived in Pinole as a young man, married and raised a family.

His most notable position was that of township constable. A son, Francis, became an attorney and practiced in Pinole for forty years.

Another typical couple were Mr. and Mrs. Christopher Ellerhorst. They arrived in 1872 as newlyweds and settled on a nearby ranch. One daughter rode a pony cart to the Sheldon School five miles from Pinole. She later came to Pinole's school as a teacher and retired in 1940 as principal. Another of the six children born to the Ellerhorsts was Annie. She became the private secretary to the superintendent of the Hercules Powder Company.

Born into an average family was Edward Downer. With only an average education but with an abundance of energy, he left his mark on west county. As a young man he became Pinole's station agent for the Southern Pacific Railroad. Downer published the town's first newspaper in the railroad's station in the early 1890s. Along with Dr. M. L. Fernandez, who lived next door to the station, Downer published the *Pinole Times*.

The Bank of Pinole opened in 1905 in this building.
Contra Costa County Historical Society

While serving the railroad the young man also became agent for an Oakland laundry, was chosen city clerk and was a principal figure in the incorporation of the city in 1903.

In 1905, still the Southern Pacific station agent, Downer opened the Bank of Pinole in the Fraser Building, once Fraser's Grocery. He was influential in founding the Pinole Light and Power Company and served his home town as mayor from 1913 to 1938.

Downer formed the Downer Land Company in 1924 to sell lots in a subdivision, resigning his appointment as postmaster at the same time and as station agent the following year. That year, 1915, he received the appointment as second vice president of the Mechanics Bank in Richmond. In 1919 he bought the controlling interest and became the bank's president.

While the fields around Pinole were alive with blue lupine and golden poppies in the spring, the streets of the town were rutted and dusty. As late as 1913 the sidewalks to the station were two-inch by twelve-inch boards, in some places only two boards wide and in a few, three wide. The board walks floated out into the bay during the storms in 1916. Only then did concrete walks appear in Pinole.

The two-story Pinole Opera House, where lodges met upstairs and the town held dances downstairs, burned down one night in 1931 along with four pianos that were in the hall.

As late as 1945, when the council ordered it stopped, cowboys drove cattle down the main street in a cloud of dust, hollering and yelling as they moved them into chutes and loaded them into cattle cars at the Southern Pacific depot.

The first Methodist Church was constructed in 1886; Saint Joseph's Catholic Church in 1889. The Pinole-Hercules Elementary School opened in 1900. The population in Pinole in 1900 was approximately one thousand persons and in 1958 was forty-five hundred. In 1985 the total came to about eighteen thousand.

Bank of Pinole in the 1930s. Contra Costa County Historical Society

The transcontinental highway ran through downtown Pinole until I-80 opened in 1958. Ca. 1939. Contra Costa County Historical Society

The heavy rains of 1958 flooded downtown Pinole. Contra Costa County Historical Society

The cartoon characters Mutt and Jeff are featured on the bill at the Pinole Theater, which was on San Pablo Avenue between Fernandez Avenue and Valley Road. Ca. 1930s. It burned down in June 1931. Contra Costa County Historical Society/Stein Collection

Lower left: Pinole; center: Hercules; upper right: Rodeo. The Bancroft Library

HERCULES

The story about Hercules goes back to 1861 when the California Powder Works established its first plant to make highly explosive black powder. The factory was two miles up San Lorenzo Creek from the ocean at Santa Cruz.

Eight years later the same company established a dynamite manufacturing facility on the then isolated sand dunes of San Francisco's Golden Gate Park.

Ten years later, the pressures of a growing population required moving the dangerous plant. In 1879 the company chose an isolated twenty-one-acre site on the shores of San Pablo Bay north of and abutting Pinole. Fields of blue lupine and golden poppies were torn up, and the work on a dynamite production facility began in 1881.

Almost from the beginning the company built housing for its employees. Foremen and their bosses lived on the "Hill" and laborers lived in the "Village." The "Village" was inhabited for 100 years. For most of that time, rent for a two-story home was only ten dollars a month, including electricity and water. Many employees came from Pinole, and that city's growth was a reflection of the prosperity of the powder works.

In 1906 the California Powder Company sold out to du Pont (E. I.) de Nemours Company. But the United States Justice Department's Anti-Trust Division challenged the purchase in 1912 as a violation of the Sherman Anti-Trust Act and made the corporation divest itself of the purchase. The new company took the name Hercules Powder Company and took

Hercules Clubhouse, ca. 1912. Contra Costa County Historical Society

control of what had grown in thirty years to a 1,300-acre plant.

Hercules' social scene began in 1910, when the company built a clubhouse for its employees. The workers themselves formed an exclusive organization, permitting "only Caucasians" to join their club. Its purpose was "to promote the social, literary, and athletic welfare" of its members.

Pinole and Hercules, only a mile and a half apart, remained allied in several activities. They shared the Pinole-Hercules Elementary School, which opened in 1907. The Pinole-Hercules Methodist Episcopal Church was founded in 1925. Even as late as 1946, when the weekly newspaper started publishing, both towns' names were in the banner, *Pinole-Hercules News.*

161

The rear-paddle wheel steamer Hercules, *built in San Francisco in 1875, delivered explosives to destinations on the Sacramento and San Joaquin rivers and around San Francisco Bay.* Contra Costa County Historical Society/ Stein Collection

Hercules Powder Company bought an additional 2,500 acres and constructed a series of gullies and revetments for safe storage of its products. It built additional housing until some ninety-seven homes stood on its ground.

Before the safety measures were taken, the life of a plant worker in a dynamite factory was a hazardous one. From 1881 until 1919, explosions killed fifty-nine men. In 1953 a single accident took the lives of twelve men. This event became a factor in the re-shaping of Hercules' future. A series of radical changes began in 1964. The company stopped making explosives and changed its name to Hercules Incorporated. It turned to the manufacture of anhydrous ammonia fertilizer, later selling this plant to Valley Nitrogen Company of Fresno. The rest of the acreage went on sale in the mid 1970s and was bought by a group of investors by the name of Hercules Properties, Ltd.

Centex Homes of California bought the first parcel put up for sale by the investors. When Centex offered its new homes for sale people lined up to buy them, attracted by the rural feeling of open space and the affordable prices. Hercules boomed with new residents.

What has happened in Hercules in the past five years is almost a miracle. The scene has changed abruptly, and what one sees today has little relation to yesterday. The townspeople walk with pride, and

well they should. Whatever it has taken to convert the old into the new, they have done.

Today the old employee housing is restored. The architecture is Queen Anne and Colonial Revival. The developer won the Grand Prize in Renaissance 1985, awarded by the National Association of Homebuilders Magazine, from among 100 contestants.

Hercules' Refugio Valley Park is the city's principal park, but there are neighborhood parks as well: Ohlone, Woodfield, and Foxboro. A bay front park is planned. It will be a twenty-acre shoreline park with trails leading to Briones Regional Park, nine miles away.

Refugio Valley Park is a beautiful eucalyptus-lined valley, stretching from the bay up through the hills. The valley serves as a "town green." The combination of deciduous and evergreen trees is an attractive feature.

In the park is a pavilion built in classical design. Columns hold up a dome roof, reminiscent of classical structures in Washington, D.C. A lake and two fountains further the resemblance. Hercules can be justly proud of its award for outstanding design of a recreational facility, received from the California Parks and Recreation Society.

High quality homes with well-manicured lawns terrace the once dry grassy hillsides. In 1985, 452 homes were built in Hercules. The population is now

Hercules, ca. 1960s.

George Collier Collection

over 10,000 and growing. A new city hall is about to be built. There are neighborhood tennis courts and two swimming pools, the responsibility of the Hercules Parks and Recreation Department. Besides the usual complement of city departments, Hercules has a Civic Arts Department, which includes youngsters in its programs.

To hold down growth in a city is one thing. To help it grow admirably is another. The people in Hercules are doing the latter, very well.

Hercules village in 1968.

Contra Costa County Historical Society

Housing in Hercules, 1986. City of Hercules Collection

Hercules' Refugio Valley Park, ca. 1986. City of Hercules Collection

The trees on the "Hill" frame Pacific Refining Company's Hercules refinery.
Ca. 1985. City of Hercules Collection

RODEO

While Rodeo's founders started the community much as other founders did theirs, numerous differences may be seen. The need for a town was created by a corporation, rather than by a farmer's selling off lots to newcomers. Rodeo did not grow because of railroad service since it did not become a regular stop on the Southern Pacific line until eight years after the first building went up.

Originally brothers John and Patrick Tormey bought 7,000 acres from the grantee's (Ignacio Martinez) heirs. Their purchase included all of what is now Pinole, Rodeo, Oleum and Tormey. The latter was given their name. In 1865, the Tormeys divided their purchase. Patrick's share covered today's townsites of Rodeo, Oleum and Selby.

Twenty-five years after the division the Union Stockyard Company bought a large tract from Patrick. They planned to make their town, where the grantee once held his annual roundups (rodeos), into the meat canning center of the Pacific Coast.

On a ten-acre plot the company built stockyards, a slaughterhouse, and a beef and pork packing plant. Employees built their homes to one side of the new operation. Pat Tormey's ranch foreman bought a few lots. He built not only his home but also the Rodeo Exchange saloon.

Three entrepreneurs who established businesses in the first year of the stockyard's operation were a Mr. Hawley, who opened Hawley's General Merchandise Store; J. D. Smith, who built two residences; and the operator of the Rodeo Hotel. The latter opened in April 1892, with publicity in East Bay newspapers. Although Rodeo was not a regular stop on the railroad, special trains brought hundreds of the curious and some prospects for inexpensive homesites. That day the Rodeo Hotel served hundreds of meals; 225 persons dined at one time.

A year after the town's founding, Rodeo had its own newspaper and in 1894 held its first local election. In 1895 volunteers organized a fire department.

But the mushrooming growth of the new town stopped in 1895, when the Union Stockyard Company went bankrupt. True, Rodeo gained more inhabitants but at a much slower rate. By the turn of the century the town was a bedroom community for employees of plants as far away as Crockett and Vallejo's Mare Island Navy Yard. The Union Oil Company at Oleum (founded in 1896) employed many Rodeo residents, as did the nearby Hercules Powder Company, the smelter at Selby and the recently opened sugar mill at Crockett. In 1898 the Southern Pacific Railroad made Rodeo a regular stop for its local trains.

In 1911 the Presbyterian Church opened its doors, helping to supply not only spiritual comfort to some of Rodeo's residents but also some social activities to even more. A few social and fraternal organizations already were meeting, but only when the first school welcomed students, in 1913, did the community feel complete.

Unfortunately, a disastrous blaze wiped out Rodeo's commercial district in 1915. The business men

Stern-wheeler Herald *ran between San Francisco's Market Street wharf and Lone Tree Point. It carried freight principally for the Pacific Patent Plaster Company at Tormey as far back as 1893.* Contra Costa County Historical Society

rebuilt surprisingly soon, and on the eve of increased travel by automobile, were ready to capitalize on the large number of travelers who came to town.

In 1914 Henry Ford had astonished labor by reducing the work day to only eight hours and increasing wages to a minimum of five dollars a day for every employee in his plants. Equally important, he brought down the price of his cars so that they were within the reach of almost everyone. Automobile traffic picked up in Rodeo, as drivers destined for Napa County, Sacramento County or any place north of the Carquinez Straits needed a place to cross over without having to drive to Stockton and Sacramento.

To capitalize on this new need, a cattle raiser who had just organized the First National Bank in Rodeo, helped form the Vallejo-Rodeo Ferry Company.

The ferry system ran two boats, twenty-four hours

a day. The Alameda-built *Avon J. Hanford* was ordered by the ferry company, but the second, the *Issaquah*, was bought in Puget Sound by the Rodeo Township. Captain Haakon Olsen sailed the ferry down from Seattle, under its own power. Two captains worked twelve-hour shifts seven days a week ferrying motorists between Rodeo and Vallejo. The ferries ran until the Carquinez Bridge opened in 1927.

Sunday outings made the ferries popular with families. Many made the crossing with picnic hamper in hand. It is reported that Saturday nights many a "young blade and his date" rode the boats back and forth. Wine and singing on the night crossings were common components of parties on ferries all over San Francisco Bay in the 1920s. One who enjoyed such crossings has left this description: "I took my girl for a ride on the ferry boat. [There was] some-

A local passenger train stopped at Rodeo in 1910. Contra Costa County Historical Society

thing romantic about it; nothing like it now. [In those days] life went on a little slower, more the speed of the Rodeo ferry."

In recent years commuters still live in Rodeo. A printing press began printing the *Tri-County News* in 1945, with Judge Joseph Longo as proprietor. A year later the *Pinole-Hercules News* was also printed in Rodeo. It ceased publication in 1972.

An important activity in the town since 1959 has been the chamber of commerce-sponsored Aquatic Festival and Bass Derby, which has attracted participants from many areas of California. The Aquatic Festival was dropped from the program after five years because of the lack of financial support from the community, but the Bass Derby is still held each October and continues to draw fishermen from all over Northern California.

The Rio Theater, with its art-deco design, was once the pride of Rodeo. It was built in 1927 and showed first-rate films for many years. Eventually television kept its former audiences at home; the theater closed two decades ago. It is open again as a teen-agers' dance hall, named the Mix.

Lefty Gomez, Rodeo native and Hall of Fame pitcher, played in the major leagues for fourteen years, compiling a 189-102 win, loss record. In World Series competition he won six games and lost none. Contra Costa County Historical Society

Rodeo and the Rodeo Marina in the 1960s. George C. Collier Collection

During the 1930s the Lincoln Highway was the name of the transcontinental highway, New York to San Francisco. It ran through Rodeo on the main street. When the same route was designated U.S. Route 40, trucks and passenger cars continued coming through the center of town. Numerous restaurants and service stations served the heavy traffic. At the single traffic light, where pedestrians could safely cross the highway, when the light turned red, lines of traffic were sometimes three blocks long.

All that changed when U.S. I-80 opened in 1958. All the cross-country truck and passenger car traffic by-passed Rodeo. Even traffic destined for Crockett and San Pablo stayed away. Before long, several restaurants and service stations had shut down, and no longer did long lines of traffic wait behind the red

Downtown Rodeo in 1941. Contra Costa County Historical Society/Stein Collection

light. The many Rodeo residents who enjoy the pace of life in a town not bothered by heavy traffic are happier for the change.

At one time in this century San Pablo Bay supported some of the finest sport fishing in the United States. As many as nine party boats, each carrying up to twenty fishermen, sailed daily out of Rodeo. In addition, no less than 150 skiffs were available for rent.

With toxic pollutants coming from industrial plants into the San Joaquin and Sacramento rivers and the bay itself, fish can no longer survice in the waters off Rodeo. Today all the party boats and all the skiffs are gone. Rodeo's once famous sport fishing grounds can draw only the annual Bass Derby, not the daily crowds which once came to town.

Selby's smelter in immediate foregound and Rodeo in far distance. Union Oil's Oleum refinery in between. Union bought the land in 1895. In those days long-distance commuting was unheard of. So, the company also built a town of homes and a clubhouse for its employees. Today the 300-acre Wickland Oil Terminal sits on what used to be Selby. George C. Collier Collection

SELBY

The history of Selby is in part the history of the American Smelting and Refining Company in Contra Costa and in part the history of a San Francisco alderman.

In 1850 Thomas Selby went into the hardware business in San Francisco, which was being supplied with goods on an irregular basis. The demand for bird shot for ammunition grew beyond his capacity to supply it. As a result he imported lead from anywhere he could get it. Supplies of the metal eventually came, by sailing ship, from England and Spain. In the meantime Selby built a shot tower at First and Howard streets, but before long, in need of greater production, he constructed a larger tower at the foot of Hyde Street. By 1870 mines in California and Nevada were supplying him with less expensive lead.

Selby dominated the market for lead products and could not keep up with the demand. He bought land in Contra Costa County from Patrick Tormey and built his first blast furnace on the shoreline of San Pablo Bay. He employed 200 men to keep the smelter going, feeding the smelter with wheelbarrows of ore. They loaded as many as seventy-four tons in twenty-four hours. Before long, after adding more furnaces, Selby had the largest smelter in the world. The company also became the largest customer of the Nortonville and Somersville coal mines.

Before the turn of the century the smelter began receiving ores other than lead. From Nevada came gold and silver ores. In 1907 the richest shipment ever received came from the Mohawk Mine at Goldfield.

The mine received $574,948 for the single shipment of forty-seven and three-quarters tons of ore.

Employees of the smelter made their homes in either of two small communities, Tormey or Selby, only a stone's throw apart. Tormey sits on an overlook of San Pablo Bay. About fifty homes are still there. In the 1930s, management, and later the English and Irish employees, occupied these bluff homes. The Mexican and Portuguese workers lived around the hill, out of sight of the bay, in Selby.

In 1958 the American Smelting and Refining Company, successor to Thomas Selby, built a 605-foot-high chimney which, with other improvements, increased the smelter's capacity to 18,000 tons of ore a month. Their deep water docks permitted ships from China, Japan, Central and South America, Mexico, Australia, Tasmania, the Philippines and Newfoundland to unload at Selby.

In 1958, 600 employees worked at the Selby smelter. The plant turned out as byproducts sulphuric acid and liquid sulphur dioxide.

When horses and cows on the hills downwind from the refinery began dying, health officials pointed their fingers at the plant. As clean-air acts were passed, Selby's fate was clear. The refinery shut down in 1971 and the 300-acre site was bought by the Wickland Oil Company for use as a terminal.

When the 600-foot-high chimney was demolished by explosives on June 14, 1973, the last vestige of Selby disappeared.

Vallejo Junction, one mile west of Crockett, was the Southern Pacific Railroad's ferry terminal for passengers crossing to Vallejo. The steamer Amador, *built by the Central Pacific in 1869, carried 300 passengers and served on this run until it was retired in 1904.*
Contra Costa County Historical Society

CROCKETT

If it hadn't been for the Northern Railway running past land owned by two farmers, there wouldn't have been any Crockett.

But the railway, which became a part of the Southern Pacific, did come, and the two farmers each built a village on land purchased from John B. Crockett. A lawyer later to become a California Supreme Court justice, Crockett received a three-mile strip of land one mile wide in payment for defending the Mexican grantee's title to his grant. The land lay along the south shore of Carquinez Strait and included all of today's Crockett.

In 1865 Crockett offered farmer Thomas Edwards

a full partnership in his property if he would rid the land of the squatters living on it. This Edwards did and subsequently named the area for his partner.

At Crockett's urging Edwards bought out some of his interest. An Alhambra Valley orchardist, Dr. John T. Strentzel, bought the balance.

Within two years Edwards laid out his town on the east end of his farm but continued farming the nearly level west end. At the same time, Dr. Strentzel (whose daughter would marry John Muir in 1880) laid out his town, which he named "Valona," to the west of Edwards' Crockett.

A manufacturer of farm machinery, John Heald,

Crockett to the left and Valona to the right. Crolona is in between. Ca. 1955. Crockett Historical Society

The causeway to Hanlon's wharf cuts across the center of this picture of industrial Crockett. C-H and the Crockett Hotel are in the center of the picture beyond the wharf.
Crockett Historical Society

moved his plant from Vallejo to Crockett in 1881 and became associated with Edwards in developing his land. Heald built a factory of brick, 300 feet long and 100 feet wide, in which to manufacture boilers, stationary and mobile steam engines, threshing machines, barley mills, grape crushers and other farm machinery. He constructed his foundry and machine shop where the California-Hawaiian sugar refinery stands today.

To the west of the present bridge tower, on Dr. Strentzel's shoreline, lumber companies built long docks for receiving lumber from coastal mills and shipping it out by rail.

A year later, Abraham Starr built what was then the largest flour mill in the world, adjacent to Heald's plant. His long docks permitted six square-rigged sailing ships to load at one time. A portion of the Starr mill still stands, incorporated into the C-H refinery.

Both Crockett and Valona filled up with houses. For the most part, workers of Irish, Welsh, English and German descent lived in Crockett. Those of Italian, Portuguese and Spanish-speaking backgrounds populated Valona. The two communities could have been miles apart for all the coming together they experienced. In spite of their close proximity, in their desire to maintain their individual cultural traits, they duplicated schools, theaters, fire departments, and even funeral parlors.

Each operated a theater. Each showed the same

The wooden sidewalk leads to the "Welcome to Crockett" arch and the county's largest hotel, the 104-room Crockett Hotel. C-H sugar refinery is on the left. Ca. 1914. Crockett Historical Society

moving picture on the same day, a runner carrying the reels between the two theaters.

In the financial panic of 1893, both Heald's and the Starr mill closed. In 1897 financier George McNear converted Starr's mill to sugar beet refining. However, farmers didn't provide McNear with the quality and quantity he needed, and he closed the plant in 1903. That same year he leased the mill to the Spreckel's sugar interests. The plant stayed closed until 1906, when Hawaiian plantation owners guaranteed a steady supply of cane. It was then reopened and has been operating ever since under the name California-Hawaiian Sugar Refining Company (C-H).

At first public conveniences were missing in the two towns. C-H soon provided a public library and

sewers, and improved some of the roads. On the level area between Crockett and Valona, the area of Edwards' old farm, the company developed a square block opposite the railroad station. It built a men's club on the middle area which became known as "Crolona," constructed an up-to-date laundry which replaced several Chinese washhouses, and built several homes for its executives.

Crockett became a company town without a company store. C-H gave the community a playground with paid directors. It kept as many as fourteen gardeners on its payroll for the town's benefit. At a Christmas pageant held annually from 1910 until 1968, every employee received a small bonus. Each child received a gift he or she had been given the opportunity to choose from the most popular gifts of the times. Each child also received a one-pound box of chocolates. The company also staged two dances with an orchestra for each. One was held at what was called "the largest dance hall in the country" (the ballroom in the Crockett Hotel). The other was held at the men's club. C-H built a swimming pool for the community and paid for five years' maintenance.

Business was so brisk in Crockett in the first quarter of this century the town required two hotels. The first was the Pinkerton, still in business as the Regal Hotel. The second, built in 1897 by the sugar company, was the Crockett Hotel, with 104 rooms and electric lights. It was for many years the largest hotel in Contra Costa County.

Crockett has been the site of two engineering feats, both trailblazers in their times. In 1901 the Bay Cities Power Company constructed electric transmission towers of unprecedented size on hills overlooking Carquinez Strait and strung cables all the way from the Sierra, bringing the largest electrical capacity to the East Bay in a single line. From Big Bend in the Sierra to Oakland, the cables were 142 miles long, a very long distance in 1901.

The first span of the Carquinez Bridge, the other major achievement of the area, was completed in 1927. Including the underwater structure, the bridge towers are the height of a thirty-three-story skyscraper. The deck is 3,200 feet long.

The first bridge to span San Francisco Bay, it was also the bridge which put Crockett's *Six-Minute Ferry* out of business. It was built by the American Toll Bridge Company, some of whose directors were the owners of the Rodeo-Vallejo Ferry Company, which bought out the ferry and retired the boat shortly before construction of the bridge was started.

Railroad passengers and automobiles used the ferry beginning in 1915. From a landing on the south shore which is now under the bridge, the boat ran across the Strait to Morrow Cove, the site of the California Maritime Academy today.

Crossing Carquinez Strait had been a problem for travelers from the time the first explorers came to the area. The record of public transportation across the river, before the railroad ran along the south shore, is not clear. However, beginning on December 28, 1879, the Central Pacific began ferrying passengers from Vallejo Junction, one mile west of Crockett, up the Mare Island Channel to south Vallejo on the *Amelia*, a coal-burning side-wheeler. The service was discontinued in 1915, the year the *Six-Minute Ferry* began.

During the Great Depression no sugar mill workers were laid off. C-H shortened its hours but kept every employee working some hours. The first of several strikes by the refinery workers' union was called in 1935. Successive strikes led C-H to reevaluate its financial support of the town. About 80 percent of its employees lived in Crockett in 1935; only 15 percent lived there in 1976.

The general increase in the cost of doing business and the declining shareholders' earnings were reasons to discontinue the previous generous support of the community. Gradually the corporation dropped subsidies, and now the town finances all of its own expenses.

Crockett is still unincorporated. Valona is still called by that name, but Crolona has disappeared. After the post office started numbering houses and delivering mail, all came addressed to Crockett. Fully occupied, the residences are home to workers who commute to jobs all around the bay.

Unfortunately, only a few small stores, once the backbone of the community, survive. Residents drive to shopping centers and malls, leaving little trade for independent local merchants.

Looking east at the Carquinez Bridge before the second span was constructed. Ca. 1930s. Don McKellips-J. E. Boynton Collection

Raising the center span into place, Carquinez Bridge, 1927. The "6-Minute Ferry" may be seen in the lower right corner of the picture. The Bancroft Library

Alexander Park and Crockett's Community Center, ca. 1922. Crockett Historical Society

Valona in the immediate foreground and Crockett in the distance. Ca. 1953. Crockett Historical Society

PORT COSTA

When the Central Pacific started running transcontinental trains in 1869, engines pulled them over the 1,000-foot-high Altamont Pass. Every ton of equipment and freight had to be lifted over the range separating Livermore and Stockton. The cost of maintaining locomotives and the extra fuel they required over this high route proved to be enormous, and engineers went to work to find a less costly right-of-way.

The railroad already controlled the line from Sacramento to Vallejo and maintained a branch serving the federal arsenal at Benicia. In 1878, it laid heavier rail on its branch from Suisun to Benicia, establishing a ferry terminal there and at its landing on the south side of the river near Bull Valley. The railroad named its second terminal Port Costa. The company built a 420-foot-long boat to ferry trains across the river. When fully loaded, the boat, which had four sets of tracks, carried twenty-four passenger cars with their road engine or thirty-two freight cars and their locomotive. Trains started using this route in late 1879.

With a world hungry for grain, California exported mountainous quantities from its fertile San Joaquin and Sacramento valleys. Now with a railroad hauling carload after carload from both valleys, deep water docks at Port Costa made that port the principal loading facility for hundreds of square-rigged sailing ships from all over the world.

Within four years of Port Costa's founding, five large warehouses received wheat and barley: the Grangers Business Association's warehouse, two miles west of the ferry dock with a 1,000-foot-long wharf; the California Wharf and Warehouse Company's docks, closer to Port Costa; and nearer the town, George McNear's immense 2,300-foot-long wharf with its two warehouses, 700 and 1,000 feet long. To the east of the ferry slip stood the railroad's coal bunker, which received coal from abroad. Farther along, the Mount Diablo bunker received coal from the mines at Nortonville and Somersville, delivering it to the few steamers on the river and to some of the railroad's locomotives. Finally, the most easterly of the grain docks were the twin Nevada Dock and Warehouse Company's giant warehouses. This facility could load as many as ten ships at one time at its 3,000-foot-long dock.

While Port Costa itself never had more than 300 residents in its permanent population, it is said that as many as 3,000 sailors, railroad employees and stevedores worked there at the height of the grain shipping season.

In 1881 thirty-nine million bushels of grain passed over Port Costa's docks. In 1882, although no roads led into Port Costa, that town loaded more grain-carrying ships than San Francisco and Oakland combined. That year four of the warehouses loaded eighty ships, and McNear's Port Costa docks poured grain into 103 more.

The town clung to the hillside, then nine sets of tracks and the ferry dock occupied all of the flat land.

Port Costa's original business district built between the railroad tracks and the river, ca. 1890. Contra Costa County Historical Society, Stein Collection

On one side the deep water defied fill and expansion, and on the other steep hills made construction hazardous. Yet the town had several hotels which fed the workers and fourteen bars to slake their thirst. The few permanent inhabitants lived and stayed on the hill side of the tracks, their bungalows close together along both sides of Canyon Lake Drive, the main road running up the canyon from the railroad tracks.

Both Congregationalists and Catholics opened churches in Port Costa. In the town's heyday the Salvation Army and the YMCA were active in the community. The early champion of the women's movement, Susan B. Anthony, temperance advocate, found Port Costa a fertile field for her views and once spoke to a gathering in the town.

Brawls were frequent and more serious crimes not uncommon. One Saturday night foray resulted in "a man badly beaten and two men arrested for stealing coal, and a sailor charged with stabbing his mate five times."

It is a wonder serious violence didn't occur more often. Hundreds of workers were hemmed into the town only two streets wide, with a Mexican population at one end of town and a Chinese community at the other. With fourteen saloons for them to patronize, mayhem could have broken out more often.

From the beginning the town caught fire with ease. If it hadn't been for the ferry boats and the yard engines with their ability to pour steady streams of river water, it couldn't have survived.

In 1899 part of McNear's 2,300-foot-long wharf caught on fire, one of his two warehouses went up in flames, and one of the wooden sailing ships moored there started burning. Sailors cut her lines and she drifted out into the river current. With her masts ablaze, her hull on fire and her tarred rigging outlining the height of the fire, she was a spectacle never to be forgotten by those who saw it.

A fire burned the greatest warehouse complex in the state next. Over the years the old wooden buildings dried by long hot summers were kindling for the smallest flame. Part of one of the immense Nevada warehouses had been used for a fish reduction plant. This use added fish oil to the dry wood, and when a fire started there, all the buildings blazed fiercely and were burned down to water level in less than half an hour.

In 1924 a million dollar fire devastated Port Costa, leveling its stores and hotels. But the town rebuilt. A double blow, which brought the business life of the

Looking west over Port Costa. Note the covered train ferry terminal at the extreme right and the turntable just right of center. Hotels, bars, and restaurants are on the right side of the tracks just beyond the pedestrian overpass.
George C. Collier Collection

town to a halt, was the opening of the railroad bridge spanning the Sacramento River, on November 30, 1930, connecting Martinez and Benicia, and the simultaneous deepening of the river channels to Sacramento and Stockton. Now steamers loaded their cargoes at those ports, and railroad trains rolled through Port Costa without slowing.

An industry which still employs 100 men was founded in 1906. It took advantage of the shale content in Port Costa's hills. One mile to the east of the town center lies Little Bull Valley. It is approximately the same size and shape as Big Bull Valley where Port

Costa is. Here "Chris" Berg and a handful of stockholders established the Port Costa Clay Products Company. Back in the 1870s the site housed a "ship chandlery and general merchandise store, three saloons and several houses which were not homes."

One month after the Great Earthquake a cattle barn became home to brick making machinery. Men mined shale with pick and shovel. With wheelbarrows, a one-mule tram car, and a shale grinding machine, the company's crew made 30,000 bricks a day. In 1922 new equipment doubled the plant's capacity. More modern machinery, installed in 1956,

Port Costa's hotels, restaurants, bars and stores on the river side of the tracks, looking east. Louis L. Stein, Jr. Collection

increased production to 200,000 bricks per nine-hour shift.

In 1964 Homestake Mining Company bought Port Costa Clay Products Company. The owner of the plant in 1986 is Port Costa Materials, Inc., employing about one hundred men the year round.

The thought of 550 freight cars of grain arriving in town in one twenty-four-hour period is just a memory. The sight of as many as four sailing ships tied up abreast, loading at one dock at the same time, is too dim to see, and the spectacle of a railroad crew shunting close to one car a minute has to be reserved for the modern classifying yards of the 1980s.

In 1941 all the usable piers went up in flames. In the town only one hotel remained open, the Burlington, and it closed in the mid-1950s. In 1968 a three-story building on the town's side of the tracks was the focal point of the community, housing thirty independent-

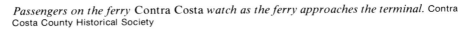

Passengers on the ferry Contra Costa *watch as the ferry approaches the terminal.* Contra Costa County Historical Society

ly owned antique and craft shops. The building was built about 1893 of stone which came to Port Costa as ballast in the holds of Australian sailing ships.

In 1986 the half-mile-long tree-shaded Canyon Lake Drive is still the location of more than twenty cottages, their residents commuting from quiet Port Costa to busier towns. Sounds are hushed in the village. Down at the bottom of the canyon, the Burlington Hotel is open again for the occasional visitor. The three-story stone and concrete warehouse is home to a cafe struggling to keep quality high and thereby attract customers from cities a dozen or more miles away.

The butcher, grocer, barber and pharmacist are all gone. The post office is open and about eight antique or craft shops occupy buildings whose walls may still echo tales of life a century ago, ever so softly.

The first of the two train ferries, the 424-foot-long Solano, *carried as many as twenty-four passenger cars with their road engine. Note the diamond-stack locomotive.* Contra Costa County Historical Society

Above: Port Costa in 1924, before the fire destroyed all the buildings this side of the two- and three-story structures. Contra Costa County Historical Society
Below: Port Costa's Canyon Lake Drive runs up the picture. Ca. 1967. The Bancroft Library

EAST COUNTY

Byron • Brentwood • Knightsen
Oakley • Antioch • Pittsburg • Coal Mining Towns

BYRON

Farmers who grew heavy crops of grain in the fertile soil of eastern Contra Costa County faced a monumental task getting their crops to market in the 1870s. The San Pablo and Tulare Railroad (later the Southern Pacific) solved their hauling problem when it completed its line from Los Banos to Martinez in 1878.

Along the tracks at a point nearest a field of hot springs, the railroad built a station, Byron. That same year (1878) F. Wilkening erected the first house close by the depot. The following year, partners Fabian and Levinsky built the first store. The farmers prospered, and more merchants came to fill their needs. Within two more years the community which centered around the railroad station, included two blacksmith shops, one harness shop, a livery stable, and a large warehouse.

Byron kept growing. Congregationalists built their church in 1883, and the I.O.O.F. Lodge members erected their meeting hall in 1887. By this time, two more warehouses housed hay and grain waiting shipment to market.

The hot springs two and a half miles southwest of the depot were known to the earliest settlers. In 1863 Lewis Risdon Mead started developing them for public use. Fire destroyed the first two buildings he erected to house visitors, but by 1882 his accommodations housed forty guests, some of them in the five cottages around the five springs used for bathing.

By now the Southern Pacific steam trains were bringing city people seeking "the cure" to Byron in ever-increasing numbers. "Only three hours by comfortable train," advertised the railroad to its San Francisco patrons. Ed Krumland, the stage proprietor, met the two evening trains at 7:00 p.m. and 9:00 p.m. His horse-drawn stages once carried thirty passengers from a single train out to the Byron Hot Springs.

The owners built a new hotel in 1904 to accommodate the health seekers. The dining room seated 150 persons and featured cut glass and silver table service. Over the next few years the owners offered additional recreational diversions for their guests: tennis, croquet, billiards, shuffleboard, and horseback riding.

Although the town's prosperity depended on its farmers, the Hot Springs accounted for much of its popularity. The former manager of the Savoy Hotel in London, England came to manage the resort. Walter Brauen, most recently the manager of Shanghai's Astor House, came to town in 1911. His position there ended one year later, when fire again came to the Hot Springs and completely destroyed the hotel.

At the time of the conflagration, Byron registered 221 voters—all men, since women did not yet have suffrage. In contrast, Brentwood's voting roll listed only 190. Byron's business district, facing the depot on the west side of the tracks, now included: Mrs. E. Hart, who offered ice cream, sodas, fruits and oranges, vegetables and cigars; Tobe Le Grand, who ran the barber shop; and Dr. J. W. Hammond, who ministered to the ailing. Peer's Saloon and Le Roy's Wild Idle Saloon filled the needs of some men. C. C.

Cutting grain in the Byron area was a cooperative effort before each farmer owned his own tractor. In this view it is likely three owners each brought a team of horses. While the lead team is five abreast the rest are hitched in threes. One of the difficult jobs on hilly terrain was the one the man on the mower had. He had to continually adjust the cutter bars to keep them parallel to the changing contour. Charles Weeks Collection

Pratt ran the Byron Bakery. Three partners, Hushbeck, Copland, and Rogers, kept a well-stocked clothing store. Mr. N. E. Grey operated the Byron Hotel, accommodating many passengers alighting from the eight Southern Pacific trains, four from each direction, which stopped each day.

Byron's population exceeded the combined totals of Brentwood, Oakley and Knightsen, and it was the only one of the four to have its own newspaper.

Farmers in the adjoining communities spent most of their money in Byron. They cut five and six crops of alfalfa from their irrigated land every year and as many as four from their dry land. Before the turn of the century, they had paid as much as sixty dollars an acre for the dry land.

The prosperity of the community necessitated a bank, and the Bank of Tracy opened a subsidiary, the Bank of Byron.

While the commercial life of the town succeeded, the spiritual had not suffered. After the Congregationalists built their church, the Presbyterians followed suit. The Seventh Day Adventists established their church soon after, as did the Methodists. The Catholic congregation formed its parish and built Saint Anne's Church.

All during 1913, concrete pourers, brick masons and carpenters worked at rebuilding the Byron Hot Springs Hotel, but it didn't open until July 1914. The four stories faithfully carried out the English architecture. The front of the building stretched out for 150 feet, with long stairs leading up to the lobby. The outer walls were of reinforced concrete covered with red brick. Window and door frames were trimmed in white.

Inside, the dining room, lobby, and all the ground floor public rooms had nineteen-foot-high ceilings. The public rooms included the mineral baths, billiard room, buffet and barber shop. A large elevator, opposite the wide front doors leading to the lobby, served the patrons.

Stately trees bordered the driveway to the hotel entrance. Many giant palms dotted the perimeter of the matchless green lawns dotted with beds of colorful flowers. Outside the ring of the palms, numerous ivy-covered cottages provided privacy for particular guests.

Trains continued to bring patrons but in decreasing numbers after 1920. By that time automobiles were owned not only by the rich. The average man searched for the unusual place to visit too. He sought the mountains with their clear breezes, the seashore with its cooling atmosphere, and not the least of all,

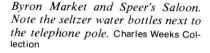
Byron Market and Speer's Saloon. Note the seltzer water bottles next to the telephone pole. Charles Weeks Collection

Above: Byron Hot Springs Hotel, 1878-1902. Charles Weeks Collection. *Below: As it appeared in 1905.* Contra Costa County Historical Society

the adventure of taking longer trips to places to which his contemporaries hadn't yet ventured.

By 1925 the Byron Hot Springs was struggling to stay solvent, and within a few years the hotel was closed.

Before the Japanese attacked Pearl Harbor, the United States War Department had designs on the empty hostelry. With the outbreak of war, they took it over, renamed it Camp Tracy, and turned it over to the Military Intelligence Command for use as a "temporary detention center."

Soon a high wire fence ringed the hotel, cottages and grounds. Outside the fencing, barracks and a mess hall went up for the use of the guard units. The

army remodeled the hotel and pump house and added a fire house and eleven cabins.

Inside the interrogation center, a division provided one unit for high ranking German officers and a separate unit for Japanese of equal rank. While under questioning, the prisoners received the best of food and treatment. At no time did the total of both nationalities exceed fifty-one. They were free to use the recreational facilities and to walk the grounds. The prisoners didn't remain long at Camp Tracy; during the year 1944 a total of 645 German and 921 Japanese officers were interrogated. At war's end, September 1, 1945, the War Department closed the camp and the Byron Hot Springs started decaying. The facilities

A Shell Oil Company subsidiary, Valley Pipe Line Company, built the Coalinga-Martinez line and eleven pumping stations, one for every fifteen miles. In this 1914 view, twenty-four mules are hauling a boiler weighing thirteen and a half tons to a station under construction near Byron. A stack of eight- and ten-inch-diameter pipe is ready for hauling to the line. Pumps pushed crude oil out through eight-inch pipe, and as pressure increased due to friction, the ten-inch reduced the back pressure having a capacity half again that of the eight-inch. Charles Weeks Collection

are privately owned now, and visitors are not encouraged.

The day of the 1906 San Francisco earthquake and fire, the man who would one day be Byron's biggest booster and the Delta's most active champion was a proofreader for a San Francisco daily paper. The next day Harry Hammond and his wife Margaret left on the first boat which would take them and boarded the train in Oakland for Byron.

In what building Hammond first set up his press isn't known, but he printed his first issue of the *Byron Times* on July 20, 1906. In August 1909 he moved his weekly paper into the vacant Green Front Building.

Hammond's *Byron Times* came out the same size as a metropolitan daily; no skimpy size pages for him. He began with a five-column four-page paper, but in 1910 he enlarged it to seven columns and eight pages and used red ink for both column headings and headlines. The paper claimed 1,500 subscribers in an area of less than 500 people (150 families?). By 1913 Hammond's weekly came out with twelve pages well filled with advertising.

Not one to "hide his candle under a bushel basket," the publisher used the masthead motto "Monarch of the County Presses," printed in bold type. Beneath the motto he ran, "If you don't read the Times you won't know what's doing." As early as 1910 Hammond boasted: "Circulation comes from every town from Richmond to Newman." At a time when only big city dailies could afford to make zinc cuts in order to print photographs and cartoons, the *Byron Times* did just that. First Hammond hired a Stockton cartoonist, a Mr. Payne, and in 1913 he employed "America's Famous Artist," Ralph O. Yardley. The front page of the July 4, 1913 issue, printed in red and blue ink on white paper, featured a large Yardley cartoon.

Hammond published the first of his 136-page bi-annual "Special Booster and Development Editions" in 1912. He printed the front and back pages in a frame of gold print on heavy coated stock. Those pages came out with print in twelve colors. Hammond mailed copies to 1,000 ticket agents of the country's biggest railroads. The booster editions publicized eastern Contra Costa County and extolled the agricultural productivity of what he named the Delta. Over the years, fifteen of these bi-annual editions were published in Byron.

Hammond's personal popularity grew as his paper grew. He beat the drums in print, advocating "Stockton the Great Hay Center." The *Times* boasted and the *Times* appealed. Before the Southern Pacific established frequent passenger service to Byron from San Francisco and from Stockton, Hammond coaxed railroad officials to improve the service. Later, "Round Trips to S.F. are now in sight" headlined one column. Finally the line did schedule service to Stockton which allowed visitors a full eight-hour day there.

When 150 carloads of sheep rolled out of Byron one July, Hammond spread the word.

Decades before organized groups demanded strict punishment for drunken drivers, the *Times* had the district assemblyman introduce a bill into the legislature which would "Punish Drunken Chauffeurs."

When an elitist group pushed for a bill which would have required a twenty-five-dollar fee for a fishing and hunting license, the *Times* trumpeted the cry, "Save the ducks for the Common People." This popular theme gave the *Times* a visible platform from

Byron's Hot Springs school, built in 1911. This is the 1914-15 student body.
Charles Weeks Collection

which, when the bill went down to defeat, it glowed for its part in the fight.

On his advertising soliciting trips around the Delta, Hammond called on farm machinery dealers and received orders for so much space he filled column after column of his eight-page, and occasionally twelve-page weekly.

In 1922 a conflagration destroyed the heart of the town's business district. Hammond lost his Green Front Building in the blaze and moved across the railroad tracks, buying the southeast corner of Mount Diablo Boulevard and Byron Springs Highway. He ordered a modern concrete brick-faced one-story building to house the *Times*.

The newspaper opened its new home in 1923, preceded by a huge celebration. About one thousand attended the opening, and about eight hundred were served at a supper illuminated by Japanese lanterns. John Gardella's band played for the celebrants, who came from miles around. A United States senator and a congressman, as well as many California officials, attended.

Hammond initiated the name "The Delta" in his early editorials, and it did its bit to bring together all the communities surrounding the state's rich agricultural district, in which no direct road to Stockton existed.

Before any road ran across the Delta, Hammond appealed for one, as well as for a paved road to Tracy. He, as much as anyone, deserves the lion's share of the credit for the state's construction of the Borden Highway which links Stockton with Byron-Brentwood. Another cause he successfully championed was for the building of the Antioch Bridge.

In 1931 Governor James Rolph appointed Harry Hammond California's state printer. He continued to publish the *Times* all through the years of his term, and when the new administration replaced him, he returned to Byron. Within a few months he died of a sudden heart attack. The final issue of the *Times* is dated June 1935.

Byron may be the only community in the country to celebrate a train wreck annually. On July Fourth in 1981, a fifty-car Southern Pacific freight train derailed and spewed massive iron coils, rails and train parts, closing Main Street for twenty-four hours.

The caption under this photograph in the Byron Times *read: "Home of the 'Byron Times,' $20,000 Structure of Surfaced Tile and Steel. Located on the main concrete highway in East Byron, where four roads converge. Building modernly equipped and fitted with store spaces. Beautiful red oleanders border the spacious parking space in the rear. To the left in the distance is the Delta home of Editor and Mrs. Harry Hammond with its two-acre demonstration orchard and gardens.—From a photograph by the Logan Studio of Stockton, Taken Expressly for the Twelfth Development Edition of the 'Byron Times.'"*

Ever since, residents have staged a colorful parade and held festivities in memory of the wreck.

The Byron Chamber of Commerce holds an annual Rail Faire, drawing an estimated 8,000 party goers between noon and midnight on a Saturday. Usually a parade of classic cars leads the floats and is followed by horse entries, marching bands, and uniformed groups. Cotton candy and barbecued beef eaters from fifty miles away join the locals in their celebration. The Odd Fellows Hall features model trains chugging and whistling along 800 feet of track through man-made tunnels and mountains.

The Hot Springs Hotel is in shambles, and the site of Harry Hammond's handsome brick building is now a vacant lot. Only a few businesses remain in Byron. Still, it will take more than the passing of a half-century to erase the memories of the town's two big reasons for being preserved in history.

Brentwood Market in 1910.   Charles Weeks Collection

Residence and farm of E. D. Grigsby, Point of Timber.
From Smith & Elliott's "Illustrations of Contra Costa Co."

Residence and farm of George Cople, Point of Timber.
From Smith & Elliott's "Illustrations of Contra Costa Co."

BRENTWOOD

John Marsh, the owner of Rancho Los Meganos, on which Brentwood would one day be established, died in September, 1856. Title to his 13,316-acre estate went to his four-year-old daughter, Alice. But her brother Charles clouded the title when he was appointed administrator of the estate, and on January 19, 1871, borrowed $30,000, giving the land as security.

About ten months later, the lender, the Savings and Loan Society (of San Francisco), forced a sale of Rancho Los Meganos to James T. Sanford of New York for $302,944, with $10,000 down. On November 1, 1871, Alice and Charles Marsh surrendered whatever interest they had.

Alice married in 1871 and moved to Oakland with her husband. He spent her legacy and later left her in disastrous circumstances.

The only thing Sanford did, worth remembering, was to sell a few acres to the San Pablo and Tulare Railroad Company. When its surveyors chose the site for a station, water tank, spur tracks and loading facilities, they selected the land for the village which became known as Brentwood, named for the town of the same name in County Essex, England, where John Marsh's roots had been. Sanford made the sale on May 28, 1877.

The railroad started running in 1878, and two businessmen moved in that fall. John Gruneaeur opened a store and Joe Carey a blacksmith shop. The United States Post Office opened the same year, and by the

The original Brentwood Hotel which burned down in 1912. Balfour, Guthrie Investment Company built a modern edifice to replace this one. Charles Weeks Collection

George H. Bedder of Brentwood, ca. 1906. Close examination of the details of this airplane's construction shows it to be of an advanced design for a pusher. Charles Weeks Collection

next spring several residences were completed.

In the meantime James T. Sanford had missed his mortgage payments. The Savings and Loan Society wasted no time, and the Contra Costa County sheriff sold Rancho Los Meganos to a man who immediately turned the title over to the Society. The date was March 16, 1878.

The new owners kept the rancho for twenty-two years. Dry land farmers arrived regularly and farmed on shares. Depending on the quality of the soil, they gave one-quarter to one-third of their crop of wheat or barley to the landlord for rent. Meanwhile shopkeepers were moving in. Soon Brentwood had a cobbler, baker, lumberyard operator, and another grocer. Three saloons were opened, and several dairymen served the village. In 1882 Brentwood could count 100 residents and enough children to support a school. The grammar school opened in 1879. In 1881 Brentwood's Methodist Church received title to its property from the Savings and Loan Society. Residents established two more churches in the next ten years, the Episcopal Church in 1885 and the Christian Church in 1890.

The Northern Railway, successor to the San Pablo and Tulare, surveyed the village, officially laying out wandering streets and homesites documenting its boundaries, and filed its map with the county in 1881. This action established the streets bounded by Railroad Avenue and Third, Spruce and Chestnut streets.

In 1890 Brentwood was declared to be the largest shipping point of wheat and barley between New Orleans and San Francisco. The two biggest shippers were Fish and Blum of Martinez and the California Wharf and Warehouse Company. They bought grain from farmers on all sides of Brentwood.

While grain came, at first, from tenant farmers, a federal statute caused tens of thousands of acres to be developed east and north of Brentwood. All through the delta, wet and dry years meant either too much water, which drowned out a year's planting, or too little moisture to grow a crop. Finally, in 1890, the Swamp and Overflow Act was enacted. Anyone willing to build dikes and drain the islands they formed could buy the result of his labors for one dollar an acre.

October 23, 1900, was the turning point for Brentwood. A group of Scottish inventors, Balfour, Guthrie and Company, bought out the owners of the Rancho Los Meganos for $200,799.43, approximately fifteen dollars an acre. In town they built a first class hotel. They underwrote the Bank of Brentwood in 1913 and the town's domestic water and sewer system.

A 1917 historian recorded his impressions of the town: "It is a neat country village with broad smooth streets and cement sidewalks. It . . . boasts a beautiful hotel built of fortified concrete, in the Mission style . . . an ornamental bank building, and a high school . . . supplemented by a manual-training school . . . "

Balfour, Guthrie spent $500,000 (in 1912 dollars) building electric pumping stations which poured irrigation water through their concrete-lined canals and into the ditches, which spread water over more than three thousand acres.

Balfour, Guthrie operated its thousands of acres under ten different identitites. In August 1917 it organized Brentwood Irrigated Farms Nos. 1 through 10. Each had its own headquarters and shops. Not all of the company's irrigated acreage was included in the ten camps. Some, suited to high yielding orchard crops, it sold off in fifteen- to twenty-acre parcels. It sold other smaller pieces for homesites and in the end recouped much of its low purchase price from these sales.

A few of the early buyers were Ethel Logan, A. C. Joslin, Ray Jones, R. F. McLeod, Thomas Hughes, John Hansen, J. A. Von Buren, Harry Osborn and R. E. Crawford. Their purchases took place between 1917 and 1927. The Liberty Union High School bought its property in April 1919.

By 1930 thousands of acres of fruit orchards were yielding heavy crops of apricots, peaches and cherries. Local hired hands tilled the soil, but imported labor became necessary for the fruit harvest. At the

A bucket brigade is trying to save this Brentwood rooming house. The first building out of sight to the left is the Bank of Brentwood building. Ca. 1912.
Charles Weeks collection

outset of the Great Depression, many farmers without income in the midwestern states loaded their families and their camping gear and headed for the Golden State. Some came for the harvest of 1931. The next year more came, and more the year after. So many destitute migrants came to Brentwood that farmers were able to get all the harvest help they wanted for seventeen and a half cents an hour. In 1934 the ranks were swelled by victims of the Dust Bowl in Oklahoma and Texas.

That year it was estimated from one thousand to fifteen hundred more pickers than were needed came to Brentwood. Cases of actual starvation were detected in some of the migrant camps. Tired, discouraged and broke, many of the pickers made their camps in vacant lots and along the railroad right-of-way.

Because of a shortage of apricots in other areas, Brentwood farmers received as much as eighty dollars a ton for their fruit, a princely sum at the time.

Organizers of the Cannery and Agricultural Independent Workers Union came out from the metropolitan area and organized pickets who patrolled in front of farm entrances for higher wages. They also harassed anyone picking fruit.

Contra Costa County Sheriff R. R. Veale deputized seventy-five armed men and issued an order to stop picketing. Deputies with a van followed convoys of strikers. The leader of one such convoy headed up a dead end road and, while turning around, the vehicles in the convoy crossed private property. Deputies arrested all of the workers. Before the magistrate, those pleading guilty were released while those pleading not guilty were jailed for three weeks.

The sixth largest grower in the area, Judge Robert Wallace, Jr., sentenced 137 strikers in one caravan to be "conducted . . . to a corral in the railroad yards, fed and escorted to the San Joaquin County line."

John A. Miller, the sheriff who followed Veale in office, offered his "Brentwood Plan" for the next harvest. By it the growers agreed: 1) Wages would be set *in advance* of the harvest; 2) Every farmer would agree to the same wage; 3) Every worker must agree to be registered by the sheriff's office and carry a registration card. Miller further exhorted the work-

This Brentwood Hotel served as headquarters for the Balfour, Guthrie Investment Company. It built the hotel after the original one burned in 1912. This one served until 1975, when wreckers removed it to make room for a service station. Charles Weeks Collection

The company's surveyors took sights on several thousand acres in preparation for the canals, pumping stations and irrigation ditches built on its land. The surveyors also staked out the domestic water and sewer lines for the system it built in Brentwood. Charles Weeks Collection

ers, "If you have any complaints, don't strike. See me!"

He said even twenty cents an hour was too low and suggested fifty cents. The two sides agreed on forty cents an hour, though about four thousand workers actually received closer to thirty cents.

Thus ended labor unrest in Brentwood. By 1940 the majority of growers had turned to labor contractors for their harvest help.

The Bank of Brentwood, established in 1913, built this building. Note the right-hand drive auto. The building is in use today as an antique store. Charles Weeks Collection

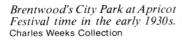

Brentwood's City Park at Apricot Festival time in the early 1930s. Charles Weeks Collection

John Marsh's Stone House

John Marsh came to California in 1836, arriving in Los Angeles. He rode on north later in the year, searching for a place to settle down. At almost the northern limits of the Mexican land grants he met a grantee, Jose Noriega, who accepted all the money he had, $500, for his 17,000-acre Rancho Los Meganos. This purchase made Marsh the first American settler in Contra Costa County.

On June 24, 1851, Marsh married Miss Abbie Tuck of San Jose. He took her to live in his four-room, earthen-floor adobe house. In 1854 he put artisans to work building the Stone House. Mrs. Marsh died in August 1855 before the workers finished construction.

In September 1856 John Marsh was knifed to death on the road just outside Martinez.

Contra Costa County Historical Society

KNIGHTSEN

Knightsen, named for George W. Knight, first appeared on the survey maps of the San Francisco-San Joaquin Valley Railway (later Santa Fe) in the summer of 1898.

The trains began running across the Eden Plain in the spring of 1900, when the railroad erected a section-house and a water tank for locomotive use and then a station. Mr. Knightsen, a nearby resident, built the first store, which housed his grocery and a post office.

Dairy farmers were already established in the area, shipping their milk and cream by the Southern Pacific to Bay Area markets. Upon establishment of the Knightsen station, the Santa Fe gained a large share of the shipments. Six dairies shipped a daily average of 2,500 gallons of bulk milk on the Santa Fe.

Eighteen ninety-eight view of Carter's threshing outfit. When drawn to a field to be harvested, the lead unit was set up as a stationary steam engine, usually fired by wood or straw. The second unit, a thresher, also stationary, threshed grain fed to it by hand by means of belts connecting it to the drive wheels on the engine ahead. The third unit is the cook's domain, a chuck wagon.
Charles Weeks Collection

Knightsen's Delta Road, ca. 1912. These first homes built in the village belonged to Bob Clark, Sam Redmond, Bill Redmond and Mrs. Heidorn. Charles Weeks Collection

The rich peat soil of the Delta yielded abundant celery and asparagus crops, and shippers built a packing plant, the first of several.

Until the mid-1920s most of the crops grown in the Knightsen area were shipped by boat from Babbes Landing, on a channel off Dutch Slough at the north end of Sellers Road.

Non-perishable crops such as hay and grain destined for the San Francisco Bay markets usually went on sailing scows. These vessels were flat-bottomed and drew so little water they could navigate in shallow streams. Vegetable and fruit crops were loaded on steam-powered stern wheel freight boats. With a shallow draft they were more sure to reach market without delay.

In only a few years trucks replaced the river boats. They came into the fields, picked up their loads and delivered them onto the customers' docks. So much less handling meant doom to the river boats, and by 1930 most had disappeared.

Unincorporated Knightsen is served by a community council in place of an elected government. People come to Knightsen to escape the crowded cities. The community has its center, a park and playground east of the Knightsen School. Its volunteer fire department, formed in 1952 by fourteen men, has three fire trucks and is associated with the Oakley Fire Protection District.

Knightsen has a Garden Club and a Sportsman's Club. The Wood Shop is on one side of the post office, and a thrift shop is on the other. Across the street, abutting a Santa Fe spur track, is the Diamond Sunsweet packing plant.

Knightsen residents have elbow room, yet live within reach of all the shopping amenities available to city dwellers.

A San Francisco stern-wheel river boat has come up a channel of Dutch Slough to load sacked potatoes at Babbe's Landing. Ca. 1920s. Charles Weeks Collection

Flat-bottom schooner-rigged scow about to depart from Babbe's Landing, north end of Sellers Avenue, Knightsen. Charles Weeks Collection

Above: Oakley's Baptist Church spire can be seen to the right. The first Oakley school is left of center. Victor Parachini-Charles Weeks Collection.

Below: Main Street, Oakley, before 1900. Charles Weeks Collection

OAKLEY

One of the three leading farmers of the area which eventually became Oakley said "no" to the Santa Fe agents who came to buy land from them for the railroad's right-of-way in 1897. However, R. C. Marsh, farmer and first postmaster, did counter with an offer to sell under rigid conditions, saying, "No, gentlemen, we will not sell you a right-of-way across the northwest quarter of Section 25, but we will *give* you a right-of-way if you will sign an agreement to put down at least a half mile of side-track, put up a small room for shelter while waiting for trains, and build us a station whenever the business will justify." The railroad signed, and transcontinental passengers began rolling through the village in the spring of 1900.

The land on which Oakley grew is predominately sand. Almond trees have flourished in it. At the turn of the century much of it sold at five dollars an acre in ten- to forty-acre plots. Until that time virtually the only inhabitants were jack rabbits and coyotes, though shrubbery gave cover for quail and wild pigeons. The land was government-grant land which James O'Hara had bought in 1887, for five dollars an acre. It was all covered with chaparral, live oak and wild daisies, which O'Hara cleared in order to plant eighty acres of almonds. Later he planted 160 acres more in nut and fruit trees. By 1912 he owned 700 acres in the area.

James O'Hara, born in Bangor, Maine, of Irish parents, has been credited with doing more for Oakley than anyone else.

R. C. Marsh did the initial subdividing, selling single lots to new arrivals. Among those were the merchants Frank Silva, Jerry O'Meara, Joseph Jesse, Henry Jannssee, and Arnold Van Kathoven. John Augusto opened the first blacksmith shop and also sold farm machinery. His brother, Joseph, established a lumber yard.

The first hotel in Oakley opened in 1908 when Mr. and Mrs. S. Dal Porto came to town. This couple came from Jackson, California, bought some acreage west of town and built their home there. After constructing the hotel they also built a town hall, which immediately became Oakley's social center.

In 1910 A. G. Ramos opened a store in which he specialized in harness of all kinds, whips, lap robes, and blankets.

A year after the Ramoses came to town, M. A. Ferrell opened another grocery store where he also sold feed and hardware.

Originally school children walked two miles west to the Live Oak School or one and a half miles east to the Iron House School. In 1904 Oakley built a new school building of its own, which sufficed until 1923, when another building, housing six teachers and about two hundred pupils, was constructed.

In 1913 a county branch library, housed in a general store east of town, offered some three hundred books to read. In 1916 the Oakley Women's Club, which was founded in 1913, bought the old Congregational Church, and the women invited the branch library to move to their building, which it did.

Fruit and vegetable wholesalers built packing sheds along the Santa Fe spur and shipped carloads of celery, asparagus and wine grapes to eastern markets. They also shipped almonds until the California Almond Growers Association established its processing plant and warehouse in the town. Then almost all the almond growers in Oakley joined the cooperative.

Field workers in the area were mostly Oriental and in the first decades of the century were paid from a dollar seventy-five cents to two dollars a day for ten hours of work, much of it stoop-labor.

Hindus, generally taller and heavier than the Orientals, had been recruited for building the dikes which created scores of islands in the Delta. Chinese settled on the larger ranches, principally to plant, till and harvest. Several towns along the Sacramento River had their Chinatowns, and Oakley had one too, albeit smaller by comparison.

Oakley's school boys unknowingly did as Shakespeare may have had in mind when he wrote, " . . . rush in where angels fear to tread." Oakley veteran Vic Parachini, who graduated from grammar school in 1912, tells of his and his schoolmates' experiences with the Orientals. "Our school was next to the Oakley Hotel. We were never sure what was going on upstairs there but later, as we grew older, we were sure it was what went on in what our parents would have called a house of ill-repute. Chinese men lived in houses behind the hotel. They had underground rooms for living and gambling.

"Downstairs I know Chinese smoked opium. In all my years I saw only one Chinese lady in town. One block off Main Street, on Ruby Street, three or four storefronts were gambling joints. Sam Kee bossed all of them. One of them sold candy and when any one of us went in for a handout we'd get a few lichee nuts or pieces of Chinese candy.

"I'll never forget the day I was in one of the stores. I'd peeked in the back room and seen stacks of twenty dollar gold pieces in front of each of the players, when the sheriff marches in. As the gamblers scurried out he seized the evidence and dragged Sam out into the street by his coat collar. The sheriff only took him across the street, gave him a lecture and let him go."

The boy congratulated the Chinaman on escaping being locked up in jail, only to hear, "He no put me in jail; if he do that he have to turn in my money."

Parachini relates one memorable experience with the Hindus. "They 'headquartered' at a camp they carved out of the tules down by the river. One day a bunch of us found them in a shot-putting contest. We challenged them to let us compete and they agreed.

This Live Oak School is the third by that name. Built in 1923, it is now a church. Contra Costa County Historical Society/Stein Collection

We beat every one of them and our hullabaloo brought a big, fine, athletic looking Hindu out of his tent. We made way when he reached for the shot. Not even warming up, only stretching a few times, he heaved the ball. It disappeared so far in the distance I don't think they ever found it. The most surprising thing about the man was that he said he had graduated from Oxford University in England. He sounded like it too. He'd been a member of their track and field team."

Fruit and vegetable packing companies built hundreds of yards of packing sheds along the north side of the half-mile-long spur track. They employed workers of Mexican descent, as many as two hundred for the season, February through September. Parachini, who worked as a telegraph clerk at the Santa Fe station for $27.50 a month in 1917, remembers the workers' annual arrival. "Many came in freight cars, loaded down with bed frames, mattresses and blankets, cooking utensils and boxes of food. It seems to me most of them came from Alameda County. Some drove old beat up trucks, their possessions filling the truck body and the overflow hanging from the side-racks.

"The packers worked fast. Crews loaded boxcars day and night. A Santa Fe engine came from Richmond every other day. Each time it pulled away forty-nine refrigerated cars to eastern markets.

"We had a mighty big fire in the 1920s when John Augusto's blacksmith shop and stock of new farm machinery went up in flames. His shop was on the corner of Main and O'Hara streets."

The Bank of Oakley, formed about 1917 by local citizens, had a relatively short career. The Santa Fe agent and the bank's cashier began speculating in the stock market in the late 1920s with the bank's money. It seemed as if everyone was gambling on the market, and stocks reached new highs day after day. When the market crashed on a November day in 1929, the bank's money didn't cover its losses. The cashier put a gun to his head, ending the shame he felt. The bank closed in 1930 and the town was without any bank for a long time, until the Central Bank opened an Oakley branch.

The Oakley Hotel was built in 1908.
Victor Parachini-Charles Weeks Collection

In 1915 the town's principal north and south street, O'Hara Avenue, except for the first three blocks off Main Street, was a loose sandy trail. O'Hara had bale after bale of straw spread over the wheel tracks, but many was the automobile which had to be towed out of the O'Hara Avenue sand. Chaparral still covered the sandy hills in 1915, coming within a quarter mile of town. At that time there were only five cross streets: Main, Acme, Ruby, Star and Home.

Shortly after World War II ended, refrigerated trucks started picking up crated vegetables in the fields, bypassing the packing sheds in town. One after another of the plants along the railroad failed to open, and as long-distance refrigerated trucking grew so the railroad's importance to Oakley diminished. Finally no plants opened and shortly thereafter the Santa Fe pulled up its long spur track.

The Oakley Municipal Advisory Council serves as the city government. In an economy move the town shares the services of a fire district.

Today the businesses in Oakley serve a much larger population—people making their homes in the new modern subdivisions. Most of the residents work elsewhere but call Oakley home.

Antioch's first brick school building, ca. 1870. D. O. McKellips-J. E. Boynton Collection

Old Antioch pottery works at about Twentieth and G streets. Another operated near the Fulton shipyards. Clay deposits in the Antioch hills made this industry viable. Ca. 1870s.
D. O. McKellips-J. E. Boynton Collection

ANTIOCH

In December, 1849, two brothers wanting to settle down approached Dr. John Marsh asking to buy a few of his Los Meganos acres. The doctor welcomed the new neighbors and sold each of the brothers, Joseph and William Smith, 160 acres on the northwest corner of his estate.

The brothers pitched their tents and broke ground for the first building at Smith's Landing. They called it "New York House," and almost at once it became the stopping place for miners sailing up or down the San Joaquin River.

Joseph died in 1850. Eager for neighbors, William sailed in September to San Francisco, where he found a company of new arrivals uncertain about where to go. The group had come around Cape Horn in their homemade ship, the *California Packet No. 2*. Smith invited Captain George W. Kimball and his brother to bring their party to Smith's Landing and offered each family a free housing site, which they accepted.

Half the group left at once for the gold fields and the rest accepted Smith's gift. He hired the men to cut wild hay on the islands across from the Landing. They piled it on a scow and sailed to San Francisco, where Smith sold the hay for sixty dollars a ton.

After a day's work as a carpenter, William Smith baked bread and doughnuts, two specialties guaranteed to popularize his establishment. Doughnuts brought in fifty dollars a day, and bread was one dollar a loaf. Within a few years, when the town had a baker, bread sold for only five cents.

Men who left their boats on the river bank, seeking companionship in the warm atmosphere of the New York House, slept on the floor for one dollar a night if they brought their own blankets. The proprietor, a former minister, prohibited the consumption of liquor on his premises.

At the Independence Day picnic in 1851 over thirty settlers came. Smith, still feeling the loss of his brother, proposed changing the name of the settlement. His words were, "Inasmuch as the first settlers [he and his brother] were disciples of Christ and that one of them has died and was buried on the land, that it be given a Biblical name in his honor." He suggested the

Early view of Antioch. D. O. McKellips-J. E. Boynton Collection

213

Empire Coal Mine locomotive in front of Antioch depot. S. H. McKellips is the engineer in the cab, and George Hawkhurst, the mine superintendent, is standing arms akimbo. Dan McKellips-J. E. Boynton Collection

Empire Coal Mine and Railroad coal loading facility at Antioch. Houseboats used for living quarters were common on the town's waterfront. Dan McKellips-J. E. Boynton Collection

name Antioch, a Syrian town where two important rivers meet, mentioned in the Bible.

Cholera hit the community in 1851. It took a father, his two sons and a relative all within a few days of each other. Several more died on board a ship anchored in the river between Antioch and Collinsville.

By 1851 steam-powered river boats ran up and down the rivers. That year the first regular service to San Francisco was established by a Captain Miller. Captain Charles Bartlett succeeded him within a year.

Antioch has a long history of successful commercial enterprise. J. C. McMaster started the trend when he established a brick making plant in 1852, using clay from the nearby hills. A year later, Martin Hamburg built a two-story house and store of the local brick.

For years, sheep raising served as Antioch's principle industry. The many miles of grazing land north of the San Joaquin River carried thousands of head, and regular transportation to and from Collinsville became a necessity. In the 1860s the steamer *Pert*, captained by the partners Turner and Cosine, ran the triangular route, Antioch, New York of the Pacific (Pittsburg) and Collinsville.

One schedule called for an Antioch departure at 10:30 a.m. and the return from Collinsville at 2:30 p.m. Subsequently, larger boats on frequent schedules, plying to San Francisco from Stockton and Sacramento and making stops at all the populated landings, replaced the smaller boats like the *Pert.*

Among the many early businesses in Antioch were the local lumber company, grain warehouses, two hotels, a farm equipment agency, several blacksmiths, a variety store, a shoemaker, a Chinese laundry, a pottery, a distillery, a copper smelter, and several general merchandise stores.

In 1865 Joel Clayton, from the town named for him, became an Antioch subdivider. He filed an ambitious map covering 122 blocks. It was almost a century before residents occupied most of them. In 1874 William Smith, representing the farmers' cooperative, Antioch Grange, filed a subdivision map of the waterfront property owned by that organization.

Possibly the first school in Contra Costa County was one contributed by a ship owner in 1851. Captain Mitchell had beached his ship on the Antioch riverbank. He removed the small ship's galley (deckhouse) and set it up on land. Twelve-year-old Adelia Kimball taught the first classes. Later Miss Martha Douglas reigned there as the town's teacher. Seventy years later, one of her first pupils, Mrs. A. B. Schott, described the classroom: "I was twelve then . . . the house was dark and small, while out of doors was big and bright, and we had fine recesses."

A small school, built after one year in the ship's cabin, served Antioch until 1869. That year the district built its first two-story building. In 1890 a new Antioch Grammar School, also two-story, began serving the community. Its pupils finished their schooling when they graduated from the elementary school since there was no high school until 1903. The Riverview Union High School District, founded that year, served Antioch, Pittsburg (Black Diamond then), Somersville, Nortonville and Live Oak.

A fire hit the town at one o'clock in the morning on March 23, 1871. It broke out in the warehouse of the

Ladies in fancy hats pose on the balcony of the Arlington Hotel while boys and girls sit in the carryall. Hotel was at 610 Second Street, Antioch. D. O. McKellips-J. E. Boynton Collection

Griffith Hotel. A stiff wind fanned the flames and in a few minutes they engulfed the livery stable, filled with hay. An eyewitness later described the terror: "It jumped across the street to McCoy's two-story shop on the opposite corner, and then his dwelling to the rear. Then it wiped out the block between 2nd and 3rd streets. By two o'clock the fire burned up two blocks and lit up the town like noonday. . . . Here, as we stood at the corner of Main Street at 2nd . . . in a

Old Antioch's planing mill on the river. Henry Beede bought into the mill in the 1870s; a fourth generation descendant is still involved in the firm. Ca. 1880. D. O. McKellips-J. E. Boynton Collection

The Antioch Cash Store was at the corner of Second and G streets. The low-bed dray was operated by Bullock Brothers. D. O. McKellips-J. E. Boynton Collection

Empire Coal Mine train leaving the coaling dock for Stewartsville. Dan McKellips-J. E. Boynton Collection

Early Antioch with Hunter's Livery Stable on the left and J. Ross's grocery and hardware store on the right. D. O. McKellips-J. E. Boynton Collection

Tyler's Hotel, Antioch. Mr. Noakes, the butcher, sold meat from the back of his wagon, at left. D. O. McKellips-J. E. Boynton Collection

The S. H. McKellips Antioch home in 1883. Built in 1882, it still stands opposite the Historic Center. D. O. McKellips-J. E. Boynton Collection

sudden brightness, a mountain of flame fanned by the rushing north wind . . . the village of terrified inhabitants running hither and thither . . . in every condition, in and out of houses, throwing and pouring every sort of article into the streets. There was scarcely a sound to be heard save the involuntary, 'Oh God!'"

Two city blocks were devastated and insurance coverage only covered $10,000, a stunning loss.

Antioch incorporated in February, 1872. The first president of the board of trustees was Russell B. Hard. Its first ordinance read, "It shall be unlawful for any person to drive or lead any horse, mule, jack, jennie, ox, cow, calf, or any other animal upon any sidewalk in town." Inasmuch as such sidewalks as existed at the time were wooden, the ordinance must have been needed.

Unusual social customs prevail today, but one has

to wonder what disturbing conditions caused Ordinance #33 to be written. It read: "[residents] are forbade to look in the direction of an opium smoker. Penalty $100." That was a great deal of money in 1872, as much as two months wages for most.

Long-lasting reminders remain of the industry which came to Antioch in 1876. That year the Empire Company started building its narrow-gauge railway to Stewartsville, up in the hills six miles south of town. A series of five coal mines eventually operated in the area. The railroad built its locomotive roundhouse at the corner of Fourth and F Street.

At first the local railroad shipped its coal by barge. Within a year the standard gauge San Pablo and Tulare Railroad Company ran through Antioch. It loaded coal into its gondolas by gravity, from overhead tracks of the Empire line.

The city had about 600 people when it incorporated and thirty years later, in 1902, still had fewer than 700. But Antioch was on the threshold of big changes. In the years before the Antioch Bridge opened (1926), two modern propeller-driven boats, the *Duchess* and *Princess*, ferried passengers and freight between Antioch, Rio Vista, Stockton and Sacramento.

The Jarvis Brothers built ships at Smith's Point before their plant became the Fulton Shipyards in 1924. During World War II Fulton completed twenty-seven vessels for the navy.

The Hickmott Canning Company came in 1920 and the Western California Canners later.

Prior to the opening of the Antioch Bridge, auto and truck travel to points north of the Sacramento River went on a long roundabout trip, either to Tracy and Stockton or to the Vallejo Junction Ferry. The Lauritzen Transportation Company answered the need with the ferry *Sherman*, running it every two hours between Antioch and Sherman Island. In 1923 the ship carried 16,000 vehicles across the river.

Athough Peter and James Brown expanded the initial paper mill, the Fibreboard Products Company and Crown Zellerbach have made Antioch an important factor in the Pacific Coast paper products industry.

The Pacific Gas and Electric Company generates electricity, burning natural gas piped in from as far away as Canada.

With these and other industries, Antioch's population grew to 28,500 in 1970. Since then residential subdivisions have provided housing for residents employed elsewhere. Now, in 1986, the city estimates its population to be over 47,000.

Antioch First Brass Band, 1884. Left to right, back row: Clarence Laverty, bass drum; Dan McKellips, solo cornet lead; Chas. Van Benschoten, cornet; Will Collis, cornet; Elmer Page, first alto; Harry Beede, first alto. Front row: Tom Sterling, tenor; Chas. Beede, second cornet; Frank Wills, first cornet; Emmett Wemper, second cornet; Star King Williams, tuba. J. E. Boynton Collection

Morning Star Hotel, ca. 1890. Contra Costa County Historical Society

The building at the left may have been at 601 Second Street. Ca. 1890s.
D. O. McKellips-J. E. Boynton Collection

The carryall met the trains, carried passengers to their homes or hotel, and was patronized much as we use a transit bus in 1986. Ca. 1910. D. O. McKellips-J. E. Boynton Collection

Antioch's El Dorado Hotel, where in the early 1900s, dead men were sometimes found behind the building on Sunday mornings. Some locals called the establishment "The Bucket of Blood." D. O. McKellips-J. E. Boynton Collection

Pittsburg's fishing fleet, ca. 1940. Called Monterey double-enders, these boats were powered by a gasoline engine and a spirit-rigged sail. They carried a two-man crew, were under thirty-two feet in length, had a retractable keel for sailing in shallow waters, and a removable rudder so that nets could be hauled in over the stern. The canneries at Pittsburg made the town a fishing port. In 1957 the State mandated the end of commercial fishing in the rivers. Pittsburg Historical Society and Museum

PITTSBURG

As early as 1849 a cabin with a tule roof lay deserted in the hills above New York Landing. Charles N. Wight, who had been living in it since 1847, took his place in history as the first Anglo to make his home at what would one day be Pittsburg.

In the fall of 1849, Colonel J. D. Stevenson and Dr. W. C. Parker bought the 10,000-acre Rancho Los Medanos from its owners, Jose Antonio Mesa and Jose Miguel Garcia, for 500 *pesos*. That year, the partners laid out the town of New York of the Pacific below the deserted cabin. At the same time the newly arrived brothers, W. W. and Joseph H. Smith, contracted to build the first house for Stevenson and Parker.

They constructed a public house, eighteen by forty feet at first, later adding twenty more feet to its south end and attaching a twenty by fifty foot tent to its west side. The structure became known as the New York House.

The next building was one owned by Dr. Forejos of San Francisco and operated by Henry F. Toy, who lived with an Indian squaw by whom he had a son. Feeling bogged down and wanting to get away, Toy traded the boy for a horse and the squaw for a Newfoundland dog, then took off and rode across the hills to Clayton, where he lived for the rest of his life.

In the spring of 1850 John Nicholls came to the New York House. Feeling the community was about to grow, he bought an old ship, the *Mount Vernon*, tied it to the river bank, and converted it into a boarding house.

Falluca fishing boats were the first used in the Delta. Italian boat builders designed them after the boats fishermen used in the Mediterranean. The houseboat served the fishermen as their residence. Pittsburg Historical Society and Museum

A few men did come—many were discouraged miners from the gold fields—but moved on when they heard about the coal mines about to open at Nortonville, six miles to the south; and the village languished.

By 1860 the Nortonville mines were shipping their coal by railroad down to the San Joaquin River and the name of the terminal was changed from New York Landing to Black Diamond. For a full decade coal left on freight boats. Then the San Pablo and Tulare Railroad ran its trains through Black Diamond and west to a connection with the Northern

Railway at Martinez, making delivery possible by rail all the way to Oakland.

In 1874 the first fishermen, Pietro Aiello and his brother Rosario, went back to Sicily after fishing the river for four years. Pietro returned to Black Diamond with his Sicilian bride in 1881. Other members of his and his wife's families followed them back. Their praise of life in the New World resulted in a large Italian population, most of them fishermen and their families, in Black Diamond. By about 1910, forty years after Pietro first came, it is recorded that almost one thousand Italians worked the rivers nearby.

While fishermen successfully fished the San Joaquin and Sacramento rivers, the Nortonville mines closed intermittently. The population of the village dropped and with it so did Stevenson and Parker's interest in their investment. They sold out to a San Francisco banker, Louis A. Pioche. Other problems beset the banker and before too long he commited suicide, but not before turning over his interest in Rancho Los Medanos to veteran railroad builder, attorney and land speculator L. L. Robinson. The new owner, much to his credit, rented ten-acre parcels to tenant farmers. He built each a home and

The five-masted bark Kobenham *loading lumber at the Redwood Manufacturing Company mill at Pittsburg, ca. 1920. The* Kobenham *was the largest sailing ship ever to come this far up the Sacramento River.* Pittsburg Historical Society and Museum

barn. Most kept a cow, chickens and a pig, and all grew a vegetable garden.

Robinson died one day when a stranger came into his San Francisco office and shot him. In 1900 his heirs sold his remaining 8,500 acres to C. A. Hooper and his brother, W. G. Hooper. Both were successful San Francisco businessmen. They paid $175,000 for the land, approximately twenty dollars an acre.

C. A. Hooper soon bought out his brother and actively sought industry to occupy his nearly ten miles of river frontage. Hooper's plan is still to be seen a century later.

Meanwhile the fishing industry was the backbone of Black Diamond. In the 1880s four canneries were buying fish from the Italian fishermen, first the Pioneer Canning Company and the Black Diamond Cannery. The other two came later, the Limberger Salmon Packers and the American Fish and Oyster Company. Frank Booth operated a small cannery on nearby Chipps Island. After a time he deserted it, going to Monterey where he became the world's largest sardine packer. He returned to Black Diamond in 1907, when he bought out the veteran J. D. Haller Company.

Beginning in 1892 a little recognized one-man boat works began producing double-ended gasoline-powered fishing boats which gradually replaced the sailing craft. Frank Seeno started the yard, which produced what became known as *Montereys*. This efficient boat became popular up and down the Pacific coast and for years was the standard for fishermen on the ocean and in the rivers. Seeno expanded his business and the yard remained one of Black Diamond's steadiest employers for years.

While the fishing industry prospered, C. A. Hooper brought industry to Black Diamond. He established his Redwood Manufacturing Company there in 1903. The Bowen Rubber Company came the same year. Six months later the town's first bank opened.

C. A. Hooper operated an electric generating plant for the town until 1910, when the Great Western Power Company took it over, serving the community with power from its hydro-electric plants at Big Bend in the Sierra.

The first Los Medanos Hotel was built on East Third Street between Cumberland and Los Medanos, ca. 1904. Contra Costa County Historical Society

This Hotel Los Medanos replaced the earlier by the same name. Built at Tenth and Los Medanos in 1917, it burned down in 1981. Pittsburg Historical Society and Museum

In 1910 the largest employer of all came to Black Diamond. The Columbia-Geneva Steel Company started on a small scale on nineteen acres, employing sixty men. It made steel castings for machinery used in dredges, ships, and in the lumber industry. Ultimately Columbia-Geneva became a part of United States Steel, increasing the firm's capacity to a 1,000-

St. Peter Martyr Church at the corner of Eighth and Black Diamond is left of center, and the rectory is to the right in this pre-1930 view. The present church was constructed on the vacant lot in this picture. The Sacramento Northern tracks are in the foreground. Pittsburg Historical Society and Museum

acre facility employing 6,000 persons at its peak.

Now the steel industry dominated the town. Its name, Black Diamond, a synonym for coal and a dead issue for twenty years, didn't suit the populace. On May 25, 1911, the residents voted to change its name to Pittsburg.

Over the years since, more and more plants have opened and a few have closed or been absorbed by larger firms. In 1912 the Cowles Chemical Company, which made a cleaning agent of silicate and detergent, opened in Pittsburg. The Stauffer Chemical Company bought out Cowles in 1965.

The forerunner of Dow Chemical, the Great West-

ern Electro-Chemical Company, opened on July 1, 1916.

More and more plants chose Pittsburg, and what C. A. Hooper had begun kept rolling on, gathering more good for the community even after he died in 1914. His company carried on until it dissolved voluntarily in 1950.

Others who came included the Diamond Flour Milling Company, Diamond Brick Company, Diamond Model Dairy, and Johns-Manville Company, which employed as many as 350 men, Shell Chemical Company, employing 250 persons, Gladding McBean and more.

Above: Christopher Columbus about to land at Pittsburg from his flagship Santa Maria *to begin a Columbus Day celebration, date unknown.* Pittsburg Historical Society and Museum

Below: Christopher Columbus, priest and officers before the 1936 parade. The large Italian population in Pittsburg began the annual event to honor their famous countryman in 1911 and still hold Columbus Day celebrations. Men in this picture are James Davi, Walter Carusa, Paul Guiliano, Joe Lucido, Larito Magna, Lupe Auguilar, Irvin Carusa, and Anthony Russo. Pittsburg Historical Society and Museum

Left, Queen Mae Latimer (Dempsey) reigned over the 1912 Columbus Day celebration. Pittsburg Historical Society and Museum

Below: Looking north over Camp Stoneman, which covers the lower two-thirds of this 1945 view of Pittsburg. To the left of Railroad Avenue is the West Garrison. Built beginning in 1942, deactivated in 1954. Pittsburg Historical Society and Museum

COAL MINING TOWNS

Nortonville's business district before the fire. Contra Costa County Historical Society/Stein Collection

Along a six-mile Contra Costa ridge, prospectors found coal outcroppings six miles south and paralleling the San Joaquin River, between Pittsburg and Antioch.

The first such find occurred in 1855, and subsequent discoveries followed every few years until 1877.

They sacked the first coal they dug out and teamed it down to the river. Ultimately three coal-carrying railroads ran down the grade to separate landings. The docks were at Pittsburg (called Black Diamond then) on the west and Antioch on the east, and the third was in between, at Pittsburg Landing (formerly known as New York of the Pacific).

The coal cars were loaded near three towns. Actually the three were clusters of mines, identified as Nortonville on the west, Stewartsville on the east, and Somersville between them.

Nortonville's Black Diamond Mine was the colossus of them all. It was a series of seven different mines, all connected underground by tunnels.

About three hundred men and boys worked in the Black Diamond, and the town's population rose to between nine hundred and one thousand people. Most were either Welsh or of Welsh parentage.

Some miners with families had large two-story, four-bedroom homes. These houses contained a dining and living room and in a few instances even an outdoor aviary.

Nortonville had the usual fraternal societies and churches and the Carbondale elementary school. This was the first school in the mining area. From Black Diamond down at the river, pupils rode horses up the hill to the Carbondale classrooms. Students from Somersville walked the one mile to Nortonville. When coal trains started running, children from Black Diamond rode them to and from school. At its peak attendance, 400 pupils attended the eight-room school.

As miners dug their shafts deeper, water seeped in, preventing excavating of the more profitable seams.

Stewartsville, with the mining company store where the combination flat and passenger car is standing.
Dan McKellips-J. E. Boynton Collection

Right: The first train crew of the Empire Coal Mine Railroad standing in front of the Antioch station. Left to right, William Bullock, Elmer Page, S. H. McKellips, Putney Reed. Dan McKellips-J. E. Boynton Collection

Below: Empire Coal Mine combination flat and passenger car is carrying passengers to Antioch. Dan McKellips-J. E. Boynton Collection

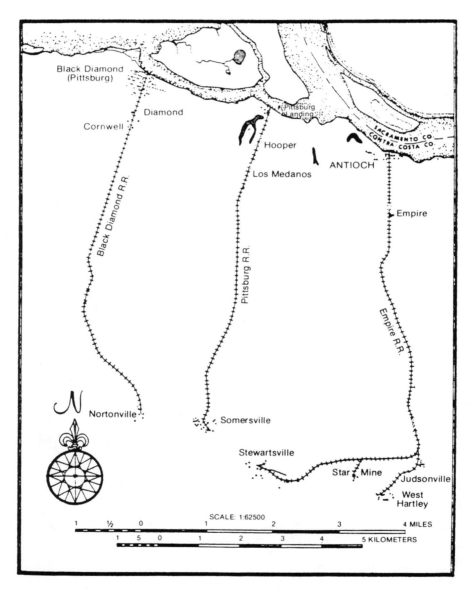

Map shows the three railroads which ran from the San Joaquin River up to the coal mines in Contra Costa County's Carbondale District. After U.S.G.S. Mount Diablo and Antioch Quadrangle maps, 1898 edition

Somersville, ca. 1878.

Contra Costa County Historical Society

Timbering the fractured rock in walls and ceilings so far underground became impractical and too expensive to continue. After yielding approximately three million tons of coal, the Nortonville mines shut down, except for one shaft, in 1885.

Somersville, the middle cluster of mines, sacked its first tons of coal in 1855 in its Union Mine. Four years later two more were producing, and in 1860 the final shaft was operational. Between 1855 and 1860 all the coal was sacked and delivered by mule-drawn teams.

One year later, in 1861, the several Somersville mines combined into one, the Pittsburg Mining Company. Its railroad down to Pittsburg Landing required eight trestles, one sixty feet high, to cross the canyons just in the upper part of its route. As in all three railroads, loaded coal cars, each carrying four and one-half tons, rolled under gravity all the six miles down to the river. After they were unloaded, a locomotive pulled a string of empties back up the grade to the loading chutes.

In 1877 the Pittsburg Mining Company shut down temporarily because of a strike over wages and an accumulation of water in the shafts. About five hundred families called Somersville home when the Somersville mines shut down.

They reopened a year later, but a lower grade of coal found less and less favor with customers. By 1902 output was negligible but enough was mined to keep the railroad in operation until 1916.

The Empire Mine, the principal mine at Stewartsville, opened in December, 1878. Its railroad, the Empire Mine and Coal Railroad Company, was the longest of the three railroads and the last to start running. It began its climb into the hills ten years after the Pittsburg Railroad started serving the Somersville mines.

Some of the extra time taken to build the line was because of the ten trestles, three of them large, and the 1,000-foot-long tunnel bored through the hills.

The trains ran from the wharf through Antioch on F Street. After climbing six miles they made a right angle turn to the west for two and a half miles more before reaching Stewartsville. In between, three branches took off, one going to the Empire, another to the West Hartley, and the last to the Star Mine. The railroad used thirty-five bottom-dump four-ton coal cars; a thirty-foot-long combination car, half passenger coach and half flat car; and several tank cars. Families rode the combination car along with freight. In wet weather they rode in the enclosed section and on clear days on the open half.

235

On his Somersville property Mr. Hobson erected a three-story house. In his garden he built a large aviary. Contra Costa County Historical Society/Stein Collection

Miners received between three and four dollars a day. Railroad engineers were paid the most, $120 a month, but firemen and brakemen usually earned only $50 a month.

None of the three towns ever had a city government or a police department, but each did have a constable. Somersville had a jail, later moved to Brentwood, and a justice of the peace. He was Sam Brown, owner of a general merchandise store. However, there was not much crime; the hard work and long hours left little idle time for the mischievously inclined.

Somersville had a grade school, which the young from Stewartsville also attended. No public high school existed anywhere in Contra Costa County before 1901. Leaving grammar school as early as age twelve, most boys went to work to help bolster the family income.

Stewartsville suffered numerous fires and near the end of its mines' lives, many of its residents moved over to Somersville.

Not only were the miners hard workers but some were very enterprising. One Somersville Welshman

Stewartsville coal bunkers. At the left is the cable-operated incline railroad used to haul supplies up the hill. Dan McKellips-J. E. Boynton Collection

Locomotive and coal cars under the loading chute at Stewartsville. Cars come out of the mine at upper left and dump their loads into the bunker. Dan McKellips-J. E. Boynton Collection

by the name of Lougher came all the way from Australia's gold fields. He built a two-story house and raised a family. He bought a farm in the area when the mines shut down and went on ranching for the rest of his life. His descendants still live in the East County.

Another immigrant who didn't speak English at first also did well. Giovanni Ginochio came to Nortonville in 1876 from a village near Genoa, Italy. He built a two-story house with four bedrooms upstairs. While mining for wages, he enlarged his home to accommodate a billiard table, a bar, and a dormitory for single men. With social contacts scarce in the community, Ginochio's house gained great popularity and his resulting prosperity made him wealthy. His descendants also still live in Contra Costa County.

The energy required to lift the coal and pump out the seepage water from the Black Diamond, whose shaft reached down 700 feet, made the cost of its coal too high, and the Nortonville mines shut down in 1885. The company moved its railroad and equipment to Black Diamond, Washington, where it mined a superior grade of anthracite at less cost. Somersville's major production ended in 1902.

Ownership of both mining properties went to a company formed for the purpose of maximizing the income from them. The Southport Land and Commercial Company, with headquarters in San Francisco, acquired approximately 2,000 acres and has sold some, traded some, and developed other property, notably along Railroad Avenue in Pittsburg. Southport has been in business for over one hundred years.

In 1922 the Hazel-Atlas Glass Company began mining silica sand at the site of the Pittsburg mine. Another sand deposit, at Nortonville, furnished foundry casting sand for the Columbia Steel Company, also beginning in 1922. It is a coincidence that both sand mines opened and closed the same years; they closed for very different reasons, however. Competition from Belgian sand glass drove Hazel-Atlas away in 1949. The Columbia Steel foundry closed its doors the same year, ending the mining at Nortonville.

For the ensuing quarter century livestock grazed Southport's property. Gradually public interest in the mines became so strong that the East Bay Regional Park District formed the Black Diamond Mines Regional Preserve in 1974.

The district bought the forty-seven-acre Nortonville townsite, and Southport made it a gift of 137 additional acres. Today the preserve covers approximately three thousand acres and welcomes visitors to its museum, the underground home, and tours through a few of the mine tunnels.

The Empire Coal Mine train is standing on the longest trestle between Antioch and Stewartsville. Dan McKellips-J. E. Boynton Collection

Reflections of a Mail Carrier

The young mail carrier between Clayton and Antioch, Leslie Mitchell, when in his late eighties in 1956, reminisced about his early days.

"My route was from Clayton to Antioch, through the mining towns off the Nortonville trail. I would be up at the break of dawn, feed Paint with hay and grain, eat my own breakfast, and saddle up.

"I would take the old stage road to the top of the hill and then take the miners' trail which led by the Nortonville School which stood in a little vale. There were more than a hundred scholars attending that little school . . . They would wave as I passed by and I would answer with a wave of the hand . . . I would ride up through Nortonville and up another hill and down through a gulch on the winding trail . . .

"There were about 600 miners working there . . . they worked in the bowels of the earth, in the smouldering pits of hell. They worked by a little oil lamp. They never knew when they went on shift just how they would come up . . .

"I would rather ride over hill and dale out where the winds blow free. I would ride on . . .

"That day has passed. The mines are closed and the miners have all drifted on. Now I have grown old, can't ride anymore, my horses are all dead or gone. It ain't far now to the end of the trail . . . Old Paint will be there by the side of the gate when the Lord waves his magic wand. Then I'll throw on my pack and ride through space to that land of the great beyond."

BIBLIOGRAPHY

Bancroft, H. H. *History of California*, Vol. VI.

Bernhand, Robert G. *Richmond*. Contra Costa Historical Society, 1965.

Blackmur, Arnold. *In Old Diablo*. Diablo, 1930.

Boeshcen, John. *El Sobrante Recollections*. El Sobrante Rotary Club, 1984.

Bohakel, Charles. *Historic Tales of East Contra Costa County*, Vol. 2. Antioch, California, 1984.

Boysen, Sue. *Some Historical Highlights of the History of Pittsburg*. Pittsburg, 1964.

Brown & Kaufman, Inc. *Early Days of San Ramon & Diablo*. 1966.

Burgess, Sherwood. *The Forgotten Redwoods of the East Bay*. California Historical Society, 1951.

Cole, Susan D. *Windows to the Past*. Richmond, 1980.

Collier, George C. *A Narrative History of Contra Costa County*. El Cerrito, 1983.

Columbus-Founders Savings. *Richmond Historical Calendar*. Richmond, 1966.

Contra Costa Times. February 23, 1986.

Griffin, Evan. *Early History of Richmond*. Richmond, 1938 and 1939.

Hansen, Earl. *East Shore & Suburban Railway*. 1961.

Homestake Mining Company. *Sharp Bits*. Lead, South Dakota, May 1964.

Hulanski, F. J. *The History of Contra Costa County*. Berkeley, 1917.

Jones, Virgie. *Remembering Alamo*. Alamo, 1975.

Kaiser Shipyards. *Fore & Aft*. Richmond, February 1, 1946.

Kensington Improvement Club. *A Survey of Kensington*. Kensington, 1966 and 1978.

Kimball & Merryman. *La Fayette—A Pictorial History*. Lafayette: Lafayette Historical Society, 1976.

Lindstrom & Griffin. *Alhambra Valley*. Martinez: Contra Costa County Historical Society, 1970.

Lyman, George D. *John Marsh Pioneer*. New York: Scribner & Sons, 1930.

Munro-Fraser, M. P. *History of Contra Costa County*. San Francisco: W. A. Slocum & Co., 1882.

Murdock, Dick. *Port Costa 1879-1941*. Port Costa, 1977.

Mutnick, Dorothy. *Horace W. Carpentier: A Man of His Times*. Lafayette, 1977.

––––––. *Some California Poppies & Even Some Mommies*. Lafayette, 1980.

Plew, Joe Ann. *Pinole—History in Pictures*, 2nd edition. Richmond, 1976.

Purcell, Mae. *History of Contra Costa County*. Gillick Press, 1940.

Rose, Gerald. "The Brentwood Plan for Agricultural Labor." Unpublished.

Roselius, Donna. "A Brief Unofficial History of Point Richmond." The Point Richmond Historical Association, 1985.

Swett, Ira L. *Sacramento Northern.* Los Angeles, 1962.

San Ramon Business Directory, 2nd edition. San Ramon, 1985.

Shell Oil Company. *Enterprise in Oil.* Martinez, no date.

Soule, Frank, et al. *Annals of San Francisco.* San Francisco, 1855.

The *Tri-Valley News.* April 16, 1976.

Wagner & Sandow. "Map of Alameda & Contra Costa Counties." 1899.

Whitfield, Vallie Jo. *History of Pleasant Hill.* Pleasant Hill, 1981.

Whitnah, Joseph C. *A History of Richmond.* Richmond: Richmond Chamber of Commerce, 1944.

Young, Andrew H. *The Improvers of Lafayette.* Lafayette: Lafayette Historical Society, 1976.

INDEX

Abbott, Dr. C. L. (Clark), 135, 151
Abbott, Dr. U.S., 135, 151
Abbott Sanitarium, 135
Acalanes Union High School District, 116
Acree's Market, 75
Adobe Restaurant, 28
Adobe Street, 28
Africa, 6
Aiello, Pietro, 226
Aiello, Rosario, 226
airfield, 48, 146
airplane, 146, 200
Alameda, 134
Alameda County, 68, 83, 90
Alameda Refinery, 134
Alamo Masonic Lodge #122, 68
Alamo Postoffice, 69
Alamo Square, 68
Alden Dell, 108
Alexander Park, 180
Alhambra Cemetery, 6
Alhambra High School, 10
Alhambra Hotel, 4
Alhambra Valley, 39
Alhambra Water Company, 10
Allen, Don, 106, 107
Allen, Judge John J., 106
Allen, Liston, 106, 107
Allen, Margaret, 89
Allinio, Pierre, 126
Alpine, The (mining company), 24
Altamont Pass, 181
Alvarado, Juan B., 140, 142
Alvarado Adobe, 141, 142, 144, 146
Alvarado Park, 135, 137
Alvarado Place, 142
Alvarado Square, 146
Amador, Señor José, 83
Amelia, 178
American Fish and Oyster Company, 227
American La France, 152
American Oriental Oil Company, 10
American Smelting and Refining Company, 173
American Toll Bridge Company, 178
American Trust Company, 31, 115

Amtrak, 136
Anderson, George, 25
Anderson, Jack, 25
Anderson, Capt. Ludwig, 39
Anderson's Lumber Yard, 40, 42
Andreasen, Vern, 85
Annie Carolyn, 40
Anthony, Susan B., 182
Antioch Brass Band, 219
Antioch Bridge, 195, 219
Antioch Cash Store, 216
Antioch Grammar School, 215
Antioch Grange, 215
Antioch Pottery Works, 212
Antioch, Syria, 214
Apache, 21
Apricot Festival, 203
Aquatic Festival and Bass Derby, 169
Arlington Acres, 122
Arlington Avenue Shopping Center, 124
Arlington Estates, 124
Arlington Hotel, 215
Arlington Pharmacy, 124
Armstrong Preparatory School, 127
Arroyo Cañada, 137
Arroyo de las Nueces, 55
Associated Oil Company, 10
Associates National Bank, 28
Astor House (Shanghai, China), 189
Auguilar, Lupe, 229
Augusto, John, 209, 211
Augusto, Joseph, 209
Australia, 238
Australian, 10, 185
Austrians, 106
Avon, 72
Avon J. Hanford, 168

Babbes Landing, 206, 207
Bacon, Samuel S., 15, 31
Baldwin, Robert, 83
Balfour, Guthrie Investment Company, 199, 200, 201, 202
Bancroft, H. H., 142
Bank of America, 58, 93, 103
Bank of Brentwood, 200, 201, 203

Bank of Byron, 191
Bank of Concord, 30, 33
Bank of Oakley, 211
Bank of Pinole, 157
Bank of Richmond, 132
Bank of Tracy, 191
Baptist Church, 142
Barnes, "Bill," 102
Barrett, George, 131
Barrett, Mrs. M. A., 86
Barrett farm, 131, 134
BART, 32, 59, 111, 115, 136
Bartlett, Capt. Charles, 214
Bartlett pears, 102
Bartnett Harness Factory, 40
Bateau, Monsieur, 40
Bates and Borland, 126, 127, 128
Bay Cities Power Company, 178
Bay Point, 16, 92, 102
Bay Point and Clayton Railroad, 29, 35, 36
Bay Point Breeze, 18
Bay Point Iron Works, 18
Bayshore Properties, 51
Bear Creek, 151
Bechtel, S. D., 137
Beckman Instruments, 85
Bedder, George H., 200
Beebe, B. F., 37
Beede, Henry, 216, 219
Beede, Charles, 219
Belding, William F., 144
Benicia, 34, 89, 181, 183
Benicia-Martinez Railroad Bridge, 11
Benicia-Martinez Vehicular Bridge, 3
Bennett, Seely J., 113
Berg, "Chris," 183
Bergeron, Vic, 128
Beringer Bros., 153
Berkeley Fire, 122, 124
Berkeley Highland Terrace, 122
Berkeley Highlands, 122
Berkeley Hills, 90
Berkeley Oil Company, 92
Berkeley Park, 122
Berkeley Police Department, 124

243

Berkeley Steel Company, 135
Berkeley Woods, 122
Bernal, Juan, 99
Berryessa, Jose de Los Santos, 5
Betts, G. F. (blacksmith), 40
Biel Hall, 16
Big Bend, 227
Big Bull Valley, 183
"Big Four," 79
"Billiard Hall," 79, 80
Bird, Harry, 105
Bishop Ranch, 85
Bishop Ranch Business Park, 85
Bishop, Thomas, 84, 85
Bishop (Thomas) Company, 84, 85
Bixby, Dr. W. E., 30
Black and Decker, 138
Black Diamond, 225-28, 232
Black Diamond Cannery, 227
Black Diamond Mine, 232, 238
Black Diamond Mines Regional Preserve, 238
Black's Cannery (Joseph), 10
blacksmith, 93
Blake, Anson, 126
Blake, Arthur, 49, 126
"Bloody Seventies," 150
Blum, Gabriel, 6
Blum's Brickyard, 40
Boeing Air Transport, 33
Booth, F. E., 227
Boquet, August, 137
Boquet's Union Saloon, 141
Boss, 45
Botelho family, 70, 100
Botts, R. H., 140
Bowen Rubber Company, 227
Boyd and Field, 71
Boy Scout Troop #126, 153
Boy Scouts, 108
Bradley House, 3
Bradley's Cash Market, 116
Brauen, Walter, 189
Brentwood City Park, 203
Brentwood Hotel, 199, 202
Brentwood Irrigated Farms, 201
Brentwood Market, 199, 202
Brentwood Methodist Church, 200
"Brentwood Plan," 202
Brevensville, 84
Brewer, William H., 21
Brewin, Eli, 83, 84
Briones Regional Park, 162
Broadway Plaza, 58, 62
Brookside Hospital, 145
Brown, Elam, 89, 90, 93, 97
Brown, James, 219
Brown, Otto, 93
Brown, Peter, 219
Brown, Richard, 129
Brown, Sam, 236
Brown, Thomas A., 3
Bruzzone, Russell, 103
Bryant, A. J., 111
Bryant Station, 114
Buchanan Field, 34
Buchanan, William, 34

"Bucket of Blood," 221
Buckley, William H., 111
Bullock Brothers, 216
Bullock, William H., 233
Bull's Head Oil Company, 10
Bull Valley, 181
Bunker, R. M., 6
Burg, Mrs. Blanche, 152
Burgess, Robert N., 47, 48, 79, 80
Burlington, The, 185
Burton School, 96
Byron Bakery, 191
Byron Chamber of Commerce, 196
Byron Hot Spring, 189, 191, 192, 196
Byron Hotel, 191
Byron Market, 191
Bryon Times, 194, 195

Caldecott Tunnel, 57, 92, 94, 111, 115
California Aerial Transport Company, 32
California Almond Growers Association, 210
California and Nevada Railroad, 99, 100, 113, 114, 118, 150, 151
California Beet Sugar Company, 45, 47
California Cap Company, 127, 130, 138, 144
California-Hawaiian Sugar Company, 49
California-Hawaiian Sugar Refinery, 176, 177, 178
California Hotel, 15
California Maritime Academy, 178
California Packet #2, 213
California Parks and Recreation Society, 162
California Point of Historical Interest, 95
California Powder Company, 142, 161
California State Printer, 195
California Wharf and Warehouse Company, 181, 200
California Wine Association, 135
camels, 6
Campolinda High School, 99, 117
Camp Stoneman, 57, 230
Camp Rockefeller, 140
Camp Tracy, 192
Camron, William, 112, 114
Cannery and Agricultural I.W.U., 202
Canyon City, 108
Canyon Lake Drive, 182, 185, 186
Canyon Park, 106, 107
Canyon Postoffice, 110
Canyon School, 105, 108, 110
Canyon Store, 106, 107, 109
Cape Horn, 213
Capwell, H. C., 58, 59
Carbondale Elementary School, 232
Carbondale Elementary School District, 234
Cardinet, George, 26
Cardinet Glen #1, 26
Carey, Joe, 199
Carothers, Dr. J. H., 14, 39, 40, 41, 42
Carpenter, Capt. A. D., 8
Carpentier, Horace W., 99, 100, 149
Carquinez Bridge, 178, 179
Carquinez Straits, 10, 168, 175, 178
Carroll, Michael, 99
Carter's threshing outfit, 205
Carusa, Irvin, 229

Carusa, Walter, 229
Casa Orinda, 116
Castro, Don Francisco Maria, 140, 148
Castro, Gabriela, 142
Castro, Jesus Maria, 140
Castro, Juan, 149
Castro, Patricio, 149
Castro, Victor, 125, 126, 149
Castro ranch, 151, 152
Catholic Church, 10, 27, 42, 191
Catholics, 182
Cave, The, 128
C. E. Long, 39
Centerville, 90
Centex Homes of California, 162
Central America, 146
Central Bank, 211
Central California Oil Company, 92
Central Contra Costa County Sanitary District, 58, 76
Central 11 Market, 153
Central Pacific Railway, 142, 174, 178, 181
Central Valley Bank, 137
Cerruti, Henry, 142
Chalet, 80
Chapeute (Sharkey), 151
Charles, Augustus, 111
Charles Hill (Road), 111, 114, 149
Charles Van Damme, 136
Cherogino, A., 25
Chevron Refinery, 131, 138
Chevron Service Station, 86
Chevron U.S.A., 85
Chicago Livestock Fair, 84
Chihuahua, Mexico, 21
Chile, 156
Chinatown, 210
Chinese, 83, 125, 127, 177, 215
Chinese boys, 127
Chipps Island, 19, 227
Chittenden, John, 124
Chochenyo, 112
cholera, 214
Choris, L., 112
Christian Brothers, 8, 102, 103, 104
Christian Church, 200
Christopher Columbus, 229
Chung, Mei, 127
Church-on-the-Hill, 91
Citizen, 156
City of Bay Point, 15
City of San Rafael, 136
Civic Arts Theater, 57
Civil War, 6
Clark, 45
Clark, E. J., 21
Clark, Robert, 206
Clarke, Raymond, 136, 139
Clark's Market, 103
Clayton Brewery, 25
Clayton Club, 24
Clayton Hall Association, 25
Clayton Hotel, 2, 24, 26
Clayton, Joel, 21, 215
Clayton, Margaret Ellen, 22
Clayton Saloon, 22

Clayton Store, 22, 25
Clayton Valley, 15, 27, 35
Close, Lillian, 75
Clyde, 18
Clyde Hotel, 18
coal, 4, 182
Coalinga, 134
Coalinga-Martinez pipe line, 193
Coffin, Oliver C., 4
Cohen's Store, 68
College Inn, 128
Collins, Francis, 156
Collins, John, 156
Collins, Mr., 26
Collinsville, 214, 215
Collis, Will, 219
Coloma, 89
Columbia-Geneva Steel Company, 227
Columbia Steel Foundry, 238
Columbus Day, 229, 230
Community Building (Lafayette), 94
Community Center (Lafayette), 96
Community Congregational Church, 15
Concord Air Field, 33, 34
Concord Chamber of Commerce, 32
Concord Elementary School, 31
Concord Hospital District, 32
Concord Inn, 30
Concord Jazz Festival, 35
Concord Mercantile, 30, 33
Concord Pavilion, 35
Concord Plaza, 30
Concord Sewer District, 26
Concord Sun, 27
Concord Transcript, 27
Condie, John, 24
Cone, Dr. F. B., 30
Congregational Church, 10, 25, 182, 189, 191, 209
Conklin's Hotel, 116
Conklin's Tavern, 116
Contra Costa, 184
Contra Costa College District, 145
Contra Costa Community College District, 51
Contra Costa Country Club, 45
Contra Costa County Flood Control District, 42
Contra Costa County Public Works Department, 58
Contra Costa County Telephone and Telegraph Company, 10
Contra Costa Educational Association, 68
Contra Costa Gazette, 6, 40, 41, 42
Contra Costa Golf Club, 49
Contra Costa Light and Power Company, 10
Contra Costa News, 6
Coos Bay, Oregon, 15, 16
Coos Bay Lumber Company, 15, 16
Cople, George, 198
Copper King, Ltd., 15
Cora, 8
Corners, The, 4, 60
Cottage Hospital, 145
Courthouse, 5, 6, 8, 10
Courter, John, 99

Cowell Lime and Cement Company, 29, 36
Cow Hollow, 23
Cowles Chemical Company, 228
Cox's Hill (Grove), 86
Crandall, J. W., 21
Crawford, R. E., 201
Crissy Field, 33
Critchett, Mr. and Mrs., 132
Crockett, John B., 175
Crockett Community Center, 180
Crockett Hotel, 176, 177, 178
Crockett Men's Club, 180
Crolona, 177
Crossroads Restaurant, The, 116
Croviotto, Henry, 116
Crow Canyon Road, 83, 85
Crown, Henry, 85
Crown Zellerbach, 219
Cuadra, Charlotte, 156
Curry, James, 24
Curtiss Eagle, 33
Curtola, Lawrence, 81
Curve, The, 116

Dal Porto, S., 209
Danville-Alamo Garden Club, 75
Danville Emporium, 74, 75
Danville Grammar School, 74
Danville Hotel, 72
Danville Journal, 75
Danville Livery Stable, 73
Danville Sentinel, 75
Danville Square, 75
Danville Women's Club, 75
Davi, James, 229
Davis, John, 126, 131
Deadfall, The, 21, 22, 23
De La Salle High School (Concord), 8
De La Salle Institute, 6, 8
de Laveaga, Edward, 115
de Laveaga, Jose, 115
de Laveaga, Miguel, 115
de Laveaga station, 113, 118
Del Rey School, 99
Delta, 194, 195, 206, 210, 225
De Martini, Paul, 25
De Martini Winery, 25
Dennickson, D. D., 21
deputy poundmaster, 105
Dexter's Service Station, 146
Diablo, 18
Diablo Country Club, 80, 81
Diablo Valley, 21, 27, 29, 39, 68, 114
Diablo Valley College, 42, 45, 51, 117
Diamond Brick Company, 228
Diamond Flour Milling Company, 228
Diamond Model Dairy, 228
Diamond Sunsweet (Knightsen), 206
Dimond Canyon, 105
Dodge, Van Mehr and Company, 122
Dohemann, Gordon H., 103
Dohrmann, Henry, 141
Don Hotel, 138
Dougherty, James, 83
Douglas, Martha, 215

Dow Chemical Company, 228
Downer, Edward, 136, 156, 157
Downer Land Company, 157
Duchess, 219
Dukes, Ida, 46
Dukes, Lucy, 46
Dukes, 45, 46
Dukes, May (Hall), 46
Dukes, Nettie (Boss), 46
Duncan, Robert, 21
du Pont (E. I.) de Nemours Company, 161
Durango, Mexico, 21
Durham, Capt. Joshua, 38
Dust Bowl, 202
Dutch Slough, 206, 207

Eagle Hotel, 40
Eagle Saloon and Ice Cream Parlor, 24
Easley, William H., 26
East Bay Municipal Utility District, 58, 76, 94, 109, 116, 150, 152
East Bay Regional Park District, 153, 238
East Bay Water Company, 122
Eastman Tag and Label Company, 138
East Richmond Hotel, 145
East Shore and Suburban Railway, 126, 135, 138
Eastyard, 134
Echman slaughter house, 127
Eddy, Harvey, 74
Eddy, Leonard, 71
Eden Plain, 205
Edwards, Thomas, 175, 176, 177
El Cerrito Fire Department, 129
El Cerrito Junior High School, 129
El Cerrito Kennel Club, 128, 129
El Cerrito Plaza, 125, 129
El Dorado, 89
El Dorado Hotel, 221
El Hambre Creek, 3
Ellen, 136, 139
Ellerhorst, Annie, 156
Ellerhorst, Mr. and Mrs. Christopher, 156
Ellis, Capt. George, 131
Ellis Landing, 131
El Paso, Texas, 21
El Rey Market, 61
El Rey Theater, 61
El Sobrante Fire District, 152
El Sobrante Improvement Club, 153
El Sobrante Library, 152
El Sobrante Postoffice, 152
El Sobrante Veterans Club, 153
El Sobrante Women's Club, 152
Elston, Jack, 89
Emeric, H. F., 131
Emeryville, 100, 114, 115, 150
Empire Company, 218
Empire Mine, 214, 216, 233, 235
Empire Mine and Railroad Company, 233, 235
Englemire, George, 67
English walnuts, 102
Episcopal Church, 200
Erath, K., 24
Europe, 10, 48

Excelsior Powder Company, 144
Excelsior Soda Works, 40

Fabian and Levinsky, 189
Fairfield, M. M., 77
Fairmount School, 128
Fair Oaks, 48
Falluca, 225
Farmers Block, 41
Farmer's Market, 47
Feather River, 68
Felice and Perrilli Canning Company, 137
Fernandez, Bernardo, 148, 154, 156
Fernandez, Dr. M. L., 156
Ferreira, W. C., 83
Ferreira, William J., 83
Ferrell, M. A., 209
ferry, 3, 9, 181
Fibreboard Products Company, 219
Fidelity Savings, 59
Fiesta de Lafayette, 96
Fiesta Market, 96, 97
Fiesta Square, 90, 96
fire, 30, 41, 42, 68, 96, 102, 122, 124, 167, 182, 184, 189, 195, 201, 215, 231
fire department (Lafayette), 94, 96
First National Bank (Concord), 31
First National Bank (Rodeo), 168
Fish and Blum, 200
Fish, Clarence, 20
Fish, Lafayette I., 20
Fish Ranch, 99, 111
Fish Ranch Road, 41, 96
Fitzgibbon, Dr. C. C., 30
Flood, Edward, 92
flood, 39, 41, 43, 47, 48, 62, 158
Ford, Henry, 168
Ford Model A, 152
Ford Model T, 50, 60, 94, 108, 129
Ford Motor Company, 131, 136
Forejos, Dr., 225
Foskett, Ellworthy and Keller, 64
Foxboro Neighborhood Park, 162
Fraser Building, 157
Fraser's Grocery, 157
French Hotel, 40
Frenchman, 24, 125, 126, 151
Friend (George) Company, 124
Fresno, 15
Fry's Market, 153
Fulton Shipyards, 212, 219

Galindo, Frederick, 33
Galindo, Francisco, 27, 42
Galindo, Maria, 3
Gallagher, Miss, 32
Galli, Mr. and Mrs. Edward, 153
Galveston, Texas, 6
Gamble Farm, 25
Garcia, Francisco, 67
Garcia, Jose Miguel, 67, 225
Gardella, John, 195
Garrett, M. M., 94
Gar Wood, 138
Gaspar family, 70
Geil Building, 92

Geldermann, Harlan S., 70
General Chemical, 138
Genoa, Italy, 238
German, 192
German U-boats, 16
GFC (fire engine), 152
Ghiglione, Frank and Rose, 94
Ginochio, Giovanni, 238
Ginochio, Mrs. Mary, 145
Girl Scouts, 108
Gladding McBean, 228
Glass, Claude, 86
Glass, David, 83, 86
Glen Terry Winery, 24
Golden Gate, 135
Goldfield, Nevada, 173
Goleta, California, 84
Gomez, Lefty, 169
Good Templars Hall, 91, 93
Grand Ball, 94
Grand Canyon Park, 135, 137
Grange Hall, 72
Granger's Business Association, 181
Granger's Warehouse Association, 8
Granger's Wharf, 6
Granite Powder Company, 144
Grant, Angus, 99
Grayson Creek, 39, 41
Great Britain, 137
Great Depression, 15, 49, 57, 81, 102, 114, 202
Great Republic (mining company), 24
Great Western Electro-Chemical Company, 228
Great Western Power Company, 10, 227
Green Front Building, 194
Green Valley, 71
Greenwood and Moran, 141
Gregory Gardens, 48
Gregory Gardens Shopping Center, 48
Gregory Lane, 48
Gregory Village, 52
Grey, N. E., 191
Greyhound, 57
Griffith Hotel, 215
Grigsby, E. D., 197
Grizzly Peak Boulevard, 122, 149
Growers Square, 57
Grubb and Ellis, 116
Gruneaeur, John, 199
Guiliano, Paul, 229
"Guymen," 112

Hacienda Homes, Inc., 115
Hale, William, 6
Hale and Fossett, 40
Hale Brothers, 40
Hall, Hiram, 50
Hall, Maria, 99
Hall, Myron Ward, 69
Haller, J. D. Company, 227
Hall-Scott, 138
Hamburg, Martin, 214
Hammond, Harry, 194, 195, 196
Hammond, Dr. J. W., 189
Hammond, Margaret, 194
Hanlon's Wharf, 176

Hansen, John, 201
Hard, Russell B., 218
Hardy, Vernon, 111
Harlan, Joel, 83, 84
Harlan, Mrs. Minerva J., 87
Harris, Reuben, 83
Hart, Mrs. E., 189
Hartz, John, 72
Hawaii, 177
Hawkhurst, George, 214
Hawley, Mr., 167
Hawley's General Merchanidse Store, 167
Haywood, Edna, 32
Haywood, Jim, 32
Haywood, Mrs. Viola, 30
Hazel-Atlas Glass Company, 238
Heald, John, 175, 177
Hearst, William Randolph, 80
Heidorn, Mrs., 206
Heinz Brothers, 15
Heinz Company, 127
Hemme, August, 68, 69
Hemme Park, 70
Henderson, Capt. Gus, 39
Hendrick, W. K., 39
Hendrick's Flour Mill, 39
Henry's Hotel, 67
Herald, 162, 168
Herald Building, 153
Hercules Civic Arts Department, 162
Hercules Park and Recreation Department, 162
Hercules Powder Company, 156, 161, 162, 167
Hercules Properties, Ltd., 162
Hickmott Canning Company, 219
Hillside Vista Acres, 108
Hilltop Mall (Road), 136, 138
Hindu, 210, 211
Hink, John, 26
Historic Center, 218
Historic Triangle, 92
Hobson, Mr., 236
Hodgkins, Charles B., 18
Hoey, James, 6
Hoffman, Henry, 67
Holy Ghost, 141
Homestake Mining Company, 184
Homestate Savings and Loan Association, 103
hoof-and-mouth disease, 144, 147
Hook, Elijah, 41
Hook, William, 45
Hook's Store, 42, 45
Hookston Station, 45, 51
Hookston Winery, 45
Hooper, C. A., 102, 227, 228
Hooper, W. G., 227
hospital, 30, 32, 145
Hough, Milo, 89
Howell, Edwin, 129
Huber, William, 126
Huchium, 112
Huffman, Harold, 152
Hughes, Thomas, 201
Hunters Home, 133

Hunters Livery Stable, 217
Huntington, Collis P., 131
Hurst, H. C., 83
Hushbeck, Copland and Rogers, 191
Hutchinson, Tallentyne, 126
Hutchinson Quarry, 126, 127

Ida, 39
Indian, 21, 112, 125, 132, 136
Inman, Andrew, 72
Inman, Daniel, 72
Inmanville, 72
I.O.O.F., 189, 196
Ione, 4
Ireland, 22
Iron House School, 209
Irvine, James, 102
Issaquah, 168
Italian, 176, 225
Iverson Banking Company, 136

Jackson, California, 209
Jacob and Levi, 141
Jannssee, Henry, 209
January Block, 29, 30
Japanese, 34, 45, 49, 102, 191
Jarvis Brothers, 219
Jason Smith's Leather Shop, 40
Jefferson, Carl, 35
Jensen, Darrell, 34
Jesse, Joseph, 209
John F. Kennedy University, 117
John Muir National Historic Site, 3, 7
Johns-Manville Company, 228
Johnston, Thomas, 21
Jones, John M., 67, 69
Jones, Nathaniel, 89, 98
Jones, R. M., 6
Jones, Ray, 201
Jones, William Carey, 99
Joslin, A. C., 201
Joslin, S. B., 222

Kaiser, Henry J., 137
Kaiser Hospital, 145
Kaiser Shipyards, 137, 146
Kamehameha, King, 155
Kee, Sam, 210
Kennedy Grove, 153
Kensington Community Council, 124
Kensington Park, 122
Kensington Police Protection District, 124
Kensington School, 124
Kensington Shopping Center, 122, 124
Keokuk (mining company), 24
Kern County, 134
Key System, 135
KGO (station), 57
Kimball, Adele, 215
Kimball, Cap. George W., 213
Kimball, G. W., 222
Kirker, James, 21, 22
Kirkwood, W. A., 25
Knight, George W., 205
Knightsen Community Council, 206
Knightsen Garden Club, 206

Knightsen School, 206
Knightsen Sportsmen's Club, 206
Knightsen Volunteer Fire Department, 206
Kobenham, 226
Kozy Kove, 132
Krumland, Ed, 189

Lafayette Chamber of Commerce, 96
Lafayette Creek, 89
Lafayette Design Project Committee, 96
Lafayette Hotel, 91
Lafayette Improvement Association, 94, 96
Lafayette Plaza, 90, 91
Lafayette Reservoir, 94, 96
Lafayette School, 92
La Fiesta Market, 96, 97
La Fiesta Square, 90, 96
La Honda Bowl, 153
Lake of the Redwoods, 99
Lake Cascade, 115
Lake Orinda, 115
Lamson, Joseph P., 105
Lander, Miss, 25
Lander and Keller, 25
Langs Drug Store, 132
Larsen, Margaret, 24
Las Juntas, 51
Las Trampas (creek), 58
Latimer, Queen Mae, 230
Laurel Glen Resort, 151
Lauritzen Transportation Company, 219
Laverty, Clarence, 219
Le Grand, Tobe, 189
Leidesdorff, William, 89
Le Roy's Wild Idle Saloon, 189
Liberty Ships, 137
Liberty Union High School, 201
Limberger Salmon Packers, 227
Limerick, 72, 84, 86, 114
Lime Ridge, 23
Lincoln Highway, 170
Lindberg, Charles, 49
Little Bull Valley, 183
Live Oak School, 209, 210
Livermore, Robert, 85
Livermore, California, 181
Livermore Valley, 89
Logan, Ethel, 201
Lommel, Dick, 60
Lone Tree Point, 168
"Long Store", 40
Longo, Judge Joseph, 169
Long's Drugs, 103
Los Angeles, 128
Los Banos, 189
Los Medanos Hotel, 227
Los Meganos grant, 114, 213
Loucks, Annie, 39
Loucks, George P., 39, 42
Loucksville, 39
Lougher, Mr., 238
Lucido, Joe, 229
Lutheran Church, 121
Lynch, Leo, 83
Lynchville, 84

Macdonald, A. S., 131, 134
Macedo family, 70
Macy's Department Store, 138
Madrone Park, 106
Magna, Larito, 229
Mahoney Field, 32
Majestic Theater, 32
Majors and Dorman, 54
Maple Grove Homestead, 111
Maple Hall, 143
Mare Island Navy Yard, 167
Marin County, 112, 127, 139
Marott, Maury, 75
Marsh, Alice, 112, 199
Marsh, Charles, 199
Marsh, John, 21, 112, 114, 199, 204, 213
Marsh, R. C., 209
Martinez, Ignacio, 5, 7, 155, 167
Martinez, Rafaela, 155
Martinez, Vincent, 3
Martinez-Benicia Bridge, 11
Martinez Packing Company, 10
Martinez School District, 8
Masonic Lodge (Alamo), 68
Masonic Lodge (Martinez), 5
Matteson, Charley, 152
Matteson, Francis E., 78
Mauvais, Romero, 24
Mauzy, Lucille Glass, 88
Maybeck, Bernard, 18
Maybeck Development, 122
McAvoy, 51, 56
McLeod, R. F., 201
McClure, Rev. David, 68
McCosker, Al, 108
McCoy's, 215
McKellips, Dan, 219
McKellips, S. H., 214, 218, 233
McKenzie, Dr. George, 30
McMaster, J. C., 214
McNear, George, 177, 181
McNeill, William, 92
McPherson, Daniel R., 71
Mead, Lewis Risdon, 189
Mechanics Bank (Richmond), 136, 137, 157
Mediterranean, 225
Meehan Hardware Store, 30
Meese, William, 83
Meese's Grove, 86
Mehran, Masud, 85
Mello family, 70
Merchants Exchange (Alameda County), 68
Mesa, Jose Antonio, 225
Methodist Church, 25, 84, 85, 86, 92, 157,
    191, 200
Methodist Episcopal Church, 10
Metropolitan Match Factory, 130
Mette and Company, 4
Mexico, 146, 173, 175, 211
Mexican government, 21
Middle Redwoods, 105
Military Intelligence Department, 192
Miller, Captain, 214
Miller, State Senator George, 58
Miller, John A., 202
Miller & Lux, 112

"Millionaire Specials," 80
Mills Field, 34
Minor, Edward, 126
Miramonte High School, 117
Mission San Jose, 105
Mission Santa Clara, 89
Missouri, U.S.S., 49
Mitchell, Aunt Polly, 67
Mitchell, Capt., 215
Mitchell, Leslie, 239
Mitchell, William, 67
Mitchell Canyon, 23, 24
Miwok, 112
Mix (theater), 169
Mohawk Mine, 173
Monterey double-enders, 224
Mokolumne River, 116
Monterey, 3
Montereys, 227
Montgomery Ward and Company, 138
Moraga, Ella, 99
Moraga, Gabriel, 99
Moraga, Jeremiah, 21 PLACE
Moraga, Joaquin, 99
Moraga, Pablo, 39
Moraga Barn, 101, 102, 103
Moraga Center, 103
Moraga Company, 101, 102
Moraga Hardware, 102
Moraga Heights, 108
Moraga Hotel, 101, 103
Moraga Land Association, 99, 100
Moraga Library, 102
Moraga Mercantile General Store, 101
Moraga Park and Recreation Authority, 103
Moraga Redwood Heights Extension, 108
Moraga Redwoods, 89, 105
Moraga Shopping Center, 100, 103, 109, 114
Moraga Townsite Subdivision, 102
Moraga Valley, 100, 102, 105
Moraga Valley Railroad, 99, 100
Morales, Aparicio, 6
Morales, Charles, 153
Morgan County and California Rangers of Illinois, 22
Morning Star Hotel, 220
Morris, J. W., 40
Morris, Judge, 24
Morrow, Dr. William, 140
Morrow Cove, 178
Mountain Copper Company, 10
Mount Diablo, 4, 15
Mount Diablo bunker, 181
Mount Diablo Country Club, 81
Mt. Diablo High School, 10, 29, 74
Mount Diablo Park Club, 80
Mount Diablo State Park, 80
Mount Diablo Winery, 24, 25
Mount Vernon, 225
Mount Zion, 24
Mount Zion Copper Company, 24
Mount Zion Mining Company, 24
Muir, Helen, 7
Muir, John, 7
Muir, Louie, 7
Muir, Wanda, 7

Muir Trestle, 11
Munro-Fraser, J. P., 142
Murderous Creek, 48
Mutt and Jeff, 159
Mystery, 131

Napa County, 168
National Association of Homebuilders Magazine, 162
National Park Service, 7
Naval Ammunition Depot (Naval Weapons Station, Concord), 16
Navellier, Louis, 126
Navy Fuel Depot, 135
Neff, Dr. F. F., 30
Nejedly, John, 58
Neustaedter Building, 30
Nevada Dock and Warehouse Company, 181
Neves, Manuel, 102
Newfoundland (dog), 225
New Lafayette Hotel, 90
New York House, 213, 225
New York Landing, 225, 235
New York of the Pacific, 215, 225, 232
Nicholl, John, 131, 135, 136, 225
Nicholl (John) Company, 136
Nicholl Knob, 131, 140
Ninety Club, 128
Noakes, Mr. (butcher), 217
Noriega, Jose, 204
Norris, Leo, 83, 84
Norris Canyon, 82
North Berkeley, 122
Northern Railway, 126, 142, 175, 200
North Pacific Coast Railroad Company, 139
Norton, Mr., 124
Nortonville, 173, 181
Nystrom, John R., 135
Nystrom, Stanley, 135
Nystrom Public School, 135

Oak Grove Grammar School, 56
Oak Grove Park, 150
Oakland-Antioch Railway, 51, 92
Oakland, Antioch and Eastern Railway, 18, 75, 76, 79, 101, 106, 108
Oakland Estuary, 89
Oakland Post-Enquirer, 153
Oakland Sunland Subdivision, 102
Oakland Traction Company, 121, 135
Oakland Transit, 126
Oakland Tribune, 108, 153
Oakland Trout Farm, 111
Oakley Fire Protection District, 206
Oakley Hotel, 209, 210, 211
Oakley Municipal Advisory Council, 211
Oakley School, 208
Oakley Women's Club, 209
Oakley's Baptist Church, 208
Oak View Park, 111
Oakwood Park Stock Farm, 79
Ocean Wave, 131, 140
Odd Fellows Hall, 15, 41, 72, 75, 195
O'Hara, James, 209, 211
Ohio Valley, 22, 79

Ohlone Neighborhood Park, 162
Old Antioch "planing" mill, 216
Oldfield, Barney, 50
Olive, John, 111
Oliver's Hardware, 153
Olsen, Capt. Haakon, 168
Olson, Oliver, 136
O'Meara, Jerry, 209
Oporto, Portugal, 154
Orinda Country Club, 115
Orinda Crossroads, 99, 111, 114, 115, 117, 118
Orinda Improvement Association, 115
Orinda Park, 112, 113, 114
Orinda Park Hotel, 112, 116
Orinda Park Pool, 115
Orinda Park School, 111
Orinda Park Terrace, 115
Orinda Theater, 103, 116
Orinda Village, 115, 116
Osborn, Harry, 201
Oxford University, 211

Pac Bell, 85
Pacheco, Don Salvio, 27, 28
Pacheco, Fernando, 27, 28, 42
Pacheco Cash Store, 44
Pacheco Creek, 25
Pacheco Flour Mill, 41
Pacheco Speedway, 34
Pacheco Tobacco Company, 40
Pacific Coast Oil Company, 134, 140
Pacific Coast Shipbuilding Company, 16
Pacific Gas and Electric Company, 80, 219
Pacific Patent Plaster Company, 168
Pacific Refining Company, 166
Pacific Telephone and Telegraph Company, 79
Pacific Vegetable Oil, 138
Page, Elmer, 219, 233
Palace Brewery, 24
Palace Hotel, 32
Panama-Pacific International Exposition, 79
Parachini, Victor, 210, 211
Park Cottage, 24
Park in Rheem Valley, 103
Park, Recreation and Parkway District, 163
Park Theater (El Sobrante), 153
Parker, Dr. W. C., 225, 226
Parr, Fred, 136
Parr Terminal, 136
Payne, Mr., 194
Paso Nogal, 48
Pearl Harbor, 57, 58, 81, 102, 124, 137, 192
Pechart, "Big Bill," 128
Pedretti, Charles, 142
Peer's Saloon, 189
Penney, J. C., 58, 137
Peralta Redwoods, 89
Pert, 214
Petrini's, 103
Peyton Chemical Company, 10
Philips, Katherine Fowler, 114
Pierce, Henry, 111
Pinehurst Park, 106
Pinehurst Road, 105
Pinkerton Hotel, 178

Pinole-Hercules Elementary School, 157
Pinole-Hercules Methodist Church, 161
Pinole-Hercules News, 161, 169
Pinole Light and Power Company, 157
Pinole Opera House, 157
Pinole Progress, 153
Pinole Theater, 159
Pinole Times, 156
Pinole Valley, 155
Pioche, Louis A., 226
Pioneer, The (mining company), 24
Pioneer Canning Company, 227
Pioneer Store, 92
Pittsburg Landing, 232
Pittsburg Mining Company, 235
Pittsburg Railroad, 235
Plaza, The (Lafayette), 90
Pleasant Hill Airport, 34
Pleasant Hill High School, 49
Pleasant Hill Market, 49
Pleasant Hill Park, 50
Pleasant Hill School, 49
Point Castro, 139
Point Isabel, 127, 138
Point Molate, 135
Point Orient, 133, 134
Point Richmond, 127, 131, 135, 136, 151, 152
Point San Pablo, 135
Police Protection District, 124
Port Chicago, 18
Port Costa Clay Products, 183, 184
Port Costa Materials Company, 184
Porter, D. C., 105
Port of Richmond, 138
"Portugee" Gulch, 70
Portuguese, 70, 141, 155, 173, 176
postoffice (Alamo), 69
postoffice (Brentwood), 199
postoffice (Lafayette), 93
postoffice (Pleasant Hill), 48
Pratt, C. C., 191
Presbyterian, 72, 167, 191
Preston, C. J., 223
Prince, William, 66
Princess, 219
Professional Golf Association, 70
Protestant, 84, 142
Pueblo San Jose, 3
Puget Sound, 168
Pullman Car Company, 135
Pueblo San Jose, 67
P-X Market, 48, 75

quarries, 126, 127, 128

railroad, 29, 33, 45, 56, 72, 75, 76, 86, 90, 92,
    100, 101, 106, 113, 126, 169, 178, 183, 184,
    185, 195, 199, 200, 209
Ramon, 19
Ramona Park, 74
Ramos, A. G., 209
Rancho El Pinole, 5, 155
Rancho El Sobrante, 149, 150
Rancho Encinalitas, 141
Rancho Laguna de Los Palos, 99, 102
Rancho Los Medanos, 225, 226

Rancho Los Meganos, 199, 200, 204
Rancho Monte del Diablo, 27, 42
Rancho San Pablo, 128, 140, 141
Rapp, Ben, 24
Red Horse Tavern, 80
Redmond, Bill, 206
Redmond, Mrs. M. E., 86
Redmond, Sam, 206
Redwood Boys, 105
Redwood Heights, 108
Redwood Inn, 105, 106, 107
Redwood Manufacturing Company, 226, 227
Reed, Putney, 233
Refugio Valley Park, 162, 165
Regal Hotel, 178
Reihn Hemme and Company, 68
Renner, "Bones," 128
Reno, 128
Reuter, Gus, 116
Rheem, Donald, 102, 103, 116
Rheem, William S., 135
Rheem Center, 103
Rheem Theater, 103
Rhine, C., 21, 24
Richmond Cottage Hospital, 145
Richmond Hardware Company, 137
Richmond High School, 116, 134, 152
Richmond Independent, 135
Richmond Inner Harbor, 131, 138
Richmond Manufacturing Company, 135
Richmond Municipal Natatorium, 136
Richmond Oil Company, 150
Richmond Pottery Company, 135
Richmond-San Rafael Bridge, 136
Richmond-San Rafael Ferry and Transpor-
    tation Company, 127, 136, 139
Riddell, Alexander, 21
Rio Grande Valley, 21
Rio Theater, 169
Rio Vista, 219
Riverview Union High School District, 215
Robert Peary, 137
Robinson, L. L., 226, 227
Roche, Patrick, 52
Rockefeller, John D., 140
Rocky Point, 111
Rodeo Exchange Saloon, 167
Rodeo Hotel, 167
Rodeo Township, 168
Rodeo-Valley Ferry Company, 178
Rodgers, Ed, 46
Rodgers, Letitia, 46
Rogers Hotel, 58
Rollingwood Subdivision, 153
Rolph, Governor Jas., 195
Romer, Jack, 141
Root, Harold, 75
Ross, J., 217
Round Hill Golf and Country Club, 70
Royal Dutch Shell Oil Company, 10
Ruscher, Joseph, 25
Russell, Maj. Samuel, 83
Russi and Sonners, 44
Russo, Anthony, 229
Rust, William, 125, 126
Rust, California, 125, 126

Rutherford, Frank, 84, 85

Sacramento, 3, 41, 181, 215, 219
Sacramento County, 168
Sacramento Northern, 19, 104, 228
Sacramento River, 3, 8, 15, 40, 162, 171, 183,
    226
Sacramento Valley, 181
Safeway Stores (Moraga), 102, 103
Safeway Stores (Richmond), 138
Safety Nitro Powder Company, 144
Saint Anne's Church, 191
Saint Anne's Park, 102
Saint Charles, 8
Saint Francis Catholic Church, 15
Saint Joseph's Catholic Church, 157
Saint Mary's College, 102, 104
Saint Mary's Station, 104
Saint Peter Martyr Catholic Church, 228
Saint Paul's Catholic Church, 141
Saklan, 112
Salvation Army, 182
San Antonio Canyon, 105
San Antonio Redwoods, 89, 105
San Bruno (San Mateo County), 34
San Fernando, 129
Sanford, James T., 199, 200
San Francisco and San Joaquin Valley Rail-
    road, 131, 205
San Francisco Bay, 178
San Francisco Ferry Building, 56, 92, 100
San Francisco Presidio, 33
San Francisco-Sacramento Railway, 32
San Francisco's Market Street Wharf, 168
San Joaquin County, 202
San Joaquin River, 162, 171, 213, 214, 225,
    26, 232, 234
San Joaquin Valley, 8, 21, 181
San Leandro, 19
San Leandro Reservoir, 109
San Pablo, 4
San Pablo Airfield, 146
San Pablo and Tulare Railroad, 189, 199,
    200, 218, 225
San Pablo Bay, 131, 155, 161, 173
San Pablo Creek, 150, 151, 153
San Pablo Dam, 153
San Pablo Dam Road, 111, 115, 116, 149, 151
San Pablo Democrat, 153
San Pablo Flat, 142
San Pablo Hotel, 141, 143
San Pablo Municipal Complex, 147
San Pablo Rancho, 125
San Pablo Reservoir, 150
San Pablo School District, 142
San Pablo Valley, 149
San Quentin Prison, 106
San Ramon Branch (Valley), 29, 33, 72, 75
San Ramon Creek, 58, 71, 72, 83
San Ramon Fire Protection District (chief),
    83
San Ramon Garage, 83
San Ramon High School, 74
San Ramon School, 85, 86
San Ramon Station, 85
San Ramon Town Hall, 84, 85, 86

San Ramon Valley, 68, 71, 114
Santa Fe, New Mexico, 22
Santa Fe Railroad, 11, 29, 51, 56, 114, 126, 131, 134, 135, 140, 205, 206, 209, 211
Savings and Loan Society, 199, 200
Savoy Hotel (London, England), 189
Schmidt, George, 126
Schmidt Village, 126
Schott, Mrs. A. B., 215
Seal Bluff, 15
Seal Bluff Landing, 15
Sears Roebuck, 58
Sebastian Querque, 21
Security Pacific Bank, 59
Seeno, Frank, 227
Selby, Thomas, 173
Semple, Dr., 3
Sequoia, 105
Seventh Day Adventists, 191
"Sharkey," 151
Sheldon School, 156
Shell Chemical Company, 228
Shell Oil, 9, 10, 193
Shell Point, 19
Sherman, Dr. Samuel, 48
Sherman, 219
Sherman Field, 35, 53
Sherman Island, 219
Sherman Oaks, 35
Sherman Oaks Subdivision, 34, 48
Sherman Anti-Trust Act, 161
ships (frigates, landing, Liberty, LST, Victory), 137
Shirpke, Andy, 15
Shreve, Benjamin, 90, 92
Shrimp Camp, 135
Sicily, 226
Sierra, 56, 178, 226
Sierra, 131
Silva, Frank, 209
Simpson's (Thomas) Saddle Shop, 40, 42
Sinclair, Tom, 117
Six-Minute Ferry, 178, 179
Skow family, 151
Smith, F. M. "Borax," 135
Smith, J. D., 167
Smith, Joseph, 213
Smith, Joseph H., 225
Smith, Kenneth, 129
Smith, Col. William M., 3, 149
Smith, William W., 213, 215, 225
Smith (C. A.) Lumber Company, 15, 16, 17
Smith's Landing, 213
Smith's Point, 219
Snelgrove, Wallace, 48
Sobrante Canyon, 152
Sobrante Valley, 152
Solano, 185
Somersville, 173, 181
Southport Land and Commercial Company, 238
Southern Pacific, 10, 18, 29, 45, 51, 56, 86, 114, 130, 131, 136, 156, 157, 167, 175, 189, 191, 194, 205
Special Booster and Development Edition, 194

Speer's Saloon, 191
Spott, Lou, 70
stage, 5, 24, 40, 90, 111, 114
Staghound (clipper ship), 155
Standard Oil Company, 127, 134, 135, 140.
    See also Chevron
Standard Oil Service Station, 116
Standard J-1 (airplane), 146
Standard Pacheco Plow Works, 40
Starr, Abraham, 176, 177
Stauffer Chemical Company, 130, 228
Stege, Richard, 130
Stege, 127, 130
Stein, Louis L., Jr., 7, 124
Sterling, Tom, 219
Stevenson, Col. J. D., 225, 226
Stockton, 21, 40, 114, 132, 181, 183, 194, 215, 219
Stone, Silas, 67
Stone Valley Creek, 68
Stone Valley Road Bridge, 68
Stow, James, 68
Stranahan, Ebenezer, 21
Stranahan, Richard, 21
Strentzel, Dr. John T., 12, 175, 176
Strentzel, Louie, 7
Such, Frank, 24, 39
Sueyras, Manuel, 156
Suisun, 8, 181
Suisun Bay, 10
Summit of Zion, The (mining company), 24
Summit Road, 89, 96
Sunset Develpment Company, 85
Sunset Nursery, 75
Sun Valley Shopping Center, 42, 53
Sutter's Fort, 89
Swamp and Overflow Act, 200
Swan, Fred, 24
Sycamore Valley, 71
Syrian, 214

Tassajara Valley, 70
telephone, 10, 74, 75
Telegraph Road, 41, 89, 90, 111
Tennent, Dr. Samuel, 155
Tewksbury, Emily, 131, 134
Tewksbury, Dr. Jacob, 131
Texas Company, 138
Thompson, Don, 116
Thompson, Peter, 93
Thompson, Ruth, 116
Three-thirty-three Club, 128
Tiger Alley, 72
Todas Santos, 42
toll collector, 81
Tonite Powder Works, 130
Toonerville Trolley, 76
Tormey, John, 167
Tormey, Patrick, 167, 173
Town Center project, 60
Town Hall (Lafayette), 94
Town Hall (San Ramon), 85, 86
Town Hall (Walnut Creek), 57, 58
Toy, Henry F., 225
Toyota, 85
Tracy, 195, 219

Trader Vic, 128
Trette, C. H., 24
Tri-County News, 169
Tuck, Abbie, 204
Tunnel Road, 30, 89, 96, 116
Tuolumne County, 39
Turner and Cosine, 214
Tyler's Hotel, 217

Unexpected, The (mining company), 24
Union Academy, 68
Union Hotel (Clayton), 24
Union Mine, 235
Union Oil Company, 93, 167, 172
Union Saloon, 143
Union Stockyard Company, 167
United Grocers Distribution Center, 138
United States Army, 6
United States Bulk Mail Distribution Center, 138
United States District Court, 99
United States government, 19
United States Justice Department, 161
United States Land Commission, 99, 149
United States Military Command, 34
United States Navy, 102
United States Post Office Department, 90, 105, 109
United States Steel Company, 227
United States Supreme Court justice, 125, 128
United States War Department, 16, 18, 192
University of California, Berkeley campus, 51
University of California Field Research Station, 138
U.S. I-80, 170
U.S. Route 40, 170
Utah Construction Company, 102, 103
"Utschvin," 112

Vallejo, Gen. Mariano G., 142
Vallejo Junction, 174, 178, 219
Vallejo-Rodeo Ferry Company, 168
Valle Vista School, 108
Valley Church of Moraga, 102
Valley Nitrogen Company, 162
Valley Pipe Line Company, 193
Valona, 175, 176, 180
Van Benschoten, Charles, 219
Van Kathoven, Arnold, 209
Variety Store, 124
Varsity Market, 75
Veale, Sheriff R. R., 48, 202
Ventura family, 70
Vessing, 48
Veteran's Hall (Lafayette), 96
Victory ships, 137
Vigorite Powder, 127
Volstead Act, 55, 127
Von Buren, J. A., 201
Vulcan Powder, 144

Wagner, Gen. Theodore, 111, 112, 114
Wagon Wheel, 128
Walker, James T., 65
Wallace, Judge Robert, Jr., 202
Walnut Creek (watercourse), 39, 41, 45, 48, 58

Walnut Creek Fire Department, 91
Walnut Creek Meat Company, 58, 64
Walrath, G. W., 39
Wampett and Wampett, 6
War Assets Administration, 34
Warmcastle, F. M., 6, 44
Warren, Earl, 128
Watson, Leland M., 49
Watt, Robert, 131
Way Side Inn, 90, 95
Welch, Widow, 3, 39, 55
Welch, William, 39
Welch Quicksilver and Mining Company, 24, 26
Welch Rancho, 39
Wells Fargo and Company, 142
Welsh, 232
Wemper, Emmett, 219
West, James, 69
West Contra Costa Hospital District, 145
Western California Canners, 219
Western Electric Company, 85
Western Pacific, 29
Western Union Telegraph Company, 41, 142
West Hartley, 235

whaling station, 135
White, Clifford, 48
White, John, 83
Wickland Oil Terminal, 172, 173
Wiedemann, Christian, 82, 84
Wiester Hay Warehouse Company, 75
Wight, Chas. N., 225
Wildcat Canyon, 121, 122
Wildcat Canyon Road, 111
Wildcat Creek, 145
Wild Idle Saloon, 189
Wilkening, F., 189
Williams, Arthur, 64
Williams, Jesse, 99
Williams, Star King, 219
Williamson, Con, 107
Williamson, George, 107
Williamson, James A., 99
Willow, The, 116
Willow Springs School District, 102
Willow Springs School #2, 102
Wills, Frank, 219
Winehaven, 135
Women's West Side Improvement Club, 136
Wood (E. K.) Lumber Company, 48

Woodfield Neighborhood Park, 162
Woodruff, Asa, 15
Woodruff, David S., 15
Woodruff, Newton, 15
Woodruff, Philo, 15
Woodruff, Simeon, 15
Wood Shop (Knightsen), 206
World War I, 211
World War II, 18, 48, 49, 53, 58, 76, 102, 108, 124, 129, 137, 145, 146, 152, 219
Wright, Tom, 141
Wright Brothers, 126, 140
Wylie, Oliver, 137

Yards #2, #3 and #4, 137
Yardley, Ralph O., 194
Yerba Buena, 105
Ygnacio Valley, 15, 23, 24, 27, 29, 35, 45, 55, 79
Y.M.C.A., 182
Yosemite Club, 128
Young's Market, 124

Zack, Professor, 26
Zeck, Professor, 26